Hallmarks: The Cultural Politics and Public Pedagogies of Stuart Hall

This provocative, interdisciplinary and transnational collection delves deeply into the educational and public intellectual hallmarks of Stuart M. Hall, a core figure in the development of the postwar British New Left, Cultural Studies at the Centre for Contemporary Cultural Studies and, later, the Open University. It opens new vistas on both critical educational studies and cultural studies through interviews with, and essays by, leading writers, shedding light on the under-appreciated public pedagogical and cultural politics of the New Left, Thatcherism and Rightist, neocolonial, diasporic and neoliberal formations in Jamaica, the UK, Australia, North America and Brazil. Cogently argued and beautifully written, the book looks to spark dialog about Hall's under-appreciated educational contributions and illuminate important aspects of his work for students and scholars in many fields.

Intimate and moving, the contributors' accounts describe Hall's diasporic formation as a courageous 'artist' and educator of cultural politics and social movements. The book shows both the reach and the relevance of his public pedagogies in the construction of alternatives to essentialist racial politics and the despairing cynicism of neoliberalism. With contributors and interviewees including Leslie G. Roman, Michael W. Apple, Avtar Brah, John Clarke, Annette Henry, Lawrence Grossberg, Luis Gandin and Fazal Rizvi, *Hallmarks: The Cultural Politics and Public Pedagogies of Stuart Hall* reveals that neither cultural politics nor public pedagogies are stable or self-evident constructs. Each legitimates and requires the other as part of a longer radical democratic project for social justice.

This book was originally published as a special issue of *Discourse: Studies in the Cultural Politics of Education.*

Leslie G. Roman is Professor of Educational Studies, Killam Fellow and Affiliate of the Institute for Gender, Race, Sexuality and Social Justice at the University of British Columbia, Vancouver, Canada. She is author and co-editor of *Becoming Feminine: The Politics of Popular Culture* (Falmer Press, 1988*), Views Beyond the Border Country: Raymond Williams and Cultural Politics* (Routledge, 1992) and *Dangerous Territories: Struggles for Difference and Equality in Education* (Routledge, 1997). Her book *Contested Knowledge* will appear shortly with Rowman & Littlefield.

Hallmarks: The Cultural Politics and Public Pedagogies of Stuart Hall

Edited by

Leslie G. Roman

Routledge
Taylor & Francis Group

LONDON AND NEW YORK

First published 2016
by Routledge
2 Park Square, Milton Park, Abingdon, Oxon, OX14 4RN, UK

and by Routledge
711 Third Avenue, New York, NY 10017, USA

Routledge is an imprint of the Taylor & Francis Group, an informa business

British Library Cataloguing in Publication Data
A catalogue record for this book is available from the British Library

ISBN 13: 978-1-138-19202-7

Typeset in Times
by RefineCatch Limited, Bungay, Suffolk

Publisher's Note
The publisher accepts responsibility for any inconsistencies that may have
arisen during the conversion of this book from journal articles to book chapters,
namely the possible inclusion of journal terminology.

Disclaimer
Every effort has been made to contact copyright holders for their permission to
reprint material in this book. The publishers would be grateful to hear from any
copyright holder who is not here acknowledged and will undertake to rectify
any errors or omissions in future editions of this book.

Contents

CONTENTS

Part 3: Articulation in theory and practice

Citation Information

The chapters in this book were originally published in *Discourse: Studies in the Cultural Politics of Education*, volume 36, issue 2 (April 2015). When citing this material, please use the original page numbering for each article, as follows:

For any permission-related enquiries please visit:
http://www.tandfonline.com/page/help/permissions

Notes on Contributors

Michael W. Apple is John Bascom Professor of Curriculum and Instruction and Educational Policy Studies at the University of Wisconsin, Madison, USA. His research centres on the limits and possibilities of critical educational policy and practice in a time of conservative restoration. Along with Stephen J. Ball and Luis Armando Gandin, he is the editor of *The Routledge International Handbook of the Sociology of Education* (Routledge, 2009).

John Clarke is Professor Emeritus of Social Policy and Criminology at the Open University, UK. His work has centred on ways in which welfare states have been transformed since the late twentieth century, with a particular interest in how the relationships between welfare, state and nation have been reconstructed. He is the author of *Changing Welfare, Changing States: New Directions in Social Policy* (SAGE, 2004) and *Publics, Politics and Power: Remaking the Public in Public Services* (with Janet Newman, SAGE, 2009).

Luis Armando Gandin is Professor of Sociology of Education at the Universidade Federal do Rio Grande do Sul, Porto Alegre, Brazil. Along with Michael W. Apple and Stephen J. Ball, he is the editor of *The Routledge International Handbook of the Sociology of Education* (Routledge, 2009). His research focuses on the sociology of education, educational policies, educational reform and the curriculum.

Annette Henry is a Professor in the Department of Language and Literacy Education at the University of British Columbia, Vancouver, Canada. Her scholarship examines race, class, language, gender and culture in sociocultural contexts of teaching and learning in the lives of Black students and Black women teachers' practice in Canada, the US and the Caribbean. She is the author of *Taking Back Control: Black Women Teachers' Activism and the Education of African Canadian Children* (SUNY Press, 1998).

Fazal Rizvi is a Professor in Education at the University of Melbourne, Australia. Much of his recent research has focused on issues of identity, culture and global mobility of students, as well as theories of globalization and the internationalization of higher education. His recent books include *Globalization and the Study of Education* (Wiley, 2009) and *Globalizing Educational Policy* (Routledge, 2010).

Leslie G. Roman is Professor of Educational Studies, Killam Fellow and Affiliate of the Institute for Gender, Race, Sexuality and Social Justice, at the University of British Columbia, Vancouver, Canada. She is author and co-editor of *Becoming Feminine: The Politics of Popular Culture* (Falmer Press, 1988), *Views Beyond the Border Country: Raymond Williams and Cultural Politics* (Routledge, 1992) and *Dangerous Territories: Struggles for Difference and Equality in Education* (Routledge, 1997). Her book *Contested Knowledge* will appear shortly with Rowman & Littlefield.

PREFACE

A remarkable gift and a daunting challenge: Stuart Hall's life and work

John Clarke and Leslie G. Roman

This book was born out of a shared desire among its editor and contributors to celebrate the life and work of Stuart Hall, who died in 2014. We wish to shed light on those dimensions which have been unrecognized, that is seeing him as an educator of many diverse publics and counter-publics. Hall's work was not the defence of cultural studies as an abstracted interdisciplinary endeavour or a Left intellectual life measured by solitary contributions inside the academy. It was an argument (or indeed many arguments) over time and in conversation with many diverse publics and counter-publics for thinking through cultural studies and the Left practices in, of and around education in their broadest sense as crucial for reading ideologies of particular historical junctures. There is no way after all to write a preface honouring the work and life of Stuart as a single entity, as the sole author. This much we have both learned from Stuart Hall.

As I (Leslie G. Roman) reached for my handy electronic pen (the word processor), I realised I could not do this alone, perhaps because finality with Stuart Hall is not possible. I reached out to John Clarke, and in a reciprocal spirit he wrote back; working from my shorthand notes, we have produced a little piece of collaborative writing. Brought together in life by Stuart's work and teaching, we found ourselves reunited in the aftermath of his death working through and indeed resisting the ethos of solitary intellectual and political work. Collaborating on a preface is a modest gesture of respect for such a generous public intellectual. Intellectual work for Hall was never meant to be distinguished by the all-too-familiar academic refrain, 'I authored this'. All of us who have contributed to this volume have been touched and moved by Stuart's life and work, often in profound and long-lasting ways. Indeed, Stuart Hall's capacity to touch and move, to engage and animate, is one of his distinctive 'hallmarks', and we hope that this book both captures and honours those qualities, even as we know that we will never quite do those things as well as he did.

There is a vital foundation for those qualities, one that linked almost all the aspects of his personal, political, intellectual and pedagogic lives. An astonishing generosity of intellect and spirit underpinned his thought and action. We can see both in his carefully critical engagement with other thinkers and theorists (from Foucault to Butler, from Althusser to Harvey, and in his returns to Gramsci). He put into practice thinking with and against the ideas of others, never presenting a critique that merely 'dismantled' but instead looked for what might be gained, what might be valuable, what might be productive in what others had dismissed. This, he argued, was a properly 'dialectical' sense of critique, and for us, as young scholars, this represented a major challenge. We had begun our studies in different parts of the world secure in the knowledge that critique meant the dismantling of other positions, demonstrating their errors, limitations and failings. Our encounters with Stuart Hall opened up a different approach to thinking critically – and that was both a remarkable gift and a daunting challenge. Both of us have consistently struggled to live up to this generosity of intellectual practice, still finding it much easier to think against positions, rather than with and against. Yet the framework of how to do both persists as one for doing intellectual work well.

'Thinking with' also marks his underlying view of intellectual work, visible in the way that he consistently sought – and promoted - possibilities of working collaboratively. His approach remains astonishingly rare among contemporary intellectual figures, who almost all take the embodied form of the single and singular great thinker offering us, more or less graciously, their latest thoughts on the world. Hall operated rather differently, consistently working in discussion, collaboration and argument: from promoting collective working at the Birmingham Centre for Cultural Studies as an organizational and political strategy – and practising it, as in the collectively authored *Policing the Crisis* (Hall et al., 1978) – through working at the Open University with its course teams as the 'collective teacher' and producing a range of innovative courses and widely used textbooks in the process, to his involvement in the creation of the International Institute of Visual Arts at Rivington Place (www.iniva.org). Though one commentator delivered the perverse judgement that Hall had not produced a single sole-authored book, what Hall did so astonishingly well was give birth to multiple publics and counter-publics, nourishing generations of artists, young scholars, activist minds and bodies politic that well exceed a single-authored volume. In place of the overly valorized sole-authored book, we point to the many books that Stuart Hall wrote – as co-author, co-editor, contributor and – not least – inspiration. Both of us have had the strange, delightful and demanding sense of hearing Stuart's voice in our heads as we struggled with some piece of work – and that voice was always cajoling, encouraging and insisting that we could do better. If a thought was still nascent, he had the capacity to draw us out to hear it and ask us to refine our ideas.

His generosity also characterized his engagement with students, whether undergraduates at Open University summer schools or graduate students at the many workshops, seminars and talks in which he participated the world over. Hall's view of doing intellectual work always necessitated a dialogic approach in which people might think together. This was profoundly conversational –dialogical, exploratory and unfinished – and was matched by his style when giving lectures or presenting ideas. Those who heard him, or have read the transcribed talks, have a sense of listening to him thinking out loud, mindful of the audience before him, working his way through puzzles, paradoxes, challenges, always on his way to try to find a better means of thinking about 'conjunctures'. Yet even more compelling are the engaged conversations that followed the lecture or talk – the 'Q & A' that was always more responsive and lively than that, animated by his willingness to take everyday people seriously, to respond to their pressing concerns and to open himself (and consequently others) to being moved intellectually and politically, as discussed by Roman in Chapter 3 of this volume.

The essays here capture some of the possibilities of such a dialogical disposition, pointing to the many sites of Hall's public, pedagogic and political work. In all of the sites that we discuss, and in so many more, he was engaged in constituting publics who might think and act against the dominant forces and formations – in the university, in schools, in the arts and all manner of popular cultural forms, as well as in struggles over national identities, international and transnational solidarities. These emergent publics or counter-publics– and their lines of possibility – are a crucial legacy of Hall's generosity and the educational cultural politics and pedagogies. They might be located in specific settings or formed around particular struggles, but they are the outcome of Hall's astonishing connective – *articulatory* – practices: the persistent search for what animates, mobilizes and connects people in refusal or resistance and the search for another– and better – way. In this vein, the artwork chosen for the cover of our volume, entitled *Self-Portrait, 2000–2014*, is by internationally acclaimed Chila Kumari Burman. Burman's work was borne of the vitality of expression which burst forth in the 1980s on the cutting-edge scene of BAM and the Asian diasporic arts inspired in large part by Hall's public explorations of the intersections of racial, sexual and cultural identities as diasporic, a process of never finished becoming. Hall worked with, mentored and inspired a number of specific arts organizations and artists and filmmakers. Burman's *Self-Portrait, 2000–2014* speaks to the instance of returning the gaze—in fact, not as a one-time affixing-of-identity event but instead as the many dynamic acts that culturally produce the social self over many years, changing and subverting stereotypical presentations of 'traditional Asian womanhood' as static, subservient, lacking in pleasure and, finally, affixed (Burman, 2015). In return, Hall praised Burman's work for its political passion and its 'ferocious energy, fierce sense of the body-as- resistance', both of which violate stereotypes of 'traditional' Asian womanhood (Hall and Sealy, 2001: 101). This is one example of the legions of artists whom he promoted but it resonates with our understanding of Hall's interventions and their long-lasting impact, a signature of his generative and generous creativity across spheres of artistic, formal and non-formal educational contexts and social movements. These for Hall were interconnected educational spaces in which to think through identities, pedagogies and cultural politics.

In this volume, we focus particularly on the sites, practices and pedagogies of both formal and non-formal education – a focus that reflects Hall's own locations (as teacher, educator and animator) and his larger understanding of popular education as one of the critical fields of the politics of culture or what he termed 'cultural politics', which also animated and thoroughly constituted his vision of cultural studies. Education has been and remains a crucial and fertile ground for the work of cultural studies. Education's many different sites, practices and processes bear witness to the articulation of relations and knowledges of domination and subordination; to the agency and capacity of publics and counter-publics to refuse and resist. In these settings, as Raymond Williams understood, the dominant is always in dynamic tension and relations with both residual and emergent cultural and political forms. Education is always a location articulated to larger ideologies, whose effects can be traced in structures, systems, pedagogic frameworks, curricula and embodied practices. Hall's work both addressed and struggled with education's many sites, contexts and practices. We hope that the essays here do justice to the generosity, brilliance and passion Stuart brought to his personal, pedagogic and political engagements, the publics and counter-publics he inspired and, in no small measure, brought to life.

References

Burman, C. (2015, October 29). Personal Communication with Leslie G. Roman by e-mail from London, UK.

Hall, S., Critcher, C., Jefferson, T., Clarke J. and Roberts, B. (1978) *Policing the Crisis: Mugging, the State and Law and Order*. London: Macmillan (second edition, 2013).

Hall, S. and Sealy, M. (eds.) (2001) *DIFFERENT: A Historical Context: Contemporary Photographers and Black Identity*. London/New York: Phaidon Press.

INTRODUCTION

'Keywords': Stuart Hall, an extraordinary educator, cultural politics and public pedagogies

Leslie G. Roman

Educational Studies, Faculty of Education, University of British Columbia, Vancouver, Canada

This special issue rethinks Stuart Hall neither strictly as a Cultural Studies scholar nor as a sociologist but rather, more broadly as an extraordinary educator of multiple and broad oppositional constituencies, publics and counter-publics. In so doing, it probes Hall's keywords for querying, contesting, and shifting the educational landscape and lexicon of culture, which previously had been wed to hegemonic essentialist notions of 'race,' nation, gender, and sexuality. Re-reading Hall as a public educator and public pedagogue, the issue recognizes how his extraordinary accomplishments, multiple counter-hegemonic projects, theoretical resources, and achievements in building diverse oppositional constituencies are now our inheritance. While some contributors of this issue show that Hall wrote about education throughout the course of his career, more importantly all show that Hall's commitments were born of political commitments to think educationally, about who constitutes 'the public,' and in whose name education's cultural politics and public pedagogies speak. Drawing upon 'keywords' of Hall's educational thinking and lexicon, we show how our understandings of hegemony and counter-hegemony do not take for granted any pre-constituted notions of culture, social subjectivity, or publics. This in turn has enormous implications for the cultural politics of education, public pedagogy, and our social future.

Tribute: political grief and appreciation

Stuart McPhail Hall was arguably the most innovative and engaged cultural theorist and sociologist of the postwar era and the key driver along with Richard Hoggart to create and legitimate the Cultural Studies – first at the Centre for Contemporary Cultural Studies and later at the Open University. Before soaring to great academic stature via Cultural Studies, he was one of the key figures in addition to EP Thompson and Raymond Williams in establishing the New Left in postwar Britain. Hailed in *The Guardian* (Butler, 2014)[1] as 'the Godfather of British Multiculturalism,' a tribute he would wear uncomfortably, Hall was also the leading light in *Universities and Left Review*, and when it was reinvented, he became a founder of *New Left Review*. He was also a major contributor to *Marxism Today*, the foremost Left British journal for many years. An astute analyst of Thatcherism, a term he invented, and more recently, a thoughtful critic of neoliberalism in the journal, *Soundings*, which he co-founded, Hall's primary legacy (albeit not yet fully appreciated) will be as an extraordinary educator and public

Figure 1.   Stuart Hall, taken in 2011. (Photo credit © Mahasiddhi)

intellectual. *Discourse* itself was affected by Stuart Hall's work, whose editors, Bob Lingard and Fazal Rizvi felt inspired to rename the journal its Australian focus to a transnational and discursive one and retitling it with the inflection of 'cultural politics' (i.e., *Discourse: Studies in the Cultural Politics of Education*) in the subtitle of the journal. Influenced by others such as Raymond Williams on the British New Left, Hall thought of culture and politics as inseparable processes and practices. This was almost entirely novel for a generation of other hard Left thinkers for whom affect and the popular were minor if nonexistent or suspect terms. Significantly, he showed us how and the ways in which the popularity of particular ideologies such as Thatcherism (which he predicted) came into being through inventing new common-sense meanings, affect and identification, thus reconstituting a dangerous and racist British imaginary. He helped ensure that the successive British fiscal crises of the 1970s, 1980s, and the present were also cultural crises 'without' normative 'guarantees' of further empire, that Britain became increasingly critical in its multiculturalism and thus, challenged the imperial unquestionable.

Hall wrote and spoke back to Britishness as white masculinist racism by mentoring several generations of diasporic and activist scholars *and* artists (Hazel Carby, Rosiland Brunt, Lidia Curti, Iain Chambers, Paul Gilroy, Angela McRobbie, Larry Grossberg, Isaac Julien, Pratibha Parmar, Paul Willis, Sankofa and Black Audio Film Collective, the Otolith Group and Smoking Dog Productions, among others) whom he taught, mentored, or inspired. Hall saw himself as bearing an intellectual and political responsibility to shape the future. Jean Fisher cast Stuart Hall as an 'artist,' not as the 'Godfather of multiculturalism' in Britain or the 'the outsider' who makes of 'England a place to think.' Jean Fisher (2014) writes that Hall's –

> ability to translate complex discourses into an accessible language and ease in front of the camera is captured for future generations both in his superb series of programmes on the Caribbean, Redemption Song, BBC2 in 1991, and in his walk-on and talking heads cameos in the film essays of Isaac Julien/Sankofa and Black Audio Film Collective, whose rich synthesis of audiovisual poetics and political analysis inspired the Otolith Group (founded by Kodwo Eshun and Anjalika Sagar. (Fisher, 2014)[2]

Evidence of Stuart Hall's mentorship of British Black and Asian artists and photographers can be found in the Institute of International Visual Art (Iniva) and Autograph ABP at Rivington Place, a building designed by architect, David Adjaye who acclaimed film-maker, Isaac Julien, mentored by Hall, also commissioned to design his film-making studio. Hall played vital roles in both these organizations, functioning for many years as their Chairs; hence, the Rivington Place Library is named after him. Yet, the best evidence of Stuart Hall's contributions goes beyond books, buildings, and tributes. If we truly believe in the capacity to create public and counter-public dialog within and across our social institutions as broader public pedagogies, then, Stuart Hall's 'legacy' as an extraordinary educator will be recalled and built upon as a living one. I cannot help but think Stuart Hall might be slightly uncomfortable with legacy talk. Yet, we intend to breathe life into what otherwise gets discussed as 'ghostly hauntings' by showing how his worldly and worldwide influence exceeded the UK and contributed to our understandings of how to challenge hegemonic cultural politics, projects, policies, and public pedagogies of education in order to articulate socially just futures – impossibly possible futures. The contributors of this special issue aim to contribute to just such a living legacy perhaps best expressed as the theory and practice of articulating publics and counter-publics.

Upon learning of his death, I had to steal myself from grief, at once, emotional, intellectual, and political. Having known him for nearly 30 years as his student, colleague, and friend, the magnitude of his loss was immediate and profound, still incomprehensible. As Annie Paul, Jamaican historian says, I now have [a] 'Stuart Hall-shaped hole in the universe' (Paul, 2014).[3] One did not have to know Stuart Hall or to have met him to have felt his impact over the years or his loss. From the outpouring of tributes and in conversations with other scholars and activists the world over, many found his death simply hard to grasp. How would our worlds look without Stuart Hall? What would our work look like had he had not provided the innovative ways of reading Foucault through Gramsci, British racism through diasporic thinking, and indeed the UK national imaginary through racialized moral panics, or youth subcultures through agency and resistance, media through desire and social subject formation?

Grief is never really consoled by passive inaction. This issue grew from the realization that to honor Hall's vision is to take intellectual action – to come to terms with what we learned from him in both theory and practice in educational and social thought. *Discourse: Studies in the Cultural Politics of Education* was among the first, if not the first journal in education of international scope to take seriously Hall's reframing of culture and politics as inseparable and as a keyword crucial in our understanding of educational practices, policies, and reforms. Stuart Hall has been a benchmark for extraordinary public intellectual and pedagogical work, an educator in the truest sense of the term. He moved fluidly between scholarship and activism as praxis, between formal and nonformal educational sites while building and contributing to progressive social movements. He did all of this with rigor, engagement of all as learners, including himself, never willing to offer easy answers or conventional wisdoms from any political ideological stance. He moved as readily to mentor and support the work of variously hyphenated Black, queer and Asian diasporic artists the world over in art galleries as he enjoyed living in the moment of jazz and political actions, always with a warm, accessible, and personal manner. He was at his best when writing collaboratively and as a lover of music, most joyous when listening to or speaking about jazz and the blues, from Miles Davis to Ben Sidran, from opera to Marvin Gaye. Through music, the arts, protests, and politics, he connected with students, artists, and ordinary people. He taught a broad, diverse, and often fractious Left who grew up in the 1950s and came of age in the 1960s, 1970s, 1980s, and yes, into the present, how to engage in spirited debate while building publics, pedagogies, and cultural politics that would become broader counter-publics and oppositional constituencies. He contributed much to our critical Left vocabularies and struggles, particularly thinking about education *and* thinking pedagogically throughout his career.

Taking up Stuart Hall's 'keywords'

Raymond Williams (1976) once suggested that certain 'keywords' define a conjuncture, forming a whole way of social thinking and life. Taking that as the starting point, the life and work of Stuart McPhail Hall certainly testify to some 60 years of cultural and social thought with his unmistakable contributions in which our critical vocabularies and keywords have shifted as a result of his public intellectual thinking, activism, and scholarship. In fact, we can no longer talk about education as strictly formal, given Hall's attention to cultural politics and public pedagogies (Giroux, 2000). This issue provides a tribute to his extraordinary educational contributions, which often go overlooked. Keywords, according to Williams, are never to be taken for granted. They often belie a history of contestation, cultural crisis, and tenacious political struggle to define or redefine their meanings. Such was the case with the words 'culture,' as well as with, arguably, 'education,' 'pedagogy,' and the very meanings of 'public' in and outside of education before Hall. Before Hall, culture was almost entirely used in its noun form often associated with either homogeneous or categorical ways of thinking about groups of people, their ideas, traditions, languages, and practices – bounded often by essentializing assumptions about national cultures, spaces, and temporalities. Even more disturbing was the way in which culture as a noun often got tethered to notions of some people's knowledge as being 'culturally deficit' while others got to speak from the unquestionable normative but legitimated centre of 'culture' as possessors of the knowledge worth knowing. In his insistence of a Gramscian materialism infused with poststructural understandings, Hall capably shifted the keywords and vocabularies of social and educational thought. Hall's 'cultural politics' has become short hand for viewing culture as a production, a process involving real agents at once discursively and materially produced at specific times and in specific places, bearing the traces of history and yet not finally inscribed in them as an anthropological or archeological finding etched on walls or carved into trinkets. Hall once said,

> culture is not just a voyage of rediscovery, a return journey. It is not an 'archeology.' Culture is a production. It has its raw materials, its resources, its 'work of production.' It depends on

a knowledge of tradition as 'the changing same' and an effective set of genealogies. But what this detour through its pasts does is to enable us, through culture, to produce ourselves anew, as new kinds of subjects. It is therefore not a question of what our traditions make of us so much as what we make of our traditions. Paradoxically, our cultural identities, in any finished form, lie ahead of us. We are always in the process of cultural formation. Culture is not a matter of ontology, of being, but of becoming. (Hall, 2005, p. 556)

With this enormous shift to culture as a 'production,' a process of 'cultural becoming,' Hall inaugurated the idea that 'cultural politics' in education do the work of 'what we might become.' They bear histories but are not finally chained to them as fixed, real, or imaginary pasts. Hall helped us to see that education is at once a site for contesting the yet unfinished practices of 'cultural becoming' and sites of struggle over power, knowledge, publics, and in whose name education registers. If cultural identities are a matter of becoming, then the question as Hall frames it is not of 'who we are' of or 'where we come from' but instead, 'what we might become?' (Ang, 2000, p. 1). Having unleashed cultural identities from their real or imaginary pasts, Hall freed critical educators to see them ever transforming in the continuous contestations of historical, political, and economic power (Ang, 2000). To his insistence that 'routes' not roots or origins are what matter was a way of rethinking racist ideologies as part of colonial histories active in the present and reshaped diasporically and globally, we find him forward-thinking and certainly beyond his own time. After Hall, psychologistic and deficit framings of culture as a noun were possible to challenge and contest as were essentialist notions of 'race.' One of Hall's greatest achievements was the reframing of culture as a theoretical concept and as a political practice in educational thinking, not just in cultural and social theory more broadly. Yet, he did not accomplish this achievement through that keyword alone. Other terms and ways of thinking contributed to his many and profoundly influential educational and political projects – terms such as conjunctural analysis, diaspora, and articulation were keywords critical to his challenge of the existing lexicon that inhabited our educational and social world. Together, these keywords of Hall's thinking have had significant implications for how we conceive of education and its relationship to cultural politics and public pedagogies – and in whose names we teach, research, think, and act.

The essays in this volume contribute to thinking about how Hall's work and keywords have challenged hegemonic projects and cultural politics in education, and in so doing ask us to think deeply about how public pedagogies, policies, and practices become interwoven with cultural formation and processes of cultural becoming. By working through and with some of his ideas and concepts such as conjunctural thinking, diasporic thinking, and articulation, we begin to come to terms with Hall's profound impact on educational thought. We do well to recall how much traditional and radical functionalism in education and social thought more widely got overturned through the interventions of Hall and those who took up and expanded his work and 'keywords' in Cultural Studies and education. These keywords sound their trumpets variously across the essays and interviews, drawing our attention and yours, dear readers, to a landscape which could not have been imagined without the extraordinary educational contributions of Stuart Hall.

We know we have just begun to scratch the surface of what is truly our extraordinary educational inheritance from Stuart Hall. This inheritance is neither exclusively academic nor disciplinary. Nor it is located politically in one theoretical tradition (e.g., materialism or poststructuralism). And yet, he was committed to a Left and progressive social justice through education and public pedagogies. Here, education means something much more broad and inclusive than any of the former disciplinary terms. Yet, having now claimed him as the critical educator he was, we ask that you build on his projects by considering how varied and wide ranging they were. Consider, for example, what education is if not the cultural politics of who can belong to the public and whose knowledge gets represented in curricula, policies, reforms, and pedagogies? Many progressive social movements have over the years taken up his analyses, and keywords, answering his generous calls and dynamic capacity to make and move publics and counter-publics for moving times with their own responses through the arts, protests, social movement writing, public thinking, and activist scholarship. If we take any direct lessons from Hall's work, it is that his intellectual generosity embodied the cultural politics of making counter-hegemonic projects: they were appealing, persuasive, and hopeful against the grain of intellectual and political solipsism. Judging from the outpouring of love and grief when various publics learned of his death, we can say his cultural politics were also not about him as a celebrity intellectual – something altogether increasingly rare in our neoliberal academy, and the worlds of art and politics. Hall's counter-hegemonic political projects were always about 'us'; his many and diverse engaged audiences the world over, whether as students, readers of his many television shows, filmic contributions, engagement of intellectual, scholarly, and political debates well beyond 'British' and 'Jamaican' national boundaries in places such as Brazil, South Africa, the USA, Europe, Australia, and many places in Asia. In many respects, 'Stuart Hall' himself could be read as keyword for our postwar era. Yet, he would be modest about making such a claim even though his projects were mighty. Some remain unfinished: this is what he would have wanted – to be seen as having built something that far exceeded the capacity of any single individual or pretense to solve single-handedly the great social inequalities of power and history: just a route (not *the* route) to a just future that we work toward collectively.

In the spirit of building upon and continuing Stuart Hall's projects, several goals inspire and animate the organization of this issue, which aims to:

(1) trace genealogically in both intellectual and political terms the continuities and ruptures in Hall's life and work, and in particular, to examine his dynamic thinking about and through materialism and Marxism, Leftist politics over time and in relation to particular struggles;

(2) explore, document and pay necessary attention to the specifically educational writing, addresses, and Hall's work over time and in key works of his;

(3) show how versatile he was at rethinking the uses of theory and theoretical traditions in the service of larger counter-hegemonic educational projects while not succumbing to relativism;

(4) signal what the conditions of reflexivity for producing public pedagogues was and have become for all of us as a result of his rethinking of materialism through post-structuralism, post-colonialism and diasporic thinking;

(5) ask probing questions about the present neo-liberal conjuncture and its implications for educational scholars/activists;

(6) converse in accessible terms through the interviews with Avtar Brah and Lawrence Grossberg about the contributions of Stuart Hall politically and intellectually in education and Cultural Studies with the aim of challenging and extending his work and his impact in cultural education, Cultural Studies, and Leftist and feminist decolonizing politics more broadly;

(7) re-invigorate through narrative, social biographical, theoretical, conceptual and empirical research, all of which occurs here, the idea that the cultural politics of becoming educators and educated are worth the struggles over whose knowledge matters in our quests for social justice.

It has been my privilege to work with each and all of the contributors to this issue. All pulled their weight in this collective issue and no one acted like a celebrity intellectual. Hall exemplified both generosity and would I believe have been proud to have this quality of dialog without celebrity narcissism. This in and of itself was gratifying and inspiring. In this regard, I believe the issue speaks best collectively – in an apt turn of phrase as 'unity in difference.' Yet, of course, there are friendly cacophonous differences of emphasis and points of view, exemplifying varying methodological, conceptual, and theoretical entrées into Hall's work and its implications for cultural politics public pedagogies. These enrich our public and counter-public dialogs. All of the contributors, though, think deeply about Hall as an extraordinary educator and draw sustenance from his dynamic thinking and intellectual activism which was the ground on which he developed our understandings of these significant keywords of conjuncture, counter-hegemonic projects of education, diasporic thinking, and articulation, and our own emerging conceptions of public education and pedagogy.

Three parts comprise the issue are organized somewhat organically by keywords Hall's work offered to the cultural politics of education to which the essays and interviews speak. Part 1 considers Hall's contributions to the conjunctural analysis or what we call 'conjunctural thinking.' Apple considers Hall in his own work over the years to analyze the conjunctures of Rightist and neoliberal politics in education. Roman also considers how Hall's varied projects hailed diverse and 'maximal publics' which were at once extraordinary educational accomplishments. She does so through four conjunctures, three of which were significant to her own personal political and intellectual formation as a critical educator. Essays by Michael Apple and Leslie G. Roman take up Hall's educational projects, publics and counter-publics, while an interview with Lawrence Grossberg in conversation with Leslie Roman considers Hall's contributions to the New Left, Left politics more generally and Cultural Studies in its formative moments at the Centre for Contemporary Cultural Studies in Birmingham and its potential international futures. He too reflects on Hall's uses of conjunctural thinking.

Part 2 considers the keywords of diaspora and 'diasporic thinking' to Hall's analyses and their importance for public pedagogies. It includes essays by Annette Henry and Fazal Rizvi, as well as an interview with Avtar Brah. Henry examines Hall's diasporic social biographical formation between Kingston, Jamaica, and London, England as part of the Windrush. Henry provides a nuanced account of the relational displacements of diasporic migration already emergent from Hall's co-constructed traumas of familial social biography and Jamaica's tripartite structure of race, color, and class. She shows us that Hall's displacements not only create his impetus to escape Jamaica for London, England on both Jamaica College and Rhodes' scholarships but also to shape his contributions to the New Left and critical public pedagogies. Rizvi, drawing on his first engagements of Hall through the later philosophical thinking of Ludwig Wittgenstein, argues compellingly that 'Hall does not so much as write about racism in or from diaspora, but rather he thinks diasporically, a notion that has significant implications for public pedagogy.' Part 2 takes up Hall's challenges to essentialist thinking about 'culture,' 'race,' 'racism,' and 'nation.' In that vein, like Rizvi, Avtar Brah's interview with Leslie Roman and Annette Henry addresses the ways in which her own diasporic formations in Uganda, Britain, the USA, and Asia (having had homes in four of the five continents), for example, have shaped her critical thinking about transnational feminist politics. An accomplished transnational feminist public intellectual, Brah challenges essentialist thinking about 'culture,' race, gender, and nation, discussing both how Hall informs her work and how she extends his 'keywords' and analyses to issues he does not consider. She considers how the politics of diaspora refracts both what she calls 'intersectional' differences and differences in the experience of migrations from different geopolitically situated nations and ideologies of racialization, gender, and color at specific junctures.

Part 3 engages Hall's concept of 'articulation' and, more particularly, the embodied theory and practice of articulation. Hall's uses of the concept of articulation draw on an interesting productive tension between Gramscian common-sense and poststructural readings of subject formation. Essays by John Clarke and Luis Gandin form the timely backbone of this part. Clarke takes a theoretically and practice-based engaged look the concept of articulation, arguing that 'it is central to the work of cultural politics, to the work of hegemony, and to his practice of embodied pedagogy' in the service of defining who belongs to the 'public.' Gandin, on the other hand, offers an empirical study drawing on Hall's key terms of articulation, common sense, and counter-hegemony to examine neoliberal reform efforts in the case of the Citizen School initiative Porto Allegre, Brazil as a specific example of the implications of the practice of articulation.

There are overlaps and departures among the contributions. There are many ways the contributions could have been organized. For example, some works could be in any of the three parts which again speaks to the success, scope, and living legacies of Hall's counter-hegemonic educational projects. A word about these editorial choices: One over-arching goal is to trace Hall genealogically in intellectual, political, and diasporic terms within, as well as across the sections organized by keywords. Another is to amplify the rich differences of approach to Hall or entrée into his work, also within and across the parts. A third was to be appealing to readers. By this I mean, offering spaces for conversation and a dialogical approach to what Hall's impact has been on education and its cultural politics through both interviews and grounded examples of his conceptual and political ideas as embodied practices, policies, and reforms. I also found that like Hall's approach to productive theoretical tensions, the essays could speak back to one other within and across the three parts of the issue. I encourage readers to take such an approach to reading and teaching this special issue. In these ways, contributors to this issue open a dialog about the political implications of public pedagogies in particular junctures.

Finally, as editor, I make no claim on behalf of the issue and its contributors to be comprehensive. I doubt any single special issue could legitimately tick the box of comprehensiveness in relation to Hall's work over some 60 years. Still, regrettably there are aspects of Hall's work we did not get to have the opportunity to engage – most notably his contributions to diasporic arts, film, and television, which could fill more than one volume. This was not for lack of trying to attract artist and film-maker intellectuals who have benefited from Hall's mentorship. Global travels and commitments of some of the artists Hall mentored prevented them from participating in the time required to think through interviewing or writing in a substantive way even after agreeing to do so. I see this as yet another reason to contemplate the inheritance of Hall's achievements in ways that exceed any one special issue. Fortunately, the essays and interviews of this issue do not sacrifice depth, richness, or nuance even though we recognize that the project of claiming Hall's theoretical, sociopolitical, and biographical lived example, as well as his cultural politics for what they are – a generous and generative inheritance and resources with which we are left to ponder and use well. Thus, this issue testifies to Hall's vision of culture and the cultural politics of education as invitations to become engaged in and creators of the varied enlivening projects of cultural production.

In his own life and work, Hall took many 'detours' – detours from Jamaica to Britain; from finishing his Oxford Ph.D. on Henry James in literature for the sake of building the New Left politics, and finally, from the luxuries of abstracted theory to grounded social movement praxis. He once argued eloquently that 'theory is always a detour on the way to something more important' (Hall, 1997). I, like others, say 'bravo' to Stuart Hall for taking all his detours, from the academy to social movement engagement, from theory to engaged praxis, from hard Left thinking to the politics of affect, memory, diaspora, and difference. All these detours were as we have discovered just the beginning of rethinking who we are and who we may wish to become as publics and counter-publics. Thinking through Hall's keywords is an embodied practice of theorizing. Though he despaired about the state of politics on the Left in the last couple of years of life, particularly those of the Labour Party in Britain, the rich insights from the corpus of his work have yet to be fully engaged for their educational implications and sustenance of the politics of hope and renewal. We hope our issue contributes to Hall's articulation of education as the practices and processes of cultural becoming – as nothing less than claiming the meaning of education and in whose names and publics we educate. Recognizing Stuart Hall's extraordinary educational accomplishments and contributing to his living legacies are a good place to begin again – perhaps we detour.

Notes

1. Retrieved from http://www.theguardian.com/education/2014/feb/10/godfather-multiculturalism-stuart-hall-dies
2. Retrieved from http://www.theguardian.com/commentisfree/2014/may/20/stuart-hall-artist-black-intellectuals
3. Retrieved from http://anniepaul.net/2014/02/10/a-stuart-hall-shaped-hole-in-the-universe/

References

Ang, I. (2000). Identity blues. In P. Gilroy, L. Grossberg, & A. McRobbie (Eds.), *Without guarantees: In honour of Stuart Hall* (pp. 1–11). London/New York: Verso.

Butler, T. (2014, February 10). Godfather of multiculturalism dies—Stuart Hall dies. *The Guardian*. Retrieved from http://www.theguardian.com/education/2014/feb/10/godfather-multiculturalism-stuart-hall-dies

Fisher, J. (2014, May 20). Stuart Hall: The artist who inspired Britain's Black intellectuals. *The Guardian*. Retrieved from http://www.theguardian.com/commentisfree/2014/may/20/stuart-hall-artist-black-intellectuals, n.p.

Giroux, H. A. (2000). Public pedagogy as cultural politics: Stuart Hall and the crisis of culture. *Cultural Studies*, *14*, 341–360. doi:10.1080/095023800334913

Hall, S. (1997). The local and the global: Globalization and ethnicity. In A. D. King (Ed.), *Culture, globalization and the world system: Contemporary conditions for the representation of identity* (pp. 19–40). Minneapolis: University of Minnesota Press.

Hall, S. (2005). Thinking diaspora: Home thoughts from abroad. In G. Desai & S. Nair (Eds.), *Postcolonialisms: An anthology of cultural theory and criticism* (pp. 543–560). New Brunswick, NJ: Rutgers University Press.

Paul, A. (2014). Active Voice: Sharp, pointed, often witty commentary on current events in Jamaica, the Caribbean, India and the world. Retrieved from http://anniepaul.net/

Williams, R. (1976). *Keywords: A vocabulary of culture and society.* London: Croom Helm.

Understanding and interrupting hegemonic projects in education: learning from Stuart Hall

Michael W. Apple[a,b]

[a]Department of Curriculum and Instruction, University of Wisconsin, Madison, USA;
[b]Department of Educational Policy Studies, University of Wisconsin, Madison, USA

Stuart Hall had a significant impact on critical analyses of rightist mobilizations in education. This is very visible in my own work, for example, in such volumes as *Official Knowledge* (2014) and *Educating the 'Right' Way* (2006). After describing an important series of lectures that Stuart Hall gave at the Havens Center for Social Structure and Social Change at the University of Wisconsin, Madison, I detail the nonessentialist position that served as the grounding of Hall's own discussion of race, ideology, and conjuncture, and how it affected so much of the critical examination of neoliberal and neoconservative reconstructions of education. In the context of laying out the tasks of the 'critical scholar/activist in education,' I then portray what we can learn from Hall about the role of the organic intellectual.

Experiencing Stuart Hall

I need to start this essay with a personal and institutional story about the University of Wisconsin that bears directly on my experiences with Stuart Hall.[1] As you will see, there are not only personal reasons for doing this, but also political and theoretical reasons. The story also serves as a grounding for much of what I say in the later parts of this article.

The Havens Center for Social Structure and Social Change is the progressive academic center at the University of Wisconsin, Madison. One of its functions is to sponsor lectures by well-known radical scholars and activists, who spend from one to two weeks giving large lectures, doing intense seminars, and meeting with individual faculty members, students, and activists. The list of people who have been invited includes powerful figures in the social sciences, political economy, literature, gender studies, critical education, cultural studies, critical legal studies, critical race theory, post-colonialism, radical science, ecology, Native American activists, and the list goes on. If I were to include even a partial list of these figures, many of them would be more than a little familiar to the readers of this journal.

I mention all of this for one particular reason. In the nearly four decades that the Havens Center has been in existence, no one has given a more popular and influential set of lectures and seminars than Stuart Hall.[2] This is an important point, for this is definitely what performers would call a 'tough crowd.' It is filled with people who are both intellectually and politically demanding and who thoroughly enjoy the give and take that accompanies serious work. And they can be very challenging.

Let me give an example. When the late and deservedly highly respected sociologist Pierre Bourdieu came to Wisconsin to give a lecture a number of years before he too passed away, for some reason he seemed to take his audience less seriously than many people expected, perhaps because he was not familiar with the long radical intellectual and political tradition associated with Wisconsin. Yet, it was an audience made up of some of the most powerful figures in class analysis, political economy, social theory, gender studies, critical educational studies, and the like in the entire nation. Perhaps it was his 'habitus,' his body 'hexus,' or his 'style,' but a considerable number of people, people who respected his work immensely, were more than a little critical of both the content of his lecture and how he presented it – and they made their criticisms clear.

This was decidedly *not* the case for Stuart Hall. The rich mix of academic excellence and political commitment created a powerful environment for serious discussion. Just as importantly, Hall's way with words, his exceptional ability to take some of the most difficult cultural and political theory and use these resources to illuminate the realities and struggles in which actors and social movements of various kinds were involved was unparalleled. He was able to publicly think through the relationship among culture, economy, and the state; the relationship between empire and race; the connections between Marxist, neo-Marxist, and post-structural approaches; how and why the Right was successful; how to think structure and agency at the same time; and how 'race' was an irreducible dynamic.

When I look at this list, I am immediately reminded of the range of his concerns and of his synthetic abilities. But having been in the audience when he gave those lectures and having been fortunate enough to spend some more personal time with him, I am also struck by his pedagogic ability. These were *difficult* issues, ones that divided – and still divide – people. And yet he brought nearly everyone in and created something for which I have called for in my own work. I (and others of course) have been deeply worried that the Left has not worked hard enough to form the 'decentered unities' that are absolutely essential to counter rightist attacks (Apple, 2006, 2013, 2014).

Yet Stuart Hall made it seem nearly 'easy.' But of course there was nothing easy about it. It was the result of his individual talent, obviously. But it was something more than this. It was an instance of Gramscian theory in practice. Hall understood the ways in which the Left was facing a 'war of position' as well as a 'war of maneuver.' He also understood, profoundly, Gramsci's emphasis on the elements of 'good sense' as well as 'bad sense' in those positions with which one might have significant disagreements and how the Right worked assiduously to connect its arguments to the elements of good sense that actors had (Apple, 2006; Gramsci, 1968, 1992, 1996). He took these theoretical/political principles seriously, employed them, and engaged in the kind of pedagogic work that created space for a critical unity to be created. It was mindful of 'difference' but at the same time demonstrated the ways in which what Nancy Fraser (1997) has called the politics of redistribution and the politics of recognition could work together against the relations of exploitation and domination in the larger society.

This was not my first experience with Stuart Hall's work. I had followed it for a very long time. Indeed, when I was writing two of my books that centered on the issues surrounding how we might both understand and interrupt the Right (Apple, 2006, 2014), Hall's analysis of Thatcherism and of the ways in which race operated at both the discursive/ideological and structural levels had a distinct impact on me. He provided some of the essential insights when I argued that behind a good deal of the Right's ideological assemblage was the creation of a constitutive outside, a set of 'raced others' who were seen as a form of pollution and danger for which only the neoliberal market could provide an answer.

This, for example, continues to be clear in the USA, where neoliberal proposals for marketization and privatization in education such as voucher plans may be couched in the language of escaping from bad state-supported schools, but the reality is that they constitute an attack on the state and on the entire public sphere. While the implications of these attacks are deeply troubling, the reality is that they have been more than a little successful in changing our common sense and in offering what are seemingly workable alternatives to even dispossessed groups. The power of the neoliberal agenda is visible in the hard and partly successful work that the Right has done in convincing many people, including some Black and Latino/Latina activist groups, that neoliberal policies offer a more realistic hope for the future of their children than, say, existing state-supported schools (see Apple, 2006; Apple & Pedroni, 2005; Pedroni, 2007).

Of course, in the face of this set of desocializing policies, the radical transformation of the public sphere into simply one more extension of the private is of no little concern. But, having said this, one should never romanticize the public sphere, as some people in critical education and elsewhere may do, since the public sphere has always been classed, gendered, and raced, with many groups being seen as less than persons and thus unable to participate in what counted as the public (Fraser, 1987; Mills, 1997). In fact, this may be one of the reasons that some aspects of neoliberal policies, with their vision of empowering the rational economic actor, may be attractive to racialized groups.

In societies where, say, Black people are tragically seen by dominant groups as irrational and dangerous – in essence as forms of pollution – the very idea of a set of policies that provides an identity *as fully rational* is partly counter-hegemonic. Thus, the reappropriation of neoliberal ideologies by oppressed people of color is actually a fascinating, and contradictory, example of the ways in which dispossessed groups disarticulate ideological positions from these positions' original site and then rearticulate them for use for their own purposes (Apple & Pedroni, 2005; Pedroni, 2007). For those of you who are familiar with Hall's work on the ways in which discourses and movements can be pulled under the umbrellas of groups that are very different from their origin, this very process of disarticulation and rearticulation sits at the heart of much of his political theory, and in large part because of his influence, certainly my own. One thing can be certain, this is not the only instance where Hall paid attention to the real world.

Hall has written critically about the complexities of all of this personally when he reflects on what being schooled around colonial forms of understanding meant to him, how the study of what were seen as the great western literary works helped create complex identities for those scholars of color who 'came home' to England (see Meeks, 2007). Hall is not reductive about any of this and points, as usual, both to contradictions and fissures that create alternative and oppositional readings of the formal corpus of 'great literature' and to the ways in which identities are partly formed around them. In this, he creatively extends a Gramscian understanding of the contradictory spaces such works provide and of the possibilities of counter-hegemonic reading and practices that are possible (see also Apple, 2014). Like all of his writings, political commitments are mixed with subtlety and a sense of complexity but always in the service of a politics of interruption of dominant structures, processes, and understandings.

Michael Ruskin (2007) captures this aspect of Hall's subtle understanding of the nature of the structures we face when he says that:

> Unless one took full note of the creative and inventive capacities of the system one was basically opposed to, one had no chance of generating an effective oppositional response to it. This has been an almost universal principle in his political writings. (p. 22)

This may be one of the reasons I personally have responded so well to Hall's writings over the years. All too much of the Left has dealt with the very real crises we are experiencing in a largely rhetorical way, but with a less than satisfactory understanding of the balance of forces we face and a none too subtle analysis of the strategic actions and alliances that the Right has built and of the counter-hegemonic actions and alliances that need to be built to interrupt them (Apple, 2006, 2013; see also Wright, 2010).

This is one of the reasons that over the past two decades I have focused a good deal of my attention on a Gramscian-inspired project that is best thought of as 'understanding and interrupting the Right.' I have argued that if you want to counter the Right's hegemonic project look very carefully at how they became hegemonic. What did they do? How did they do it? Like Hall, I want us to take very seriously the fact that 'conservative modernization' has involved a vast, and partly successful, social/pedagogic project of changing common sense, a project in which not only class but also race plays a constitutive part.[3] Only by taking 'full note of the creative and inventive capacities of the system one was basically opposed to,' only then could those of us in education begin to think through what was possible (Apple, 1996, 2006, 2014).

As Hall showed early on in his critical analyses of the rise of Thatcherism, issues of 'law and order' and the repressive forms of authoritarian populism that they spawned and that were spawned by them had much of their grounding in 'race.' Economic anxieties were *dialectically* connected to an entire history of racializing discourses and practices. They were not the automatic workings of economic dynamics, although they were clearly connected to these dynamics. They were both produced by and themselves produced a creative ideological process of disarticulation and rear-ticulation, a process that required hard political and ideological work on the part of rightist movements.

But even given the power of his arguments about race and the growth of the Right, Hall was very clear here as well about his commitment to avoid essentializing categories. For there was not one kind of racism, always static, always predetermined. Rather, racism was plural. Once again historical specificity must be recognized. As he puts it:

> Racism [should not be] dealt with as a general feature of human societies, but with historically specific racisms. Beginning with an assumption of difference, of specificity rather than of a unitary, transhistorical or universal 'structure' … one cannot explain racism in abstraction from other social relations …. One must start, then, from the concrete historical 'work' which racism accomplishes under specific historical conditions – a set of economic,

political and ideological practice, of a discursive kind, concretely articulated with other practices in a social formation. (Hall, quoted in Brah, 2007, p. 76)

Or as he says elsewhere:

No doubt there are certain general features to racism. But even more significant are the ways in which these general features are modified and transformed by the historical specificity of the contexts and environments in which they become active. (Hall, quoted in Grossberg, 2007, p. 105)

Hall is not a romantic here, nor does he see the world in only discursive terms. Racism(s) can be and are utterly damaging and murderous. But the key for any concrete analysis of the current balance of forces is how racism is constructed and employed in supporting dominance in a specific historic conjuncture. And here the resonances with previous generations of anti-colonial writings are present, with their focus on the specifics of empire, identity, and subaltern struggles. Such a conjunctural understanding provided much of the grounding for the analysis I noted earlier that Tom Pedroni and I did of the ways neoliberalism was partly taken up by racialized groups as a strategic form of identity construction and interruption.

Lawrence Grossberg, one of the wisest of the commentators on Hall's corpus, catches Hall's methodological impulses perfectly when he says that in Hall's critical interrogations of race, like in all of his writings:

[T]he appropriate level of analysis – and theorizing – is always at the level of specific contexts, or what he sometimes calls conjunctures. It is the level at which any social reality is overdetermined, existing as a configuration of relationships that are constantly open to re-articulation. At this level of the concrete, relations are themselves articulated, not into a simple unity but into a condensation of differences, an articulated unity. Analysis at this level involves mapping the 'redisposition of elements with a configuration.' (Hall, quoted in Grossberg, 2007, pp. 99–100)[4]

This is a fundamentally Gramscian interpretation, one that understands race and racism as fully embedded in reality in much the same way as, say, Critical Race Theory sees race as a constitutive dynamic, not an add on (Gillborn, 2008; Ladson-Billings, 2009; Leonardo, 2009a, 2009b). But it also insists that the workings of race can best be understood as part of a larger social formation that is a 'complexly articulated unity' (Grossberg, 2007, p. 107). Such a social formation is made up of fractures and conflicts, with multiple axes of power. There is a constant process in which dominant groups seek stability through diverse practices. All of this constantly involves processes of struggle, compromise, and negotiation. And, once again, all of this cannot be understood without a keen sense of the issues and relations surrounding 'intersectionality,' the complex and often contradictory ways in which differential power relations relate to and struggle with each other (Bhopal & Preston, 2012; Gillborn, 2008). It is this very principle that has guided much of my work on the classed and raced relations that are produced in and by educational policies and struggles as well.

In terms I have used elsewhere that do not quite capture the specific complexities about which Hall is talking, simply because the concepts remain at too abstract a level, the problem is how to think through the relationship between the economic, the political, and the cultural and how at the same time to also think through the specific relations of exploitation and domination – and struggles against them – in each of these spheres (Apple, 2012).[5]

This sense of complexity and of difference does not make Hall into what Charles Mills (1997), himself an eminent critical analyst of race, a 'university postmodernist.' As Mills says, even though at times Stuart Hall seems sympathetic to some postmodern and post-structural claims about, say, identity, difference, and discourse, 'he is wary … of the self-indulgences and academic language games of university postmodernism' (Mills, 2007, p. 136). But clearly, neither is Hall a traditional kind of Marxist. His is a heterodox, not orthodox position, something for which I too have a good deal of sympathy. Indeed, I do not think that it is possible to understand and interrupt the relations of exploitation and domination in education without taking such a position (Apple, 2013).

I have noted that Stuart Hall has had a profound influence on critical scholarship in an entire range of fields – and most certainly on me and others in critical educational and cultural studies. His influence on people such as myself is not odd. After all, in many ways, not only has he been a teacher, but he has always been about 'education' in the very broadest sense of that term as well. As many readers will already know, he spent much of his academic life as the director of what was then the University of Birmingham Center for Contemporary Cultural Studies and then as a professor at the Open University. The first institution produced some of the most powerful books ever published on the politics of culture, on empire, on the intersections of class, race, and gender, and on so many other crucial issues. It sought to redefine the terrain of how we think about identity and cultural struggles and the institutions that now define them both historically and now before it was closed through a deeply controversial act of 'restructuring' by the university in 2002.

In terms of the second, with all of its very real contradictions the Open University has also been a crucial site of cultural politics in its own right. As a site where the conflicts over what counts as 'tradition,' over official knowledge, over who can and should know it, the Open University at least partly has at times and in certain areas embodied what Raymond Williams (1961) so nicely called 'the long revolution' (although important parts of that set of historical commitments have been lost or made simply rhetorical by the Open University more currently).[6] Like Williams, Hall always recognized that 'culture is ordinary' and that insurgent movements have cultural preconditions and involve intense battles over recognition.

Stuart Hall's focus on the politics of culture, on the ways in which the media work, on the creation of nationalism and identity, on the role of the intellectual – all of this was clear throughout his work. His post-retirement efforts as chair of the International Institute for the Visual Arts (inIVA) had as a centerpiece a commitment to 'ethnic' perspectives on the visual arts, thereby once again demonstrating his continuing concern with the question of voice and representation and with diasporic imaginations. Furthermore, Hall's activist and organizational work on art and the creation of places for alternative and counter-hegemonic narratives and representations is crucial. It reminds me of what education can be and often is, when it is not turned into a factory for the production of paid and unpaid labor, for the reproduction of racializing processes and outcomes, or for the production of statistics of educational defeat that seem to be so beloved among the new managerial measurement gurus who act as experts for hire for neoliberal and neoconservative agendas in education and social policy.

The alternate view of education in its broadest sense, one that is linked to insurgent voices and to struggles against the relations of dominance and subordination in all of their lived complexity was central to Hall's project. This is popular education as it should be thought about –as embodied in people, movements, and institutions that can go well beyond the corridors of officially sanctioned spaces and places.

Stuart Hall and the tasks of the critical scholar/activist

Given what I have said so far, in the last part of this essay I want to speak more generally about what it is that figures such as Stuart Hall do for us and for the larger field of education. In the process, I will argue that Hall was and continues to be a model for those of us in education who take on the role of the 'public intellectual' or as I say elsewhere the *critical scholar/activist* (Apple, 2013).

As Hall – and such figures in critical education such as Paulo Freire – recognized, serious theory about culture and politics, about curriculum and pedagogy, and about education inside and outside of schools, needs to be done in relation to its object. Indeed, this is not only a political imperative but an epistemological one as well. The development of critical theoretical resources is best done when it is dialectically and intimately connected to actual movements and struggles (Apple, 2006; Apple et al., 2003), and to the *specific* conjunctural balance of forces and their histories and possibilities that exist.

Speaking specifically to a sociological audience, what Michael Burawoy (2005) has called 'organic public sociology' helps us understand this and provides key elements of how we might think about the nature of these connections and commitments. In his words, but partly echoing Gramsci as well, in this view the critical sociologist:

> works in close connection with a visible, thick, active, local, and often counter-public. [She or he works] with a labor movement, neighborhood association, communities of faith, immigrant rights groups, human rights organizations. Between the public sociologist and a public is a dialogue, a process of mutual education ... The project of such [organic] public sociologies is to make visible the invisible, to make the private public, to validate these organic connections as part of our sociological life. (Burawoy, 2005, p. 265)

This act of becoming (and this is a *project*, for one is *never* finished, *always* becoming) a critical scholar/activist is a complex one, but it helps us understand some of the many contributions that Stuart Hall made. Because of this, let me say some things about the role of critical research and the critical researcher in education. My points here are tentative and certainly not exhaustive. But they are meant to begin a dialog over just what it is that 'we' should do.

In general, there are nine tasks in which critical analysis (and the critical analyst) in education must engage (Apple, 2013):

(1) It must 'bear witness to negativity.'[7] That is, one of its primary functions is to illuminate the ways in which educational policy and practice are connected to the relations of exploitation and domination – and to struggles against such relations – in the larger society.[8] Hall's analyses of neoliberalism are exemplary in this regard.

(2) In engaging in such critical analyses, it also must point to contradictions and to spaces of possible action. Thus, its aim is to critically examine current realities

with a conceptual/political framework that emphasizes the spaces in which more progressive and counter-hegemonic actions can, or do, go on. Documenting these spaces and the agentic possibilities and actions that already exist needs to be done at the level of individual experience and at the institutional level. This is an absolutely crucial step, since otherwise our research can simply lead to cynicism or despair. What consistently characterized Hall's efforts was its cogent account of the creativity that the Right employed in working off of and on the elements of good sense that people had and on the possibility that domination was never 'automatic.' Interruptions were possible at every level. This was a key element in much of what characterized the work of the Center for Contemporary Cultural Studies both during and after Hall's period of leadership.

(3) At times, this also requires a broadening of what counts as 'research.' Here I mean acting as critical 'secretaries' to those groups of people and social movements who are now engaged in challenging existing relations of unequal power or in what elsewhere has been called 'nonreformist reforms,' a term that has a long history in critical sociology and critical educational studies (Apple, 2012). This is exactly the task that was taken on in Freire's descriptions of his pedagogic work with oppressed people in Brazil (Freire, 1971), in the thick descriptions of critically democratic school practices in *Democratic Schools* (Apple & Beane, 2007; see also Gutstein, 2006; Watson, 2012) and in the critically supportive descriptions of the transformative reforms such as the Citizen School and participatory budgeting in Porto Alegre, Brazil (see Apple, 2013; Apple, Au, & Gandin, 2009; Apple, Ball, & Gandin, 2010). When accompanied by truly cooperative work with those individuals and groups who are building successful programs, institutions, and alternatives, this increases the power of such descriptions. Through his own writing and the many books that emerged from the Center for Contemporary Cultural Studies and the Open University, real alternatives, real struggles now and in the past, were constantly being documented whether in social movements, in the actual uses of cultural commodities, and in lived cultures and institutions.

(4) When Gramsci (1992, 1996) argued that one of the tasks of a truly counter-hegemonic education was not to throw out 'elite knowledge' but to reconstruct its form and content so that it served genuinely progressive social needs, he provided a key to another role 'organic' and 'public' intellectuals might play. Thus, we should not be engaged in a process of what might be called 'intellectual suicide.' That is, there are serious intellectual (and pedagogic) skills in dealing with the histories and debates surrounding the epistemological, political, and educational issues involved in justifying what counts as important knowledge and what counts as an effective and socially just education. These are not simple and inconsequential issues and the practical and intellectual/political skills of dealing with them have been well developed. However, they can atrophy if they are not used. We can give back these skills by employing them to assist communities in thinking about this, learning from them, and engaging in the mutually pedagogic dialogs that enable decisions to be made in terms of both the short-term and long-term interests of dispossessed peoples (see Burawoy, 2005). This commitment to 'giving back' and doing so in a way that also showed respect for the knowledge and new perspectives that were being developed is clear in Hall's corpus. He was not a

'vulgar populist' who felt that theoretical, empirical, and historical resources and the continual development of new resources had no place in the long revolution.

(5) In the process, critical work has the task of keeping the multiple traditions of radical and progressive work alive (see Apple et al., 2009, 2010). In the face of organized attacks on the 'collective memories' of difference and on critical social movements, attacks that make it increasingly difficult to retain academic and social legitimacy for multiple critical approaches that have proven so valuable in countering dominant narratives and relations, it is absolutely crucial that these traditions be kept alive, renewed, and when necessary criticized for their conceptual, empirical, historical, and political silences or limitations. This involves being cautious of reductionism and essentialism and asks us to pay attention to what Fraser (1997) has called both the politics of redistribution and the politics of recognition and to what Lynch, Baker, and Lyons (2009) call *affective equality*. This includes not only keeping theoretical, empirical, historical, and political traditions alive but also, very importantly, extending and (supportively) criticizing them. And it also involves keeping alive the dreams, utopian visions, and 'nonreformist reforms' that are so much a part of these radical traditions (Apple, 2012; Jacoby, 2005; Teitelbaum, 1993; Wright, 2010). 'Purity' should not be our goal. Instead, we should be guided by an openness to expanding the critical understandings we need to more fully cope with the range of dynamics and their intersections that are so destructive in our societies. As I noted at the outset of this article, I can think of no one who better exemplifies this openness better than Stuart Hall. If the Right has been so successful in part because it has been willing to build alliances across some of its substantive differences, so too should the Left (Apple, 2006, 2013; see also Apple & Buras, 2006).

(6) Keeping such traditions alive and also supportively criticizing them when they are not adequate to deal with current realities cannot be done unless we ask 'For whom are we keeping them alive?' and 'How and in what form are they to be made available?' All of the things I have mentioned above in this taxonomy of tasks require the relearning or development and use of varied or new skills of working at many levels with multiple groups. Thus, journalistic and media skills, academic and popular skills, and the ability to speak to very different audiences are increasingly crucial (Apple, 2006; Boler, 2008). This requires us to learn how to speak in different registers and to say important things in ways that do not require that the audience or reader does all of the work.[9] As his lectures at Wisconsin and his many interviews and more popular writings demonstrated, Hall was nearly unparalleled in his ability to do this.

(7) Critical educators need also to *act* in concert with the progressive social movements their work supports or in movements against the rightist assumptions and policies they critically analyze. This is another reason that scholarship in critical education implies becoming an 'organic' or 'public' intellectual. One must participate in and give one's expertise to movements whose aim is the transformation of both a politics of redistribution and a politics of recognition. It also implies learning from these social movements (Anyon, 2014). This means that the role of the 'unattached intelligentsia' (Mannheim, 1936), someone who 'lives on the balcony' (Bakhtin, 1968), is not an appropriate model. As Bourdieu (2003, p. 11) reminds us, for example, our intellectual efforts are crucial, but they

'cannot stand aside, neutral and indifferent, from the struggles in which the future of the world is at stake.' From his early work, to his participation in the writing of the *May Day Manifesto* in the 1960s, to his efforts in *New Left Review*, to his writings about the social and economic crises afflicting minoritized peoples, to his later challenges to neoliberalism and to the Left's at times too mechanistic understanding of it, to his tireless work at the OU in clarifying issues surrounding identity, nationalism, and so much more – and the list could go on and on – the signifiers of 'balcony' and 'Hall' cannot easily be used in the same sentence.

(8) Building on the points made in the previous paragraph, the critical scholar/activist has another role to play. She or he needs to act as a deeply committed mentor, as someone who demonstrates through her or his life what it means to be *both* an excellent researcher and a committed member of a society that is scarred by persistent inequalities. She or he needs to show how one can blend these two roles together in ways that may be tense, but still embody the dual commitments to exceptional and socially committed writing and research and participating in movements whose aim is interrupting dominance. The fact that this journal and many others are now publishing special editions on Hall, that numerous articles on his work and influence are now appearing across traditional boundaries (see, e.g., Blackburn, 2014), and that his work and career are celebrated in the popular press and at events sponsored by political movements, signifies that many people who also refuse to stand on the balcony see him as a model.

(9) Finally, participation also means using the privilege one has as a scholar/activist, as a 'public intellectual.' That is, each of us needs to make use of one's privilege to open the spaces at universities and elsewhere for those who are not there, for those who do not now have a voice in that space and in the 'professional' sites to which, being in a privileged position, you have access. This can be seen, for example, in the history of another program at the Havens Center at the University of Wisconsin, the 'activist-in-residence' program, where committed activists in various areas (the environment, indigenous rights, housing, labor, racial disparities, education, and so on) were brought in to teach and to connect our academic work with organized action against dominant relations. (In many ways, Hall's participation in the Havens Center served as a bridge between the academic and the activist programs.) Or it can be seen in a number of Women's Studies programs and Indigenous, Aboriginal, and First Nation Studies programs that historically have involved activists in these communities as active participants in the governance and educational programs of these areas at universities. I cannot speak to Stuart Hall's contributions here. But given what I have already said in this section and in the earlier parts of this essay, I have little doubt that Hall would be in strong agreement with this commitment and the set of institutional policies it creates.

These nine tasks are demanding. In most areas, and certainly in the field of education inside and outside of its formal setting, no one person can engage equally well in all of them simultaneously. Confronting the realities of education in a deeply unequal and often uncaring society so that we can *collectively* take them seriously will never be easy. What we can do is honestly continue our attempt to come to grips with the complex intellectual, personal, and political tensions and activities that respond to the demands of this role. Actually, although at times problematic, a concept that Hall himself helped us think about in complex ways – 'identity' – may be a more useful term here. It is a better way to conceptualize the interplay among these tensions and positions, since it speaks to the possible multiple positioning one may have and the contradictory ideological forms that may be at work both within oneself and in any specific context (see Youdell, 2011). And this requires a searching critical examination of one's own structural location, one's own overt and tacit political commitments, and one's own embodied actions once this recognition in all its complexities and contradictions is taken as seriously as it deserves.

I can think of no one who embodied the personal and political struggles to engage in these tasks better than Stuart Hall. Indeed, it is important to note that when I was originally thinking through these tasks in the context of critical educational studies, perhaps it is also a sign of the influence that Hall had on me that the person who came to mind repeatedly was Stuart Hall.

A final personal statement

As Paul Warmington (2014) has so clearly documented, there have been other notable diasporic leftist intellectuals of color who have understood the role of the popular in the formation of identities and in the politics of empire and whose work has carved out paths that have enabled many people to go forward both politically and intellectually, among them, for example, CLR James (see also Grimshaw, 1992; James, 1993). Stuart Hall himself would have recognized that he was not a solitary figure, but a member of a long historical trajectory of diasporic critical public intellectuals – a role in which both of these terms needed to be acted upon. Like many people, I hope to have shown in this essay that I too owe a considerable debt to this tradition and especially to Hall. And one of my continuing responsibilities is to keep this tradition, and the ways in which Hall pushed it further, alive and vital.

Interestingly, in a recent essay about my own work over the years, a well-known sociologist of education stated that I was a 'public intellectual' and compared me to figures such as Stuart Hall (Ball, 2007). Whether it is true or not is up to others to decide. But there is no doubt in my mind that this is the nicest compliment any progressive scholar/activist can receive. Hall indeed was (yes, it is still so very hard to use the past tense) a person who those of us who are deeply concerned with the intimate connections between culture and power both inside and outside of education – and with radically transforming these relations – could use as a cogent model for our own efforts. It undoubtedly will be difficult, but I and many others will certainly continue the struggle to do so.

Notes

1. Portions of this essay are drawn from Apple (2013) and Apple (2008).
2. Hall was awarded the Lifetime Achievement Award by the Havens Center in recognition of his powerful influence and deep connections with counter-hegemonic understandings and movements. There are of course a large number of books devoted to Hall that have been published. To name just a few, see Morley and Chen (1996), Davis (2004), Proctor (2004), and Meeks (2007). The list gets more extensive by the year.
3. The list of Hall's writings that strongly influenced me – and continue to do so – is extensive, but among the most important were Hall (1980, 1983, 1985, 1986a, 1986b, 1988) and Hall and Jacques (1983). Among other things, his later work on neoliberalism and the creation of alternatives in the journal *Soundings* is also crucial and continues to influence me and many others.

4. Hall's arguments about the complexities of race and on the ways in which such rearticulation work in contradictory and at times partly progressive ways both historically and now has influenced a range of discussions in multiple disciplines and multiple nations. See, for example, the influence of his work in discussions of the history of gender, race, and slavery in the Caribbean in Green (2007) and of the lived experiences of popular culture and the politics of the body in Niaah and Hope (2007).
5. There are of course specifically Althusserian echoes here.
6. However, important parts of the tradition of thinking about the complex theories and politics of a more conjunctural analysis that Hall embodied at the Open University are kept alive and extended by many people there. This is evident, for example, in the important work on the changing nature of the state and the nature and effects of neoliberalism. See the analyses of John Clarke and Janet Newman, such as Newman and Clarke (2009), Clarke, Newman, Smith, Vidler, and Westmarland (2007), and Clarke and Newman (1997).
7. I am aware that the idea of 'bearing witness' has religious connotations, ones that are powerful in the west, but may be seen as a form of religious imperialism in other religious traditions. I still prefer to use it because of its powerful resonances with ethical discourses. But I welcome suggestions from, say, Muslim critical educators and researchers for alternative concepts that can call forth similar responses. I want to thank Amy Stambach for this point.
8. Here, exploitation and domination are technical not rhetorical terms. The first refers to economic relations, the structures of inequality, the control of labor, and the distribution of resources in a society. The latter refers to the processes of representation and respect and to the ways in which people have identities imposed on them. These are analytic categories, of course, and are ideal types. Most oppressive conditions are partly a combination of the two. These map on to what Fraser (1997) calls the politics of redistribution and the politics of recognition.
9. I would hope that it should go without saying that these skills and values should be deeply present in one's teaching as well.

References

Anyon, J. (2014). *Radical possibilities: Public policy, urban education, and a new social movement* (2nd ed.). New York, NY: Routledge.

Apple, M. W. (1996). *Cultural politics and education*. New York, NY: Teachers College Press.

Apple, M. W. (2006). *Educating the 'right' way: Markets, standards, God, and inequality* (2nd ed.). New York, NY: Routledge.

Apple, M. W. (2008). Racisms, power, and contingency. *Race, Ethnicity and Education, 11*, 329–336. doi:10.1080/13613320802291207

Apple, M. W. (2012). *Education and power* (revised Routledge Classic edition). New York, NY: Routledge.

Apple, M. W. (2013). *Can education change society?* New York, NY: Routledge.

Apple, M. W. (2014). *Official knowledge: Democratic education in a conservative age* (3rd ed.). New York, NY: Routledge.

Apple, M. W., Aasen, P., Cho, M. K., Gandin, L. A., Oliver, A., Sung, Y.-K., … Wong, T.-H. (2003). *The state and the politics of knowledge*. New York, NY: Routledge.

Apple, M. W., Au, W., & Gandin, L. A. (Eds.). (2009). *The Routledge international handbook of critical education*. New York, NY: Routledge.

Apple, M. W., Ball, S., & Gandin, L. A. (Eds.). (2010). *The Routledge international handbook of the sociology of education*. New York, NY: Routledge.

Apple, M. W., & Beane, J. A. (Eds.). (2007). *Democratic schools: Lessons in powerful education*. Portsmouth, NH: Heineman.

Apple, M. W., & Buras, K. L. (Eds.). (2006). *The subaltern speak: Curriculum, power, and educational struggles*. New York, NY: Routledge.

Apple, M. W., & Pedroni, T. C. (2005). Conservative alliance building and African American support of vouchers: The end of Brown's promise or a new beginning? *Teachers College Record, 107*, 2068–2105. doi:10.1111/j.1467-9620.2005.00585.x

Bakhtin, M. (1968). *Rabelais and his world*. Cambridge, MA: MIT Press.

Ball, S. (2007). Reading Michael Apple – The sociological imagination at work. *Theory and Research in Education, 5*, 153–159. doi:10.1177/1477878507077726

Bhopal, K., & Preston, J. (Eds.). (2012). *Intersectionality and 'race' in education*. New York, NY: Routledge.

Blackburn, R. (2014, March–April). Stuart Hall. *New Left Review, 86*, 75–93.

Boler, M. (Ed.). (2008). *Digital media and democracy: Tactics in hard times*. Cambridge, MA: MIT Press.

Bourdieu, P. (2003). *Firing back: Against the tyranny of the market 2*. New York, NY: New Press.

Brah, A. (2007). Feminism, 'race' and Stuart Hall's diasporic imagination. In B. Meeks (Ed.), *Class, politics, race and diaspora: The thought of Stuart Hall* (pp. 73–82). London: Lawrence and Wishart; Kingston: Ian Randle.

Burawoy, M. (2005). For public sociology. *British Journal of Sociology, 56*, 259–294.

Clarke, J., & Newman, J. (1997). *The managerial state: Power, politics, and ideology in the remaking of social welfare*. Thousand Oaks, CA: SAGE.

Clarke, J., Newman, J., Smith, N., Vidler, L., & Westmarland, L. (2007). *Creating citizen-consumers: Changing publics and changing public services*. Thousand Oaks, CA: SAGE.

Davis, H. (2004). *Understanding Stuart Hall*. Thousand Oaks, CA: SAGE.

Fraser, N. (1987). *Unruly practices*. Minneapolis: University of Minnesota Press.

Fraser, N. (1997). *Justice interruptus*. New York, NY: Routledge.

Freire, P. (1971). *Pedagogy of the oppressed*. New York, NY: Continuum.

Gillborn, D. (2008). *Racism and education: Coincidence or conspiracy*. New York, NY: Routledge.

Gramsci, A. (1968). *The modern prince and other writings*. New York, NY: International.

Gramsci, A. (1992). *Prison notebooks, volume 1*. New York, NY: Columbia University Press.

Gramsci, A. (1996). *Prison notebooks, volume 2*. New York, NY: Columbia University Press.

Green, C. (2007). Unspeakable worlds and muffled voices. In B. Meeks (Ed.), *Class, politics, race and diaspora: The thought of Stuart Hall* (pp. 151–184). London: Lawrence and Wishart; Kingston: Ian Randle.

Grimshaw, A. (Ed.). (1992). *The C.L.R. James reader*. Oxford: Blackwell.

Grossberg, L. (2007). Stuart Hall on race and racism: Cultural studies and the practice of contextualism. In B. Meeks (Ed.), *Class, politics, race and diaspora: The thought of Stuart Hall* (pp. 98–119). London: Lawrence and Wishart; Kingston: Ian Randle.

Gutstein, E. (2006). *Reading and writing the world with mathematics*. New York, NY: Routledge.

Hall, S. (1980). Popular democratic vs. authoritarian populism: Two ways of taking democracy seriously. In A. Hunt (Ed.), *Marxism and democracy* (pp. 150–170). London: Lawrence & Wishart.

Hall, S. (1983). The great moving right show. In S. Hall & M. Jacques (Eds.), *The politics of Thatcherism* (pp. 19–39). London: Lawrence & Wishart.

Hall, S. (1985, May/June). Authoritarian populism: A reply. *New Left Review, 151*, 115–124.

Hall, S. (1986a). Popular culture and the state. In T. Bennett, C. Mercer, & J. Woollacott (Eds.), *Popular culture and social relations* (pp. 22–49). Milton Keynes: Open University Press.

Hall, S. (1986b). Variants of liberalism. In J. Donald & S. Hall (Eds.), *Politics and ideology* (pp. 34–69). Milton Keynes: Open University Press.

Hall, S. (1988). The toad in the garden: Thatcherism among the theorists. In C. Nelson & L. Grossberg (Eds.), *Marxism and the interpretation of culture* (pp. 35–57). Urbana, IL: University of Illinois Press.

Hall, S., & Jacques, M. (1983). Introduction. In S. Hall & M. Jacques (Eds.), *The politics of Thatcherism* (pp. 6–16). London: Lawrence & Wishart.

Jacoby, R. (2005). *Picture imperfect: Utopian thought for an anti-utopian age*. New York, NY: Columbia University Press.

James, C. L. R. (1993). *Beyond the boundary*. Durham, NC: Duke University Press.

Ladson-Billings, G. (2009). Race *still* matters: Critical race theory in education. In M. W. Apple, W. Au, & L. A. Gandin (Eds.), *Routledge international handbook of critical education* (pp. 110–122). New York, NY: Routledge.

Leonardo, Z. (2009a). Pale/ontology: The status of whiteness in education. In M. W. Apple, W. Au, & L. A. Gandin (Eds.), *Routledge international handbook of critical education* (pp. 123–136). New York, NY: Routledge.

Leonardo, Z. (2009b). *Race, whiteness, and education*. New York, NY: Routledge.

Lynch, K., Baker, J., & Lyons, M. (2009). *Affective equality: Love, care, and injustice*. New York, NY: Palgrave Macmillan.

Mannheim, K. (1936). *Ideology and utopia*. New York, NY: Harvest Books.

Meeks, B. (Ed.). (2007). *Class, politics, race and diaspora: The thought of Stuart Hall*. London: Lawrence and Wishart; Kingston: Ian Randle.

Mills, C. (1997). *The racial contract*. London: Cornell University Press.

Mills, C. (2007). Stuart Hall's changing representations of 'race'. In B. Meeks (Ed.), *Class, politics, race and diaspora: The thought of Stuart Hall* (pp. 120–148). London: Lawrence and Wishart; Kingston: Ian Randle.

Morley, D., & Chen, K.-H. (Eds.). (1996). *Stuart Hall: Critical dialogues in cultural studies*. New York: Routledge.

Newman, J., & Clarke, J. (2009). *Publics, politics and power: Remaking the public in public services*. Thousand Oaks, CA: SAGE.

Niaah, S., & Hope, D. (2007). Canvasses of representation: Stuart Hall, the body, and dancehall performance. In B. Meeks (Ed.), *Class, politics, race and diaspora: The thought of Stuart Hall* (pp. 218–248). London: Lawrence and Wishart; Kingston: Ian Randle.

Pedroni, T. (2007). *Market matters: African American involvement in school voucher reform*. New York, NY: Routledge.

Procter, J. (2004). *Stuart Hall*. New York: Routledge.

Ruskin, M. (2007). 'Working from the symptom': Stuart Hall's political writing. In B. Meeks (Ed.), *Class, politics, race and diaspora: The thought of Stuart Hall* (pp. 19–44). London: Lawrence & Wishart; Kingston: Ian Randle.

Teitelbaum, K. (1993). *Schooling for good rebels*. Philadelphia, PA: Temple University Press.

Warmington, P. (2014). *Black British intellectuals and education: Multiculturalism's hidden history*. New York, NY: Routledge.

Watson, V. (2012). *Learning to liberate: Community-based solutions to the crisis in urban education*. New York, NY: Routledge.

Williams, R. (1961). *The long revolution*. London: Chatto & Windus.

Wright, E. O. (2010). *Envisioning real utopias*. New York, NY: Verso.

Youdell, D. (2011). *School trouble: Identity, power, and politics in education*. New York, NY: Routledge.

Conjunctural thinking – "pessimism of the intellect, optimism of the will": Lawrence Grossberg remembers Stuart Hall

Leslie G. Roman

Educational Studies, Faculty of Education, University of British Columbia, Vancouver, Canada

Lawrence Grossberg, a key figure in Cultural Studies, both in the USA and internationally, reminisces about Stuart Hall as a political intellectual and teacher. He talks about Stuart Hall's impact on him, as well as on Cultural Studies, education, and the Left more generally. The interview traces how Hall and Cultural Studies have been taken up, not only in the UK and the USA but also in other parts of the world. Grossberg points out some of the misunderstood aspects of Hall's intellectual and political contributions, and perhaps more importantly, how Hall taught him and others on the Left to think and act conjuncturally, defining new practices of intellectual work as cultural politics. Grossberg, together with Leslie G. Roman, thinks about the difficult state and future of Cultural Studies and education in the current context. The interview concludes with a moving homage about Hall's legacies as an extraordinary teacher and public intellectual.

Notations:

LG: Responses by Lawrence Grossberg
LGR: Questions asked by Leslie G. Roman

Political grief and formations of political selves

LGR (Leslie G. Roman): Your homage to Stuart Hall speaks about your loss of him as "political grief" and not just the more familiar "emotional grief." I was moved by that uncommon description. Can you speak to the ways in which you and no doubt many diverse publics experienced his loss as "political grief"?

LG (Lawrence Grossberg): Wow! It's always difficult when you're called upon to explain poetic images. For many people, certainly for me personally, Stuart, in many dimensions, embodied a unique way of being in the world politically. He lived his life and personal relations as part of that way of being, through his commitments to political struggles, education and the art world, as well as to intellectual work; they were all a piece of the whole. They created a kind of totality greater than the sum of its parts.

His life – and loves of many sorts – was defined as a kind of political act of being in the world. More than any single person I have ever encountered, Stuart embodied a way of being a political subject I try to emulate.

Part of that political way of being in the world was to really embody, in ways that I have never quite been able to comprehend. "Comprehend" is not quite the right word because I do understand it intellectually – that motto coined by French writer, Romain Rolland and then developed[1] by Gramsci that he loved so much, commonly formulated as "pessimism of the intellect, optimism of the will." Stuart lived that.

Stuart was critical of and disappointed by what was happening in the world – that, even given the constraints under which we must operate at any moment, we too often failed to see the possibilities, and so we continue to make the world not only inhumane but increasingly inhumane.

Yet, at the same time, he never let anger and pessimism rule his life. He always found the openings. He always believed that his function, his role, his position was to turn that intellectual pessimism toward the possibilities that the world offered to us, to make it a better place. His is the loss of a political subjectivity that I don't see much of in the world, embodying it through his laugh, voice, presence, generosity, and words, as well as his intellect, scholarship, and politics.

Many, who knew Stuart personally, loved him. Equally important, many who didn't know him personally still loved him. I think we mourn the loss of a man and a particular political subject.

Relational genealogies: from the New Left to Cultural Studies at Birmingham

LGR: I very much relate to what you have just so beautifully described. The subjectivity you described is uncommon and rare in the academy, not just now, but especially now, but in my entire history as an academic, rare.

LG: And it's not just in the academy, you know? I am hard-pressed to find political leaders, whether political figures or subjects on the Left who can mobilize – who have that kind of – I think people too quickly and easily characterize it, dismiss it, worship it as charisma. It wasn't charisma in the normal sense of the word because it was a kind of earned charisma. It was an embodied pedagogy, which, in the end, made people respect Stuart in ways that very few other political intellectuals or activist leaders have been respected.

Few people ever criticized or argued with him from anything but a position of extraordinary respect and admiration. In part, it was because Stuart never assumed he was right that the question had been answered and the book was closed. He knew that things were always changing and always more complicated, so he was always open to further thinking, to more conversation, to listening to what other people might contribute to his thinking.

It seems to me everyone today is so certain of what they know, whether it concerns political strategies, ethical norms, or intellectual theories. Stuart was only ever convinced about three things: the world is more complicated than we think, and our politics have to deal with that complexity; knowledge does matter; and the intellectual's responsibility is to contest the growing inhumanity of the world. This all adds up to a different attitude toward our own "certainties": we have to approach our ideas, our understandings, and our politics, with greater humility and to approach others with greater generosity.

LGR: Would you describe how you came to know Stuart and over what period of time you knew him, and speak to this juncture for those who haven't followed this history?

LG: I went to college during the height of the "counterculture" and the anti-war movement, and I was active in a wide range of struggles. Because of the draft, I decided to leave the country, and some of my professors pointed me toward the Centre as an intellectually interesting and politically sophisticated place. They had known Richard Hoggart when he had spent a year at Rochester. They didn't exactly know what was going on there. They didn't quite know what Cultural Studies was. They didn't know Stuart Hall at all. But they knew that this was a place where intellectual work and politics came together and where innovative and experimental kinds of projects were being put forward. And they thought this would be a good place for me. So I went.

I showed up in the fall of 1968 at the Quonset hut on the outskirts of the campus of the Birmingham University, and found myself in the middle of a wonderful and chaotic conversation that was creating Cultural Studies. With Stuart and Richard Hoggart's encouragement, I also started to do my own research on the politics of popular music. But I left England after about a year because I was one of the leaders of a strike at the university, and the media did not take kindly to "outside agitators." So I left with an itinerant anarchist theater community. When I finally returned to the USA, I asked Stuart where to go to grad school, and he said the only person he knew Cultural Studies in the USA was Jim Carey at the University of Illinois. So I went, and discovered I was in communication studies. I didn't know there was such a field.

I maintained occasional contact with Stuart until I finished my Ph.D. and started teaching, and then I renewed real contact with him, and began a friendship not only with Stuart but with his family as well. His wife Catherine had been wonderful to me during my time in Birmingham (she was very present and very pregnant with their first child during the strike). Stuart became my mentor, my hero, and my dear friend, and he introduced me to the larger community of Cultural Studies people, primarily that group from the mid-1970s, often thought to be the high point of the Centre – John Clarke, Dick Hebdige, Paul Gilroy, Angela McRobbie, Dave Morley, and many more. Many have become close friends and are the seeds of my intellectual community.

When we organized the Marxism and the Interpretation of Culture in the summer of 1983 at the University of Illinois (including a six-week summer school and the conference that led to the book, *Marxism and the Interpretation of Culture*, edited by Cary Nelson and Lawrence Grossberg, University of Illinois Press, 1988), Stuart was the first person I invited. At the time, although he had been to the States a few times and knew a few people – and some critical education scholars knew his work (and some of the work of the Centre) – he was relatively unknown. But that summer, Stuart stole the show. By the time we organized *Cultural Studies – Now and in the Future* at Illinois in April 1990, Stuart was obviously the person who people wanted to hear and to meet.

I started visiting Stuart and Catherine regularly (it was on one of those trips that I met my wife). I did some interviews, and helped him edit some essays and interviews. Jennifer Slack and I edited his lectures from the Marxism summer school. One chapter on Althusser was published, and it looks like the entire book will finally be published.

I don't know what else to say, except that [voice halts and chokes up], his death made me reflect upon the fact that I've known Stuart and Catherine since 1968 and their kids for their entire lives. They are probably the people I have been closest to for the longest period of my life outside my own family. In a sense, Stuart was my oldest friend, although I wouldn't have said in 1968 that we were close friends. But they treated me wonderfully and opened the door to eventual friendship. It was a friendship that was multidimensional, political, intellectual, pedagogical, and emotional.

LGR: Yes. It's hard to really fathom what that loss means to you. That's why I wanted to ground the question around your political formation and – how your grief is political. How was 1968 essential to your own political formation? Also, from your knowledge of Stuart's role at the Centre in Birmingham and his ways of working intellectually and politically with students, why was his mentorship so profound and effectual?

LG: Let me start with my own political formation before turning to Stuart's. I have to say that I was raised in a progressive Jewish family, so Leftist politics was in my bones. But I was largely shaped by the 1960s, a time of multiple, intersecting, and sometimes contradictory struggles, strategies, and even political fantasies. It had no specific ideological-theoretical form, but it addressed issues of class politics and urban politics, of the politics of everyday life and of popular culture, of difference and community. All were woven together into what is loosely referred to as the counterculture. It was complex, contradictory, very messy, constantly changing – and always operating with and on the popular.

I went to the University of Rochester in 1964 to enter the emerging field of biochemical genetics. I was a science nerd, although not quite as weird as the Big Bang Theory. But two things disrupted my neat plans. First, I didn't particularly like the scientists that I had gone to study with; they turned out to be too intellectually narrow. I wanted to read Nietzsche and Spinoza and C. Wright Mills, and they wanted me to read *The Journal of Genetics*. So they drove me away from science and fortunately, I found a great group of professors invested in philosophy, intellectual and cultural history, and politics, who shaped my thinking. I wrote an honours thesis on the relation of politics and music in the counterculture. Second, I got politicized, partly through my love of popular music, especially the folk music I started listening to in Greenwich Village, which was right near my high school. Music became a gateway for me, as for others, into political struggle and all sorts of other things.

Stuart's early formation was very different. You can see something about his formation in and by colonial and racial politics in some of his interviews. This will become even clearer in the book he was working on when he died (which Catherine and Bill Schwarz are working to complete). This no doubt shaped the ways he engaged – even wrestled – with other political questions and subjects, and with Marxism, after he arrived in England. It is this conversation which, in some ways, defined the agenda when he helped found the New Left in the 1950s. As he said, he arrived in England as a colonial subject, but after deciding not to go home, his politics and subjectivity were reconfigured in complicated ways. This is probably not the place to go into detail about the English New Left, but it shaped Stuart's broad sense of both politics and Cultural Studies. And through Stuart, it certainly reshaped my own political formation, building on, crystallizing my own perhaps idiosyncratic sense of the counterculture.

What did Stuart teach me? He taught me that ideas matter; that we need to invent a new cultural politics (I'm not sure what we would call it) appropriate for the present. Such a politics would have to be built upon new and better analyses of the political, economic, social – and cultural relations! Both the politics and the analyses would have to embrace the complexities, multiplicities, and contradictions that define our social reality and therefore, both had to reject the easy binaries (even the strategic ones) that make our job too easy. Such a politics would have to be a "popular politics," resonating with, speaking to and even, constructing broader constituencies; and finally, that such a politics had to operate, at least in part, at the level of the conjuncture (as opposed, for example, to the epoch or the particular situation). Stuart taught me to embrace complexity and differences, and to think conjuncturally, theoretically, analytically, and politically.

All this may help explain why Stuart was such an extraordinary teacher and mentor. As many people have said, he tried, and succeeded more than most of us, to live and practise his commitments in every sphere of his life. I don't want to make it sound like he was perfect – he wasn't – but he did practise what he preached more than anyone I have known. But he never assumed that his was the only way or necessarily the best way. He did not want to make people fit his expectations. Instead, he wanted to help people become whatever they wanted to become. It was not that he would not argue or criticize, but he never assumed that he necessarily deserved the last word or that he could solve a problem by himself. Institutionally, the Centre kept evolving under his "leadership," as power was distributed first into the working groups and, after the strike at the university, into collective decision-making. Stuart was passionate, brilliant, a riveting speaker, generous, caring. He believed that everyone mattered and what we were doing mattered, and he believed that how we did it mattered.

LGR: It's so different from how Cultural Studies was interpreted in large part in the USA.

LG: I think it has to do with fervently believing that what you are doing matters, and therefore knowing that the risks – of failure, of rejection, of repression – are worth it. Maybe I can start with Richard Hoggart, the founder of the Centre, who is not appreciated as much as he should be. Richard died a month after Stuart. We don't often talk about how much imagination and courage it took for Richard to create the Centre. I mean, it was very weird at the time. His fellow colleagues in the English Department had no idea of what he was doing or why he would want to do this, why he would invest his growing stature as an English professor in this kind of project. But for Richard, it was very much about the importance of knowledge in political transformation. Hoggart deeply believed having good knowledge was absolutely necessary if we were to take control of our own history rather than allow ourselves to be set "adrift on the ties of social change."

Cultural Studies at the Centre was always articulated to politics, but not necessarily any particular politics. But I do not think that people at the Centre confused what they were doing with politics – knowledge may be power but it is not inherently political. Cultural Studies existed to produce knowledge in the service of political struggle. And it embraced complexity and difference. There were lots of different theoretical, intellectual, and political interests and positions constantly fighting with each other at the Centre. It was never homogeneous, there was never a "Centre" position, and people did not assume that they knew the final answers because there were no final, no complete answers. This was not merely a gesture, a kind of footnote; it was an attitude at the heart of Cultural Studies.

Therefore, the Centre was a place of innovation, experimentation, and risk-taking. For a long time, it did not have a fixed reading list or curriculum. Faculty, staff, and students were making it up as they went along; and they pushed themselves to find ways of actually doing the kind of collaborative, collective interdisciplinary research that was needed. In fact, when I was there, we attempted such a project. We started out thinking we would study English women's magazines, and we ended up studying one story ("Cure for Marriage") in one issue of one magazine. Unfortunately, Stuart's final report was lost, and the project has remained unknown. Stuart asked me to do something with the files he kept, to make the work visible, so it is one of my future projects.

The people at the Centre were collectively trying to develop new intellectual and pedagogical practices that went against the norms of the research university at the time. But it had not gone as far as it was about to go. The events of 1968 at Birmingham and other universities, and the emerging social protest movements and political experiments in England and elsewhere pushed the people at the Centre, including Stuart, to consider how they should and could even further radicalize some of the practices at the Centre.

The Centre increasingly invested its greatest effort and power in a series of working groups, and it began to rethink how it governed itself, making the decision-making process more and more inclusive (unbeknown to the those embodying the hierarchical powers of the university) ranging from the apparently trivial decisions about how much paper to buy for the mimeograph machine to the vital decisions about which students to admit. Think about it, students were interviewing other students to decide who to admit – because if you are committed primarily to the working groups, then the question was more about whether someone would be part of the conversations, whether this person had the passion and commitments (as well as the intelligence of course) to work with others at the Centre, than about some kind of professionally or professorially pre-defined set of qualifications, distinctions, etc.

LGR: What was the University of Birmingham's response to what was happening at the Centre? Was it, as I've seen on website for the conference marking the 50th anniversary of the Centre, retaliatory towards Stuart?

LG: I wasn't there for most of its history, although, even when I was there, Hoggart used to talk about the fact that the administration was not very happy about the existence of the Centre. They [the Administration] put it, literally, as far away from the center of the campus as you could get, in an old World War II Quonset hut, they refused to give it any financial support at all. Over the years, they tried again and again to either bring it into conformity with their notions of how academic units, i.e. disciplines, are supposed to act, which means in a disciplined way. This place was neither disciplinary nor disciplined. They understood this even without understanding exactly how radical the Centre actually was, without actually knowing what it was doing on the ground, as it were. They tried repeatedly to control it by restructuring and institutionalizing it. They tried to close it down a number of times. They tried merging it into a department; the name kept changing; they kept trying to imagine it out of existence and sought various ways and pressures to make that actually happen. They certainly didn't treat Stuart well – or Richard Johnson or Michael Green or any of the people who were the directors at various times. I don't think they treated the graduate students or the undergraduates well, even though the program was pedagogically one of the most popular and innovative and successful at the university. In the process, they screwed over the students – and the faculty, many of whom had outstanding reputations. Eventually, they succeeded in erasing any presence of Cultural Studies at the University.

LGR: I think your answer is most definitely "yes."

LG: Yes. And there was certainly a lot of resentment, displeasure, and even anger expressed at the 50th anniversary conference that the Centre archives were going to be housed at the Birmingham library after the way Birmingham had treated the Centre.

LGR: So why put them at Birmingham?

LG: For two reasons. One was that creating an archive takes work and resources. And that means individuals willing to do the work and gather the resources, with the knowledge and intelligence to do it really well. At Birmingham, Matthew Hilton and Kieran Connell have taken on this task.

Second, Stuart decided, after many conversations, with many people, including me, about where to put his own archives as well as the Centre Archives that they should be at Birmingham. He knew it was not a great solution but it was the best solution he could come up with. Some people disagreed and still disagree. Others who were involved in the Centre in different capacities will have to decide for themselves what they want to do.

LGR: When you think about political formation, and the kind of work that Stuart did on identity as a process of becoming a future with imaginary and real pasts, as Ien Ang so eloquently puts it in her essay "Identity Blues" in your co-edited collection *Without Guarantees* (Ang, in Gilroy, Grossberg, & McRobbie, 2000, pp. 1–13), a festschrift that honours Hall on his retirement from the Open University, what do you believe is the biggest misconception about Hall's political formation?

LG: This takes us back to the question you asked a moment ago, about the different genealogies of Cultural Studies in Britain and the USA. I'm not comfortable talking about how Stuart's work or Cultural Studies has been taken up more broadly and interpreted in other parts of the world (where, I will say, it is often both more interesting and more in line with my own understandings). The academy in the USA in general (and certainly back in the 1970s was) was very different and that is at least one of the lines determining the different development of Cultural Studies and the different receptions of Stuart's work, although of course there are some wonderful Cultural Studies intellectuals and interpreters of Stuart in the USA. Still, the academy here is so much larger and more professionalized, so much more dominated by elite universities and by the sheer size and power of the disciplines in general and of particular disciplines. It's hard to be an intellectual without succumbing to the demands of the academy. Moreover, the impact of the counterculture was largely expressed in very different terms, and to a large extent, the dominant oppositional ways of imagining the relations of knowledge and politics, of theoretical and empirical work, are very different. As Stuart himself pointed out, in the USA academy, there is a greater split between theory and empirical work, and the result is that each is fetishized by different academic constituencies. And further, there is a strong tendency among some Left intellectuals to assume that doing intellectual work is itself inherently political, a form of political practice.

I think this contributes to two misconceptions about Stuart. One is to separate his work, his intellectual work and his ideas from the rest of his life. And then one celebrates him because he was both a brilliant analyst and theorist – and a political activist. I want to go back to where I started – these were inseparable. It's not just that his political activism, his art activism, his pedagogy, were somehow expressions of his ideas: they were imbricated, intricately interwoven in ways such that you don't understand his ideas if you don't understand what he was doing politically, aesthetically, artistically, in support of

Black film programs, in support of Black artists, in support of pedagogical projects, and vice versa. Even in the early days of the Centre, Stuart spent lots of time consulting with, trying to help people produce things that could go out to schools, to help schools. People don't think about why his first book, *The Popular Arts*, co-authored with Paddy Whannel (Hall & Whannel, 1964) was a pedagogical project. They're not just addendums to his ideas, derivable from his ideas. They shape his ideas. As Nick Beech, who was Stuart's assistant in the last years of his life and might have been, informally, Stuart's last student, reminded me: you don't understand his ideas unless you understand the rest of his activities.

LGR: Yes. Well put.

LG: And the second misconception, which also follows almost necessarily from the way that USA academy works, is to think that Stuart had a position, had a theory, for example, of identity as difference. There's an interview where Stuart actually says that people misunderstood him because they think he is offering some kind of general theory, rather than understanding that theory is a tool defined and deployed conjuncturally. Hence, for Stuart, there is no final theory; one just keeps on theorizing in relation to the changing conjuncture. Or they assume he is addressing their questions rather than always trying to understand a conjuncture. So he says that he was never really writing about questions about "race" as an identity, but rather as a subject position. He says that *Policing the Crisis* (Hall, Critcher, Jefferson, Clarke, & Roberts, 1978) is not a book about race. It is a book about a society that is raced and thus, is a conjunctural study. He was never interested in race, per se, as an abstract identity, but in how race was deployed, constructed, articulated in relationship to a complex structuration of power. And in that sense, then, he never ever offered a generalizable theory. Yet, he was read by many in the USA into other positions and arguments, about essentialism and anti-essentialism, that were never exactly his own. He was read as offering one of the first and most rigorous articulations of a theory of difference. But then Stuart turns around and says that while such an understanding is important and useful at a certain moment in order to contest certain kinds of political strategies, now thinking about "race" as difference is not a very helpful, progressive analysis. Other forces have taken up difference and transformed their potential political and analytical efficacy. So, we need to think past even notions of hybridity (since hybridity is all there is). Cultural Studies is always about contexts and conjunctures. This becomes very explicit in the book he was writing during his final illness. Thinking about contexts as conjunctures forces us to embrace the complexity of articulations, the multiplicity of and contradictions among the struggles, demands, determinations, etc. It's always about context and complexity, all the way down as it were. In other words, Cultural Studies (and theorizing) are radically contextual practices. This is very clear in his brilliant essay on Marxist method, where theories are understood to develop out of contexts, in response to contexts. The more universal a theory is claimed to be, the less useful it is in the conjuncture. Yes, Stuart thought identity was always becoming, always hybrid, but that is the starting point, not the conclusion. What is missing is the conjunctural analysis that specifies just what is happening, and how.

To read Stuart as a general theorist of anything misses just how radical and extraordinarily original he was. For example, his brilliant essay on "deconstructing the popular" (in Samuel Hall, 1981) is often read as if it were a theory of the popular, but I think it is a conjuncturally specific intervention into a particular moment when the popular had to be taken seriously. And unfortunately, people do not take the last line seriously enough, when Stuart says that popular culture is one of those places where a socialist opposition might be constructed: "That is why 'popular culture' matters. Otherwise, to tell you the truth, I don't give a damn about it."

Stuart was never a student of popular culture per se. Instead, he was a student of political struggles in particular contexts. One of the first things I say to my students is that people are going to ask them what their theory is. Are you a Derridian? Are you a Deleuzian? Are you a Foucaultian? Are you a Gramscian? And the answer to that question from Stuart Hall's perspective is that I'm not any single or permanent thing. I am trying to understand the context better. And I have a set of tools. And if you tell me the problems posed by the context, I'll tell you with which tools I might start. And for Stuart those were usually Gramscian, with some Foucault and Derrida thrown in, maybe some Lacan. Feminist theory was crucial, Fanon was crucial. But, you know, it was not that he had a theory. It was that he had tools to understand a context and to understand the political struggles of that context, and to find some possibilities for opening up more and more hopeful struggles in that context.

LGR: I was very struck when reading the tributes how they were simultaneously homages and yet, full of erasures and categorical thinking. Very few tributes really understood both the depth and breadth of his radical politics and the diversity of his constituencies. In a BBC radio interview, John Clarke noted with understandable critical irreverence that those tributes which referred to him as the "Godfather of Multi-culturalism" had missed the point because such a distinction was "too nice." That isn't the way Stuart would have thought of his work.

LG: Well, he didn't invent multiculturalism. He had –

LGR: He had an intervention into multiculturalism.

LG: Yes, and he had a somewhat limited support of it, given certain positions and certain conjunctures, you know? For example, the Greater London Council and Ken Livingston's work – Stuart supported the way in which multiculturalism was articulated there in those particular projects. But it was not as if –

LGR: [Completing his thought in concurrence] [t]here was some kind of great embrace of multiculturalism.

LG: Yeah, as if this was a solution to the problems of racism or ethnocentrism, you know? When he intervened into a big project on multiculturalism in England, the Parekh report, what he said was that with all its "multiculturalism," England remained a racist society.

LGR: His intervention was not a great embrace of liberal multiculturalism.

LG: It doesn't surprise me that people appropriate Stuart into all kinds of universalizing theories. It didn't surprise me that people appropriate Stuart into the great defender of multiculturalism, whether to celebrate him or to dismiss him, because we all know multiculturalism is a liberal failure. It didn't surprise me that people constructed him to fit their own agendas. But it saddens me because I think they are missing something of the heart of Stuart as a political intellectual.

In a sense, Stuart understood and taught me early on that intellectual work is no different from any other work in the sense that, as Cultural Studies and other formations have taught us over the past 50 years, people do things with cultural texts that you could never have predicted. Just think about how people have universalized his rearticulation of the concepts of encoding and decoding for understanding the media, arguments which appeared in many different versions of what people assumed was the same essay, into a general theory of media reception. Stuart taught me that people are going to do that to your work just as much as they're going to do it to the popular culture texts that they consume. And you can't take responsibility for everything people do with your ideas. It is one of the failures of academic self-consciousness that we think of our own texts, and those that matter most to us, as somehow sacred, protected from the unpredictability of interpretations; there is only the right interpretation and everything else is capricious and mistaken. We might not be able to tell you the true reading of a movie but we can tell you the true reading of Foucault. Right?

You know, some people blamed Stuart for Blairism because of his analysis of Thatcherism and his critique of the Left, including the Labour Party. They said that Blair was doing what Stuart had called for. Really? Not at all. Did Stuart approve of Blairism? Not a chance in Hell. And he wrote some of his most devastating political analyses and critiques about Blair and Blairism. On the other hand, there were Blairites who read Stuart and Stuart's allies and thought that their arguments justified what they were doing. I have no doubt there were some. It doesn't mean that Stuart is to blame. It means that our intellectual texts have no more sacred status than all the other texts we study.

I suppose I could be accused of treating Stuart's work as sacred texts here, but I think there is a legitimate question of whether you are reading someone into your own certainties, or allowing him or her to challenge you, whether one's reading repeats what you already know, or surprises you. For example, I have this argument with some Foucaultians who end up making Foucault sound like Derrida. "But then I didn't need Foucault." If I could get to the places I want, you know, thinking about racial differences or racism without Stuart, why do I need Stuart? On the other hand, if I read Stuart this way, I get to new places. I get to other places. I get to places that I haven't imagined, or at least places that are more complicated than those we have inhabited. And that's a good thing. So it seems to me a more productive reading.

LGR: When you think about those tributes, how have you wrestled with the misconceptions yourself? Or is your position that there weren't any misconceptions?

LG: There are lots of people who misread Stuart, both in terms of what he was doing and his arguments; but there are a lot who did not misread him and found creative ways to take up specific arguments he made. There are better and worse readings of his work and his life, although there will always be disagreements. There are some questions and issues that are unresolved in Stuart's work. But what I took away from all the tributes was that in my 50 years as an intellectual, I don't think I've ever seen a response to the death of an intellectual like that provoked by Stuart's death. The tributes were from all over the world, from many disciplines. They were full of love, talking about the man as an individual, talking about his generosity, his compassion, his humility. They talked about him as a teacher, acknowledging how he took the time to answer their email or their letter, or to talk with them after a lecture, how he empowered them to do their work and take the risks that they might not have otherwise taken. They talked about him as a scholar and intellectual, as a political critic and activist, as someone who valued the arts as a necessary political activity.

You know, hundreds of people from all over the world wrote obituaries that said, "I've never met the man, but he was my mentor." That is what Stuart empowered in people. I took great hope and faith from that response. Even when I disagreed – when someone like Tariq Ali said something that really pissed me off – in the end I said:

> but that's less important than the fact that all these different people, even people who have built a career, in a sense, by opposing Stuart, even if not so explicitly, have had to acknowledge his position, his contribution, his very being in the world as a unique and significant political intellectual.

I was awash in the love that, it seemed to me, said, "This was a unique person." Many people love their mentor, and mentors die. Many of my colleagues and friends, when they heard Stuart had died came to me and said, "We're very sorry to hear Stuart died. I lost my mentor, too, a year ago. I know how you feel." And I wanted to say to them, "Well, I appreciate your kindness and the gesture. I appreciate the similarities that come from losing a mentor." But it's not the same!

Public intellectual, extraordinary educator

LGR: What do you think that Stuart contributed to the concept of public pedagogy and being a public intellectual scholar?

LG: Wow, that's a big question.

LGR: It is, but I have been contemplating how he was an extraordinary educator. For me, that describes him better than public intellectual, which almost has a rarified quality to it.

LG: Yes, that's a good point, and I think that's true. And I think if you've seen John Akomfrah's sometimes moving film, *The Stuart Hall Project*, one of my criticisms might be that it is about Stuart Hall, the public intellectual and not Stuart Hall the public pedagogue, public teacher. Let me say two things, one at a kind of abstract theoretical level. Nick Beech asked me recently where I thought Stuart falls on the balance between thinking about political agency and political constituency. I think that the drive in so much contemporary theory, especially so-called *post*-Enlightenment thought, and so much of contemporary autonomous politics, is all about agency. But Stuart's politics were always about constituency. Maybe that was in part because, as he always said, unlike other political-intellectual formations, Cultural Studies never had the luxury or privilege of imagining it had a pre-constituted political constituency.

Notice how close that is to his description of the New Left in England. He describes its political project as the attempt to mobilize a popular politics by mobilizing a constituency or multiple constituencies into a political discourse and a political materiality. It's not vanguard politics, which a lot of so-called radical democratic politics still are in some ways because the vanguard acts as if it knows the solution in advance, and because you already have to agree with them to be allowed into the democratic process.

Stuart often said that we have to move people from where they are toward better possibilities, but in that process we are moving with them, so that we ourselves are changed, reshaped as we reshape the popular constituencies of political change.

LGR: And I think that insight is what made him such an extraordinary educator.

LG: Yes. And finally, I would add, he did not assume that you could ever know in advance with whom you were speaking. Your responsibility as an intellectual/teacher was to help people to create a collective sense of their own position in history. It is a kind of dialog, a mutually engaging attempt to transform the organization of social existence, to transform the nature of public constituencies. Is that a pedagogical project? Seems like one to me. It seems more specific than simply being an intellectual or even a public intellectual because it's about engaging in a particular kind of conversation, not one in which "we know what's going on in the world, just listen to us," right? Moreover, it's a conversation aimed at creating new kinds of collectives, new kinds of publics, and at expanding the field of conversants of all sorts, including intellectuals located in any number of different social sites; it takes the intellectual into a wider space of discursive possibilities. You don't have to be an academic to be an intellectual. Stuart often spoke about organic intellectuals and it was his dream, in some ways, to create organic intellectuals who would give expression to emerging social constituencies. I think that his dream was to be an organic intellectual. What I have been saying is that he was as successful as one can imagine at living this dream.

Neoliberalism and the academy

LGR: Speaking now from the position of "pessimism of the intellect," in the current neoliberal context, whether in Britain or the USA, it's very difficult to imagine how scholars who are extraordinary educators are going to be produced. Would you speak to some of the constraints and possibilities for, say untenured scholars in today's neoliberal academy to hang onto and practise the kind of extraordinary, organic intellectual work that his life and practice embodied. Many of my junior (I detest the word) colleagues bemoan the fact that it is no longer safe to do community-engaged work as an academic. How would you advise them?

LG: I would say three things. First, there are spaces that still exist for people who are doing extremely interesting, innovative, experimental, politically risky sorts of things. They may be rarer than they were, although I'm not sure about that. They may be harder to find. But they are there. There are always people struggling to do these kinds of things. But you have to look for them. The second thing I want to say is – and I hope you will see this in the light of the third thing I'm going to say – that doing interesting, important and politically significant work is risky. It was risky 50 years ago. I get a sense sometimes that people think that previous generations didn't have any risks. I mean, do they not know the stories of all the feminists, of all the critical race theorists, of all the gay and lesbian scholars, of all the anti-colonial scholars, of all the Cultural Studies scholars, of all the political intellectual work, all the innovative work, all the interdisciplinary people, all the collaborative work that was done in which people got fired? People were not promoted. People didn't get the prestigious jobs. People didn't get the pay raises. A lot of them left the academy. Some of them took jobs in shitty places. And either continued to produce great work or continued to be great teachers, or just gave in to their cynicism, right?

To speak personally, when I went out on the job market, everyone except for Jim Carey and Stuart Hall said, "You'll never get a job. Don't do this. You can't write a dissertation on Raymond Williams and Martin Heidegger." This was back in 1968. No one gave cared a whit about Heidegger in the USA or had ever heard of Raymond Williams. No one knew what Cultural Studies was. Theory was still largely invisible. No one cared about popular music. I took a risk because both Jim and Stuart asked me why I wanted to be an intellectual. The first job I got was not a very good job and I was forced to teach mass communication effects research, not exactly something I had any interest in.

I know that the "market" has collapsed, the possibilities have diminished and the constraints have grown more powerful. But the question still holds: why do you want to be an intellectual? It isn't the neoliberal university that has invented the risk of doing political intellectual work or interdisciplinary work. It has made it harder than before. However, if you don't want to take risks, I don't know what you should do with your life but you shouldn't be doing Cultural Studies in or outside of education –

LGR: That is the most wonderful answer to that question.

LG: Thanks. On the other hand and here's my third point, we should not place the burden on untenured younger faculty to take all the risks. What pisses me off is not the fact that young faculty don't seem willing to take the risks, seem to assume that we had no risks, "I'm not going to get a job if I do interdisciplinary work." Of course! People said the same thing to me. That doesn't piss me off as much as the fact that the faculty who have lived through that shit and survived, seem now to be unwilling, even from a position of greater security, to actually engage in the struggle that would transform the university and not make young scholars go through the exact same battles that we went through. That is to say, what pisses me off is the cynicism with which older politicized faculty have greeted the neo-liberal university, in which we end up either cynical or resigned or we become nostalgic for that university that screwed so many good people. Why should we be nostalgic for or want to go back to the universities of the 1960s and 1970s, which excluded feminists, interdisciplinary scholars, political intellectuals, etc.?

Let's reinvent the university. Let's use our weight and power to create new spaces, to advocate, for example, for the possibility of joint dissertations of interdisciplinary degrees, for new forms of tenure and appointments. Let's use our weight to re-imagine the university and not just bemoan the neoliberal university. But how do we transform the university? The university is a historical invention. It was made by human beings in response to certain kinds of conjunctural demands, constraints and possibilities. Why can't we struggle toward a university that reinvents education and knowledge production, opening new spaces of possibility in ethical and political, as well as economic and epistemological terms? Remember what I said about Hoggart and the creation of the Centre.

We might begin by thinking about how to create publics that understand what we do and that support us. I wonder why it is that we assume not only that people should value what we do, but that should pay for it. I am sure that many do not. But even before entering into that struggle, which the conservatives have managed so well, how many of us are even capable of explaining why what we do matters to broader constituencies? We have to find better ways of speaking with people, reconstituting the forms of public discourse and valuation, and re-constructing publics. And that means educating ourselves as well in those conversations.

LGR: And that doesn't go on as much as it should between academics and non-academics.

LG: It doesn't go on at all, as far as I can tell. University administrators (and some faculty) increasingly parrot the neoliberal (not a term I like) incantation of innovation and entrepreneurialism, and offer the university as capable of solving any community's problems. Their idea of engaging with communities is that communities say, "We have a problem, solve it." And then there are those who confidently speak from the high ground of elitism, either asserting the intrinsic and universal value of knowledge, or the practical benefit of exposure to high or even mid-cult (cultural) capital. But as I said, I am not sure we know how to defend our own critical and imaginative work, how we defend to people who, in the first instance, do not see its immediate value. How do we say that we are trying to offer a better understanding of what's going on, and a more compelling vision of the problems we face, and a richer sense of the possibilities for solving these matters, which might lead us to a different future?

LGR: Some of the tributes that have been written by your generation and mine read like mourning ourselves.

LG: I understand what you mean. We were, are, a generation that, in a sense, thought we could change the world. And we thought that the work we were doing as political intellectuals was a vital part of that process. Disappointment probably does not quite capture a sense of how we have to look at the world today and ask what went wrong. It's not coincidental that at the end of his life, toward the end of his life, Stuart was depressed not only because of the success of conservative and capitalist forces, but also because of what he called the state of the Left.

But in the spirit of Stuart, it is okay to be intellectually pessimistic about our own careers and what we may not have accomplished. But it is also incumbent upon us to find the possibilities of optimism. We have to ask ourselves why we have failed, why there is no effective political opposition. How has the intellectual Left contributed to this state of affairs? While I don't really like the vocabulary of "blame," we have to take some responsibility, as political intellectuals, for the absence of an effective Left opposition in many parts of the world, especially the North Atlantic. How this has come about and why, in the face of generations of political intellectuals who think that they are changing the world? How can we be so wrong? Let me add, in a moment of shameless self-promotion that this is what my next book will be – it will be called "Is this any way to change the world?"

LGR: I suppose my reinterpretation in the months following his loss was that mourning should translate as a kind of responsibility to future –

LG: Yes. I agree. The only way to honor his memory is to continue in the work of "pessimism of the intellect and optimism of the will," of telling better stories about what's going on in ways that enable new constituencies of popular opposition to emerge and struggle to produce another future, another world.

Note

1. This phrase originates from French writer, Romain Rolland, who coined it. Gramsci then took it up extensively in his speeches to and with workers' circles about the Paris Commune, Marx, Romain Rolland, the French Revolution and the emancipation of women. See Sanctucci, La Porto, and Hobsbawm (2010, p. 121). Thank you to Dennis Dworkin and Iain Chambers for pointing this out. Like many, I had assumed mistakenly that Gramsci was the originator since the phrase was popularized as his alone.

References

Gilroy, P., Grossberg, L., & McRobbie, A. (Eds.). (2000). *Without guarantees: In honor of Stuart Hall*. London: Verso.

Hall, S. (1981). Notes on deconstructing 'the popular'. In R. Samuel (Ed.), *People's history and socialist theory* (pp. 227–240). Boston, MA: Routledge & Kegan Paul.

Hall, S., Critcher, T., Jefferson, T., Clarke, J., & Roberts, B. (1978). *Policing the crisis: 'Mugging' the state and law and order*. London: Macmillan.

Hall, S., & Whannel, P. (1964). *The popular arts*. London: Hutchinson Educational.

Hall, S., Critcher, C., Jefferson, T., Clarke, J., & Roberts, B. (2013). *Policing the Crisis: Mugging, the State and Law and Order* (2nd ed.). Basingstoke: Palgrave Macmillan.

Nelson, C., & Grossberg, L. (Eds.). (1988). *Marxism and the interpretation of culture*. Urbana: University of Illinois Press.

Sanctucci, A., La Porto, L., & Hobsbawm, E. (2010). *Antonio Gramsci*. (G. Di Mauro & S. E. Di-Mauro, Trans.). New York, NY: Monthly Review Press.

Making and moving publics: Stuart Hall's projects, maximal selves and education

Leslie G. Roman

Educational Studies, Faculty of Education, University of British Columbia, Vancouver, Canada

An extraordinary educator and public intellectual, Stuart Hall's career as a scholar, activist, teacher and mentor has touched almost every field in the social sciences and humanities. Paradoxically, education rarely claims him as an educator. Stuart Hall's refusal to see publics as given, fixed or settled matters with clear or final demarcations and boundaries allowed him to move pedagogically and politically between and among different constituencies and sites of formal and non-formal education, policy and praxis, arts' groups and social theorizing in larger national and transnational spaces as places for public thinking, teaching publics and, thus, for making what I will call 'maximal selves'. Indeed, his praxis articulated Michael Warner's queering of our theoretical understandings of publics and counter-publics, addressing and registering affectively and effectively with variously hyphenated communities. I will show how his formation as an intellectual worked with uncomfortable diasporic differences of his own 'minimal selves' to suture together alliances with specific marginalized groups as part of his extraordinary commitment to education as public thinking and teaching publicly. It is only until we understand him as an extraordinary educator that our tasks and inheritance from Hall's varied projects become appreciable.

Extraordinary educator: queering publics and counter-publics

It is Hall's educational praxis of social change and justice embodied in word, deed and movement among multiple sites of activist intellectual work that he bridged which made him an extraordinary educator. In this chronicle, tribute and scholarly essay, I move rhetorically between letter writing – an epistolary voice – to Stuart Hall and scholarly voice, a relational genealogical strategy to honour affectively and politically what I have learned from him. Stuart Hall was my mentor, professor and friend, someone I had known for almost 30 years when he died 10 February 2014. My debt to him cannot be voiced in strictly scholarly terms and writing conventions. Such a task calls upon different registers of voice and affect, steals our educational inclinations from the fully rational, modern and cold tonal register of the scholarly impersonal voice.[1] It invites us to engage ourselves and others from the subjectivity of the heart, active listening, dialogue, critical consciousness and emotional openness to third-space alternatives, and ultimately to the movement across the personal, impersonal and the scholarly.

What made Stuart Hall so unusually gifted and imaginative at making and moving publics? Though the concept of the public is vague, the question becomes: how do strangers in transitory contexts recognize each other as belonging to 'our' world? What makes addresses or hails recognizable to specific groups? To answer these questions, I turn to Michael Warner's far-reaching analysis of the contradictory and often ambiguous oppositions of the public/private distinction. In *Publics and Counterpublics* (2002), Warner draws on post-structural, feminist and queer theorization of the concept of the public in modern liberal thought to show how vexing and yet necessary it has become. As the concept of the public extends to new contexts, politics and media, the meaning of it changes in ways that can be difficult to uncover. Warner makes distinctions among three uses of the word *public* too often falsely conflated as 'the public': (1) a 'social totality' such as a nation; (2) 'a concrete audience such as a crowd witnessing itself in visible space, as with a theatrical public'; and of most interest to him, (3) 'the kind of public that comes into being only in relation to texts and their circulation' (2002, pp. 49–50). This third sense of 'public' distinguishes itself from the public as a totality and registers a specific audience bound to an event commonly evoked and understood, but its rules are never explained. Warner explains these 'rather odd' rules of publics in which, they are: (1) 'self-organized, exist[ing:] by virtue of being addressed'; (2) 'a relation among strangers'; (3) 'addressed in both personal and impersonal terms'; (4) 'constituted through mere attention'; (5) 'the social space created by the reflexive circulation of discourse'; (6) 'act[s:] historically according to the temporality of their [texts':] circulation'; and (7) 'is poetic world-making' (2002, pp. 50, 55, 57, 60, 62, 68, 82). Warner believes that counter-publics act in the same way but through discourses that address those strangers not as just anybody but as somebodies marked by their participation in this kind of discourse; members of the dominant groups are presumed to not want to be mistaken for the kind of person who would participate in this kind of counter-public discourse or 'scene' (p. 86). Unlike feminist post-structuralist Nancy Fraser, Warner insists that a counter-public does not have to be subaltern, as Fraser postulates, but can be understood as 'a scene for developing oppositional interpretations of its members' identities, interests, and needs' (2002, p. 86). Counter-publics possess awareness, whether conscious or not, of their subordinate statuses in relation to dominant culture (Warner, 2002, p. 86). Warner's distinctions are well placed to explain how Hall made and mobilized publics across sites, texts in circulation, events, contexts and communities:

Still life and noise

Dear Stuart,

I learned of your death in the wee hours of february 10, 2014, while wired to the screen through an activist anti-racist student and faculty list-serve. The night was still. Among the most profound of all my illustrious mentors and professors (and I have had the best from Michael W. Apple, Dorothy E. Smith to informally, fazal Rizvi), you will never leave me. No matter how expected, given your debilitating kidney disease, weary body racked with pain and fatigue, your loss is untimely. While your death leaves me breathless, your life and work fill my lungs with critical oxygen. After several minutes of indescribable shock, I reach for your immediate traces in my life – the last of your many emails and correspondences, the notes I took in your seminar still saved and used all these years. I scramble determined to locate your presence in the one of black and white photos given to me by Dennis Dworkin of your interviewing Jesse Jackson. I saved that photo all these years. I cannot locate it. As if there could ever be one text, anchor point or memento that would console me, I become seized in the search for it. Into which box had I packed it?

Instead, I find among my mementos, the book you gave me upon the end of your time in Madison Wisconsin, as my professor. The book you selected matched my doctoral work (Roman, 1987, 1988), an ethnography of Punk working and middle class young women and their music, resonated with my spirit and your own political convictions, entitled *Noise: The Political Economy of Music* by Jacques Attali (1985). You inscribed it: 'Dear Leslie, with love – I hope this is good – which is just as well, since it's called, "*Noise*!!" Love, Stuart.'

In the stillness of the wee hours, life is still. Still – life, death. I feel the urgency to speak with Dennis. I email Dennis Dworkin, now a History professor at the University of Nevada, who experienced with me some of the same history-making events with you – from listening to you at the *Marxism and the Interpretation of Culture Conference* (1983), and later, to hanging out in Madison and in Chicago, witnessing at your invitation to Dennis and me, your interview with Jesse Jackson to be published in *Marxism Today* (Hall, 1986). Then, the next day all three of us went to hear Bishop Tutu speak. Dennis and I both feel the urgency to speak to one another, to relive, grasp the magnitude of your loss, and mourn together. Stuart, I almost cry out, I always read to my students Marge Piercy's poem, "To be of use" which reminds me of your confident passion in teaching:

To be of use

The people I love the best
jump into work head first
without dallying in the shallows
and swim off with sure strokes almost out of sight
(Piercy, 1982, p. 106).

Swimming: a teacher is made, not born

In the most memorable and instructive interview of Stuart Hall, at least for my purposes to (re)claim Stuart Hall as an extraordinary educator, sociologist Les Back (Hall & Back, 2009) helps the Left recover a little known episode in Stuart Hall's formation as a public intellectual, as an ordinary Secondary Modern teacher. It was posthumous news to me that Stuart Hall was ever a Secondary Modern school teacher, in fact, more to the point, he was a recurring supply teacher for the same school and aptly refers to himself as part of a 'reserve army of labour' (1983) composed mainly of newly migrated foreign workers of colour in a predominantly white working-class boys' Secondary Modern school in Kennington.

In the 1950s, Les Back tells me that the school in which Stuart Hall taught was populated predominantly by white working-class English-born, as well as Scottish and Irish migrants with very few black pupils (Back, personal communication, 2014). Yet, the neighbourhoods of Kennington and Brixton were populated as well by a significant wave of Caribbean migrants to Britain who were part of the Windrush of Caribbean migrants in 1948. When he had first come to Oxford just after the War (1951–1957) on scholarships from both Jamaica College and Rhodes, during the Windrush, he played in a jazz band with Caribbean migrant bus drivers who were saxophonists and conductors. Then, he moved to London during the post-Suez Crisis and Hungary to found *Universities and Left Review*. It was the first time in England when working-class students had access to higher education (Phillips, 1997).[2]

Though the historical details of this early part of his being an educator are at once, contested and sketchy, what is most riveting is Hall's recollection of becoming a teacher. In a most self-deprecating and humorous manner, Hall reveals his first teaching job was a default option, as it is for many, and likewise, he was made a teacher through mistakes, not born one. He did not swim with 'sure strokes' and found that 'while he loved teaching, it was a completely harrowing time' (Hall & Back, 2009, p. 271). Second, his teaching takes place in the larger context of his activist intellectual and political work at other sites, notably, but by no means all-inclusively, of editing *Universities & Left Review* (later to become the *New Left Review*). Like many students who leave university not knowing what they will do, Hall chooses teaching while still considering whether to return to Jamaica:

> I thought, well, what can you do? Practically, nothing! I couldn't then drive, so I couldn't drive a milk float. You can teach. So I got a job in a secondary school as a supply teacher, and you're sent round to different schools, but my school was unable to retain any of its supply teachers, or indeed, its teachers. So once I'd got in there they never let me go. I was a

supply teacher in a school at the Kennington Oval, for quite a while, about three or four years, and I used to leave there, get on a train, go to Soho, and edit the journal, and go back on the night bus – try to wake up in time to get to the Oval for the opening of class. (Hall & Back, 2009, p. 671)

It was an epiphany for Hall that he found another medium for his voice and passion in teaching, despite recognizing how naive he was at the job itself:

> I loved teaching though it was a completely harrowing experience for me. First of all I couldn't keep discipline. I was very young still and had no experience of teaching. I'd never been taught to teach so I just walked in. I was given a class, which was 4FX. This was a Secondary Modern school so everybody in it had already failed their 11 Plus … So, this is kids right at the bottom of the pile. What was I to do with them? So I said, 'What are you going to do when you leave school?' 'Oh sir, we're going into the print.' Their fathers all worked then in the print – that was the only route into print. So they didn't see any reason why they should ever study anything again … Well, I'd teach them. I tried to teach them English Grammar. Can you imagine? Gerunds, commas, and semi-colons. [Laughter] (Hall & Back, 2009, p. 671)

Hall scrambled to make a relevant curriculum in the context of the contradictions among his students' lives, the lowered social class expectations for them and his own inexperience. Back (2014) relayed to me in an informal interview and personal correspondence that "'Secondary Modern'[3] confers a whole series of charged cultural and class meanings'. The British school system in the 1950s was a 'tripartite pyramid structure' with the Secondary Modern schools at the bottom, Grammar Schools topping it and Technical Schools in the middle (Clarke, personal communication, 2014). Hall's mostly white working-class students were expected to follow their fathers into the printing industry – the only route available to them. However, due to racialized trade protectionism in the printing industry, this route was closed to the offspring of Caribbean migrants who were part of the UK's post-war 'boom' resulting from the 1948 Nationality Act to revitalize the urban centres of England such as Kennington. Instead, Caribbean migrants found themselves relegated to service jobs in hospitals or the transportation sector, driving buses and working in railway development. Hall commented to Les Back that very few Black students attended the Secondary Modern School where his first teaching occurred (Back, personal communication, 2014).

Hall faced an extraordinary situation, teaching with no formal experience and then realizing in this moment most novice teachers' worst fear – being observed by one's supervisor, Head teacher or principal while 'making it up' for the first time. He recalls:

> I had to teach them geography, and one day the geography master came in and said 'This is interesting. You're-teaching them about the trade wind, except that you've got the south-east and north-west wrong way round on the blackboard'. [Laughter]
> I was so naive, I'd left it there. I tried to get them to act *Romeo and Juliet.* Craziness – just completely crazy and made up out of my head really. But I also had to take them swimming and do life-saving. I'd never life-saved anything in my life, so I was terrified. I said, 'Before we go to the pool, we're going to practice life-saving in the hall upstairs' [Laughter]
> These kids, all lying in the hall, saving one another, while I read the book. Eventually of course, I had to take them to the pool. I was sure one of them was going to drown, I was absolutely certain, but they didn't … It was a very rich experience; but not for very long. (Hall & Back, 2009, p. 671)

When I first read this humorous episode, I smiled, asking: 'Was that the great Stuart Hall, making such mistakes, noticing that his kids peeled off from school, finding little reason to return after swimming only to be dismissed?' Then, I thought, good teachers can laugh at their own mistakes and learn from them. Great educators remember their mistakes and relish their inventive capacity to make it up as the moment requires, something he would later say was the secret to the successful creation of The Centre for Contemporary Cultural Studies – teaching and learning with others from their own impromptu assemblages.

Hall's time enjoying teaching his Secondary Modern students came to an abrupt end once the Notting Hill and Nottingham riots began and after his 'subject' of writing about diaspora 'found' him, not by choice but by being racialized as 'Black' in the British context through British forms of 'homegrown' racism (Henry, 2015). One day, Hall followed the boys into West London by train only to discover they had been harassing Black women and getting into a bit of an 'argy-bargy'. On their return to the classroom, Hall pointedly queried them, challenging their racism but not their sexism. The 'kids' in his school were like a first alert system for Hall of the racial conflicts about to occur:

> [M]y first awareness that something was happening in Notting Hill was before the riots, by kids in my school alerting me. So when we got back to school I said, 'What are you doing up there?'
> 'Oh, you know' I said, 'Why are you shouting at them?' 'Well, they're taking our women.' I said, 'What do you mean? If only you had had any women!' [Laughter]
> 'They're taking our things,' etc. So I said, 'Do you mean these?' And I pointed to several Black kids in the class and they looked at them as if they'd never seen them. 'No sir.'
> 'They're one of us.' So I said, 'What about me?' 'No sir. Not you. Them.' It was a very important experience to me. Incredible. (Hall & Back, 2009, p. 672)

The exchange was a telling form of powerful racializing and racist ideology of the exceptions made though the affinities and connections between Hall and the white students in the class, exceptions they also declared to Hall they made for their Black classmates. Yet, such contradictions of racism also can become the brutal flipside. Hall went onto to discuss just such a conjuncture when the racism 'simmering underneath finally gets spoken', and later 'erupts in straightforward open aggression and violence'. He spoke of the instance of British High Tory and Member of Parliament, Enoch Powell espousing that the Windrush 'immigrants' were eroding the social cohesion of Britain, expressing anti-immigration views and anti-immigrant moral panic (Hall & Back, 2009, p. 672). The classroom exchange left a mighty impression on Hall, who over many years referred to it in critical discourses and texts he circulated for different publics and counter-publics – from speeches to the National Committee for Commonwealth Immigrant[4] to writing for *Universities and New Left Review*. Here, we see a mobile educator who clearly realizes that education itself exceeds formal schooling and that its public pedagogies reach different audiences and constitutes different polities across meaningful sites of what he would later dub, 'cultural politics'.[5]

Hailing educational publics and counter-publics through diaspora

In 1959, Hall wrote a modest duet book review, 'Absolute Beginnings'[6] for the *Universities and Left Review* which sums up the sorry shape of class conflict and racist tensions between the white secondary modern teachers and the often foreign-born supply teachers of colour. Most striking is the fact that Hall framed himself professionally as an educator and one who speaks back to the profession and its staff, drawing on a structural critique of Secondary Modern Schools as deeply impacted by an intertwined classism and racism. He astutely observed that the Secondary Modern teachers 'suffer an acute lack of morale' which goes 'consciously overlooked because such teachers are in such short supply' (Hall, 1959, p. 17). Hall reports not only that the teachers 'despise the areas in which they teach', but also the 'homes from which their students come' and the personal problems the young people bring with them. While the white teachers maintain 'a safe distance between themselves and the school – protected from the realities of urban life by the green belt and suburban line', he wrote how this internalized self-disrespect gets foisted onto the mostly foreign born migrants of colour who are, like him, the supply teachers whom he refers to as the 'shock troops in the front line of the class struggle in secondary education' (Hall, 1959, p. 17):

> It is most disturbing to count up the number of young teachers who would like their self-respect and their status to be protected by the agile and relentless use of the headmaster's cane. In many cases, Sec. Mod teachers invert their affronted sense of status into an attack upon the supply teachers. How much of this is due to professional jealousy, how much to the fact that supply teachers are often foreigners – Australians, West Indians, Indians, Pakistanis, etc. – is difficult to judge. But the thing is there, and fostered at national level too (witness the disgusting sentiments expressed at a recent conference of the Schoolmasters' Association), in spite of the fact that, without the present numbers of supply teachers, many Secondary Modern schools would fold up tomorrow. (Hall, 1959, p. 17)

Here, in the text that circulates of *Universities and New Left Review* Hall hails a public in a manner that embodies three of Warner's (2002) conceptions of the public. In the first, he speaks reflexively as an educator, addressing others who might identify with his materialist critique of classist racism and neo-colonialism at work in the school system. In the second, he signals a deeper structural critique of such practices in Britain as a nation – a 'social totality'. Third, not content to let the events of his Secondary Modern teaching go unremarked, he publishes and publicly speaks about them, creating a counter-public discourse through which others marked as 'foreign born' supply teachers could recognize themselves as appreciated addressees. Through Hall's involvement with the New Left Club's activism against the racism in Notting Hill, he also met 'Michael X' (Michael de Freitas), a Trinidadian who migrated to London in 1957, who had taken on the name 'Michael X' after the US Black Power Movement and founded the Racial Adjustment Action Society, a Black Power Commune in North London. Hall's deep knowledge of 'Michael X' shows what Clarke argues (2015) that he took political encounters with activists, the ordinary public or his students from the starting place of the learners, engaging their extramural curricular interests for the sake of creating public pedagogies to redress the racism and other oppressive experiences diasporic peoples encountered.

For Hall, to write about diaspora, racism and 'race' as a 'floating signifier' was to trouble and queer the familiar white masculinist English nation as more diverse than the official discourses cared to imagine. Diasporic thinking was both a loss and a starting place for new identifications, not just the emergent condition of post-colonial modernity (Chen, 2010). Migration, bits of different cultures intertwining while nostalgic for the displaced first national home and yet realizing that one can neither go home nor be at home in the new country of 'settlement' – a constant state of displacement and not quite belonging, was a new place from which to forge creative alliances, cultural politics and the potential for counter-hegemonic movements. He worked as part of the New Left not only on creating what we now would call anti-racist coalitions but also tenants' organizations in London, as well taking on leadership roles such as speaking at the Campaign for Nuclear Disarmament in Trafalgar Square in 1958. This was public conjunctural thinking, teaching publicly – making publics and moving publics.

Well before he came to Madison, Hall taught liberal arts at Chelsea College (1961–1964) and co-authored with Paddy Whannel (Hall & Whannell, 1964), a book for teachers and students, *The Popular Arts* published by Hutchinson's Educational Division, which would become a cornerstone text for the cultural studies to emerge at the Centre for Contemporary Cultural Studies. Whannel was the Education Officer for the British Film Institute and had been himself a teacher in British schools for nine years previously. Hall was hired as a 'research fellow' under Richard Hoggart at the Centre for Contemporary Cultural Studies, and later became its Director. It was not fully operational until 1964 but the Centre's 'philosophy of teaching' decentered the texts of heralded authors and instead offered students an interrogatory way of finding their own subjectivities, voices and counter-hegemonic politics in relation to querying key texts.[7] These students included among notable others, Lucy Bland, Rosiland Brunt, Hazel Carby, John Clarke, Paul Gilroy, Angela McRobbie, Charlotte Brundson, Rosilind Brunt, Larry Grossberg, Iain Chambers, Lidia Curti, Pratibha Parmar, Paul Willis, and many more, who became the primary progenitors of Cultural Studies. By 1979, without a Ph.D. but already an accomplished and internationally acclaimed scholar, he would be asked to become a Professor of Sociology at the Open University (Evans, 2014a, 2014b) and would write one of the most important critiques of the how the Right worked its articulations on education ever written, aptly titled, "The Great Moving Right Show" (Hall, 1979).

The long seminar: historical imagination and Stuart Hall's pedagogical revolution

People often ask me, 'What was it like to be a graduate student of Stuart Hall?' The first thing I say is, 'Well, I only had Stuart for my professor in one short course but it turned out be to the longest seminar of my career, in fact, my life'. In the fall of 1985, 8–26 September, to be exact, on the advice of Michael Apple, my Ph.D. supervisor, and with my prior excitement of having heard Stuart Hall speak at the *Marxism and Interpretation of Culture* conference in Urbana, Illinois, I enrolled in Hall's one credit seminar offered through the University of Wisconsin-Madison's Sociology Department and, more specifically, the Class Analysis programme. While formally titled, 'Critical Sociology 994', it was really a transformative course on the concept of ideology as articulated by Hall's dialogue with the readings through his work and with us. I have told my students over the years since that the course should have been titled 'Articulating Ideology: Stuart Hall Re-works Marx, Engels, Althusser, Foucault, Freud, Gramsci, Mouffe and Laclau'. It was a sociological history of ideas and concepts. Yet, it was also more than that, and best encapsulated in the notion of dialogue. Hall had been invited to be the Eugene Havens' Memorial Scholar and in conjunction with his larger talks open to the public at the University of Wisconsin, he taught this graduate seminar for four weeks. Each of the seminar weekly readings and discussion were then followed and punctuated by one of four public talks – to which the word 'lecture' does not do justice. So emblazoned in my memory, it is nearly effortless to recall the palpable excitement and intensity of Hall's teaching and public seminars. As an educator, I have rarely heard or felt anything like the intellectual and political engagement with which he capably handled ideas and debates that seemed stuck. Hall had a way of offering alternatives, unsticking polarities in theoretical traditions and most of all, not being wed to theoretical traditions as identities in and of themselves.

In class, the roster (Hall, 1985f, n.p.), which I still possess reflected that we were a mixture of 17 registered students (and several more unregistered) from different countries, fields and disciplines, including from my class list, one from Political Science, six from Communication Arts and Mass Communications, eight from Sociology, one from Educational Policy Studies (me) and one from Social Work and there were other non-registered students from Curriculum and Instruction, History, Journalism and English, as I recall not reflected on the roster (Hall, 1985f, n.p.). If bodies in the class from different fields and countries mean anything, they certainly attest to Hall's reach as a scholar and intellectual who was being read before students arrived (Hall, 1985f, n.p.). The word had gotten out!

The quality of the engagement among students and with Hall and the readings much like a musical score of a rich jazz composition followed a very unconventional logic. Entering the class, I expected something like a classical approach to the readings. Students with a wide and diverse engagement in activist social movements – from the underground railroad in Central America to anti-Apartheid in South Africa, from a literacy campaign for low-income elderly migrants and people of colour to feminist fugitives from masculinist Marxism – found themselves not just taken seriously but truly to be the real texts and subjects of the course. Whereas in most graduate courses, the appetite to have students read the canon, do the literature review, or refine their methodologies, Stuart Hall's approach was something different. Each week we were expected to prepare an 8- to 10-page essay responding to his takes on the readings – his were set up as a critical dialogue with the readings. What was novel (to this day) was that our ideas were critical to his own intellectual formation; as students we were not there to parrot him but instead to challenge his thinking in an against-the-grain manner which took our own activist and diasporic experiences seriously. For example, I recall that it was no longer out place for me to discuss my own work in the Sanctuary Movement with refugees from El Salvador and Nicaragua, in which I was journalist-cum-witness covering the trial in Tucson, Arizona, of the indicted Sanctuary workers and interviewing refugees who had escaped certain death in Central America only to find themselves captive detainees in INS (Immigration and Naturalization Service Centers). Nor was it seen as less than scholarly academic rigour to link my earlier work in Freirian adult literacy with low-income housing tenants to Hall's own reworking of Gramsci's understandings of war of position. Most of the students were activists involved in one or more social movements from around the world with stories to share in light of experiences and in relation to the readings. I recall a very lively exchange among students over just how far the militancy should go in South Africa, and whether Foucault had anything to offer a radical democratic and revolutionary struggle. My notes also describe a heated debate among students over the oppressiveness of marriage and Marx's incapacity to figure issues of the gendered division of labour in the family, reproductive work and domestic labour into his critique of capitalism. It was not long before the students in the class became colleagues with one another and were as memorable and engaging as he was. For example, when an idea Hall had written about did not sit well with a Black activist student who had worked in South Africa, it was Hall who had to rethink out loud what was wrong with the concept he had developed up until that point. We got to see how Hall would respond on his feet so to speak and then, rewrite an argument based on learning from us. Moreover, we became the primary and the advance audience for Hall's Havens' lectures. We would arrive at the public lectures as though we were not transitory lumpen but rather, the royalty of Cultural Studies and Sociology! In some instances, when Hall sharpened an argument about 'ideology', 'hegemony' or 'articulation', we knew we were the rightful co-shapers of the finer point. This, I experienced as writing in progress for the service of honing one's audiences and publics – writing purposely and speaking passionately as part of intellectual movement work: going public meant leaving behind the ethos of the solitary scholar and the one who would become famous for selfish good.

As I read through the course syllabus (Hall, 1985e, 1985f, n.p.), my notes (Roman, 1985), I cannot help but note that this period would be approaching Hall's mid-career as an educator and public intellectual. While for many, the readings and figures he drew upon may seem like a distant affair, the way he taught them still remains incredibly prescient and present for me. However, I must note, higher education in the USA in the 1980s marked a transition from Reaganism to neoliberalism and the indentations of that were articulated in structural demographics of doctoral education: precious few doctoral students could afford to do Ph.D.'s exclusively as full-time students unless they took out huge loans or were funded through scholarships. It has gotten only worse since. I was among the former group, largely without significant scholarships. Funding was becoming extremely competitive when compared with the 1960s and 1970s. While Hoggart and Hall had already established the Centre for Cultural Studies in Birmingham as part of the New Left, in the US context, Cultural Studies was some years later just finding its 'feet'. Hall was of course much more than its translator; he was its embodied diasporic intellectual scholar activist and 'midwife'. In this case, rearticulating Cultural Studies within the USA required a subtle and sophisticated intellectual public pedagogue. In Hall such a public pedagogue had arrived. To be able to talk about materialism and class politics, let alone racism and populist ideologies such as Thatcherism, was ponderous, wondrous, exciting and dangerous. Each of his four public 'lectures' created palpable effect among the audiences that they were moved. The talks were framed as questions which he posed to the audiences much as he did in our classes, which have long stayed with me:

(1) 'Is there a Materialist Theory of Ideology?' (Hall, 1985a, Monday, September, 9, 3:30 p.m., 8417 Social Sciences)
(2) 'The Structuralist Critique' (Hall, 1985b, Friday, September, 13, 1985, 3:30, p.m., 8417 Social Sciences)
(3) 'Is there a Theory of Ideology in Gramsci?' (Hall, 1985c, Monday September 16, 3:30, p.m., State Historical Society)
(4) 'Towards a Theory of Articulation' (Hall, Monday, September, 23, 1985d, 3:30 p.m. 8417 Social Sciences)

Audiences did not just linger afterwards, they engaged Hall and he them. The 'question periods' were seminars unto themselves. Perhaps, this had something to do with how Hall regarded audiences, not as passive recipients but as people who might have doubts about what he was saying or have deep resonance with some elements of his ideas and not others. He did not take audiences or his students for granted. I recall Hall's audiences for these large talks included feminists, neo-Marxists, post-structuralists, non-academic union members, various student sub-cultural groups – a group of Latino, Caribbean and South African anti-Apartheid activist students, and I had scribbled on one page, 'Hey, so and so and so and so [names deleted for anonymity's sake] from the Punks are here!', international students of many diverse backgrounds, racially and nationally. His oratory skills were incomparable – a mixture of being adept at making sometimes dense or abstract ideas come alive and being a scholar's scholar, cautious to root ideas in their larger historical and political context without succumbing when questioned or challenged to easy solutions or either-or thinking.

I recall someone asking Hall to explain whether and how Thatcherism was different from Reagan's populism – something to the effect of – 'Was Reaganism just another version of Thatcherism?' This was followed up by, 'And, would you comment on the state of working-class conservatism in the US context?' (Audience comment quoted in Roman notes, Hall, 23 September 1985). Hall's answer was not what I believe some expected. He first spoke about the very historically specific dynamics of racism in the USA that would have made Reaganism's populist historical formation different from Thatcherism. Then, he reframed its forms of populism in the US context where the history of slavery and Civil Rights' movement had 'outed' the movement from invisible marginalization to the Black Power movement well before such a movement had articulated itself in Britain. Lastly and famously, he involved the questioner with intelligent regard and turned the question back to the audience and the questioner: and then, he asked the questioner whether Reaganism could be seen in this context instead of British Thatcherism. My notes said, 'Reaganism is a collective historical subject and project' – and further, that it is 'specifically important to ask yourselves how Reagan established strong elements of the Republican Party to become the popular party?' (Hall, 23 September 1985, pp. 6–8 in Roman, Hall Lecture 4 notes, 'Towards a theory of articulation'). Then, this surprising critique came forward from Hall:

> Usually, radicals see the working classes as inherently conservative on women's rights, pro-nuclear family ideology, interested in the control of crime and have themselves a relatively short-lived attachment to labour with short-lived interest. I find fault with this view. There is no essential conservative or revolutionary subject. We must use the 'notion of contradictory subjects' in order to understand for example, how and why Thatcherism is successful in politics, and where the Labour Party has evacuated, neglected or left out particular issues from politics. In the UK, the Labour Party has tended to treat these as non-political issues or as partisan issues. This already concedes a vast political terrain to the Right. Labour gave up on the comprehensive school once it was established with the Black Paper's stand on back to basics, aligning the Conservative Party with working class parents with a political force missing from the Labour party. This was hegemony. Thatcherism appears to address the real interests of working class parents, refers to them as 'aspiring parents', 'law and order parents', 'mothers against abortion', etc. and this becomes a composite personality. The question is: 'How does a particular ideology become popular and win hegemonic consent across different social movements?' We need to explain how diverse social classes come to speak a non-partisan discourse of the New Right, which includes familialism, nationhood, etc. so as to refract and destabilize other discourses and harness them to a new social project and ideological basis. This is what articulation means and why it is central. It puts the focus on the work of different ideological elements to harness the themes of 'hard-working family', 'policing crime' and condensing Black people into signifiers for 'criminals' in the context of the US's own populist contradictory conservative projects. (Hall, 23 September 1985; Roman, 1985)

The logic was clear, 'policing crime', 'familialism' and the racist racialization of Black people in the UK (or anywhere for that matter) were not inherently or exclusively problems of working-class conservatism and furthermore, the Left should understand that articulation works best when consent is won across class, racial, gender formations and different social movements. Hall invited us to use our working knowledge of US political politics to query what made Reaganism work as a conservative populist ideology. Some may have thought he was here to tell the audience from the British experience what we might anticipate in the US context. Not so. While it was clear connections could be made from the racialization of Thatcherism to the racialization of Reaganism, Hall's conceptual work on the concept of 'articulation' was not a theory of simple duplication from place to place. In order for the articulation of hegemony to be secured, it had to take hold of people's common sense and speak to them in a vernacular that resonated, all the while reconstituting new elements of common sense.

Having electrified the audience on this his last of the four lectures or talks, he left us with questions about how the Left might disarticulate the assembled New Right project. The last part of his talk, he spoke about the articulation of subjects not being universal or strictly psychoanalytically rooted, but as what he called:

> the languaged subject [through which] we go on or make sense of the world in addition to using language and psychoanalytic processes in a system of narration and processes of condensation, the latter of which comes from Freud. The contradiction is that we must engage in the dominant hegemonic discourses to disarticulate them and make them belong to a new discourse. For this, we must understand unities of struggles and the need for the plurality of differences in social movements, in our work, theoretically and politically. (Hall, Monday, 23 September 1985)

After Hall spoke on this the last of his four lectures; 'You could hear a pin drop'. A millisecond later, the audience gave an ovation. Something unforgettable and transformative had occurred:

Stuart,
    Did I ever tell you that what I learned from you walking across the spaces of the classroom, the public lectures, the private conversations and yes, the dance-floor in the aftermath of our final class with all the students and Dennis, dancing to Marvin Gaye and musing politics in my shared rental apartment in Madison? I learned that Left scholarship, feminist, anti-colonial politics, and social movement work were all of one cloth, though they had different audiences and discourses: they could be at once hard work and occasionally, fun. They could challenge dominant propertied notions of marriage and ways of doing scholarship.

Public thinking, Jesse Jackson and the Rainbow Coalition

In the fall of 1986, I got the phone call of my life up until this point. It was Dennis Dworkin, excitedly telling me that Stuart was about to fly to Chicago and interview Jesse Jackson for *Marxism Today*. Hall had invited Dennis, who was an amateur photographer and also already interviewing Stuart for his dissertation (Dworkin, 1990) on the New Left in England,[8] to accompany him to photograph the interview and asked him to bring me along to the interview. Now, this kind of extraordinary access to witnessing history and being a small part of a renowned public intellectual's life was nothing unusual for the Stuart Hall both Dennis and I and countless others got to know. However, suffice it to say it was entirely extraordinary for both us and remains so. Jackson had just campaigned and lost his first bid for the Democratic nomination for the US Presidency in 1984. However, Jackson still had strong support in the National Rainbow Coalition, which had grown in size and influence. Jackson outspokenly criticized Reagan's policies for disinvesting in domestic government spending, particularly in the urban centres, causing further unemployment, white flight to the suburbs and cuts to health care and education. In the meantime, Jackson pointed out that Reagan's policies supported corporate investments abroad in the infamous tax-free import-export zones outside the USA, where labour safety and environmental regulations did not pertain and workers from Third World countries were exploited. Jackson had international prominence as well as being a leading voice for the USA and the world in anti-Apartheid struggles and had recently appeared in London, England to protest in a demonstration 12,000 strong in Trafalgar Square with anti-Apartheid Labour Movement activists and Members of Parliament, as well to meet with and appeal to Prime Minister, Margaret Thatcher, to release Nelson Mandela from prison and stop Apartheid.[9] Jackson's Rainbow Coalition consisted of African-Americans, Native Americans, working mothers, Jewish progressive people, small farmers, sexual minorities and other groups hit hardest by Reagan's policies. Hence, for Hall this robust instance of a counter-hegemonic coalition had to be documented and its key animator interviewed. Uniquely gifted at anticipating such milestones and then

Figure 1.   Stuart Hall interviews Jesse Jackson for *Marxism Today*, 1986. (Photo credit ©Dennis Dworkin).

Figure 2.   Stuart Hall interviews Jesse Jackson, 1986. (Photo credit ©Dennis Dworkin).

translating their importance for larger publics, Hall seized the moment to catch a plane to Chicago. He bunked on a futon at Dennis Dworkin's place, while I took a bus to Chicago from Madison. Dennis was to interview Hall for his doctoral thesis and I was to join them the next day for the historic interview with Jackson.

Together, the three of us drove to the People United to Service Humanity (PUSH) office, the headquarters for the Chicago Rainbow Coalition at the time located somewhere on West 43rd St and North of Hyde Park and not the same Southside address as it is now. Hall's intermediary for this interview had been former graduate student of his from the Centre for Contemporary Cultural Studies who worked with the African National Congress (ANC) in South Africa and was now working with Jackson's Coalition. From the PUSH office, we were then driven by an African-American woman, who had been the key scheduler of and woman behind the scenes to three generations of African-American leadership (Reverend Ralph Abernathy, Reverend Martin Luther King and now Reverend Jesse Jackson Sr.). She was an impressive statuesque woman who was the knowledge-keeper, Ms Lucille Lohman, having been with PUSH in all its organizational forms. I recall later regretting that I had not interviewed her! She gave us an impromptu seminar in the car on what made each generation of African- American leadership so significant to the Civil Rights' history in the USA – all this on route to Jackson's middle-class home on the south side of Chicago. There, behind tight security, we were ushered into a palatial waiting area. I recall seeing a large armoire lit up with glass shelves, displaying trinkets, trophies, statues and regalia from Jackson's various trips around the world. We could see whenever the door opened a crack to the living room, cameras, lights and stands, and overhear but inaudibly Jackson being interviewed. We would learn when the reporters left some two hours later while waiting that the prior interview was for *Ebony* magazine. They filed out, and in we came. Dennis carried his photography gear and historical sensibilities. I brought my sociological curiosity and acute attentiveness.

Once in the room, it became apparent that Jackson was flanked by an entourage of staff composed mainly of young adults, the future of America's best hopes for racial equality and social justice from a variety of different social backgrounds. They were there to advise him, keep him on task and on message for the interview. Jackson sat to my right in a wing-backed decorative chair, his body angled towards Hall and yet still facing the camera. Jackson himself looked framed by a large portrait of himself from his younger days hung just above the centre of the fireplace mantel (see Figure 1). Hall was seated to my left. Dennis, the photographer, crouched to the left of me and moved about to shoot the photos for *Marxism Today* (Hall, 1986). Jackson's advisor (featured in Figure 2) was sprawled out on the floor and moved around, so it was sometimes difficult for Dennis to get his shots, though the photos featured here are taken from different angles in the same room.[10] On the wall and side tables framed photos of Jackson's family, one with one of his sons in dress whites of the military, another with another son on the football field and others including framed family portraits decorated the room. I remember feeling a mix of awe and rare honour. Like any major politician hosting media in their homes, Jackson understood the symbolic power of this representation of his family as 'all-American' for the media. Later, we later learned this was mock family room understandably staged for the media; the real one was downstairs. Hall had informed us that one of his South African anti-Apartheid activist students from the Centre for Contemporary Cultural Studies now working for Jackson, had persuaded Jackson to grant the interview – something of significance in a former Presidential candidate's demanding schedule. Such was the stature of Hall in the transnational diasporic intellectual counter-public.

Uniquely combining the voice of a critical researcher-cum-journalist and activist scholar, Hall had come well prepared. Under the headline which would soon read: '**STUART HALL INTERVIEWS AMERICA'S LEADING BLACK POLITICIAN**', he opened the interview that would be published introducing the future readers of *Marxism Today* to Jackson:

> Former Martin Luther King lieutenant and civil rights organizer was active in equal rights, voter registration and affirmative actions before emerging in 1984, from a host of possibilities, to become America's first black presidential candidate. His appeal to the black, Hispanic and Asian communities to join women, the poor, gays, liberal progressives and peace activists to form a 'Rainbow Coalition' challenged the Democratic party establishment in 1984 (and nearly upset the Hart and Mondale candidatures). Combining shrewd political judgment with the charisma of the black prophetic tradition, Jackson is now the leading progressive figure in national American politics. (Hall, 1986, p. 6)

The formal interview began with two tape-recorders ready – showing Hall's preparation as a researcher for the possibility that one might not work. As Figures 1 and 2 show, Hall had an engaging style of visual and aural communication, speaking with his hands, as well as erudite inviting Jamaican and British inflected voice:

SH: You are the first black to run for the presidency. Can you recall what the sorts of political calculations were in your mind when you decided to stand?

JJ: The conservatives and the liberals are often two faces of the same coin. They are going in the in the same direction, with the same presuppositions about economic policy, foreign policy and race relations. After all, neither a Democrat nor a Republican led the movement to end apartheid laws or for the right to vote. Martin Luther King led that. Those who want to change must accept neither personal gains from conservatives or be satisfied with public grants from liberals but must fight for liberation that represents the direction of those who are locked out must take. Fundamentally, liberation represents a change in direction. [Clarification of speakers mine] (Hall, 1986, p. 6)

I could not believe my ears. Did I just hear a recent almost successful major and the first African-American candidate for the 1984 US Presidency critique the two-party system in the USA with the devastating observation that neither party had the moral guts to oppose Apartheid? Jackson's reference to Martin Luther King's activism needs to be heard in relation to his prophetic words about the platitude that the political parties have become 'two faces of the same coin'. In particular, he pointed to Martin Luther King's activism as the source for challenges to the Apartheid in South Africa – as exemplary of the inspiration, commitments, actions and social movements that fuel change to the existing political system. Like Hall, he shared the belief that progressive social movements which took their ideas to the streets, often outside the existing political parties or rather within larger publics had the edge on creating conditions of equality and social justice.

Once fully underway, though, the interview took on fast-paced verbal repartee with a subtle undertow of the limitations of Jackson to embrace openly a seriously full-blown anti-imperialist and anti-capitalist critique. This was not from Hall's lack of pushing Jackson. It was the nature of US politics that reined Jackson's responses into an increasingly tight net in which most of his answers still had to sound acceptable to prospective voters in the conventional two-party vernacular, which embraced liberalism, 'free-market capitalism' and a redemptive vision of USA. Hall attempted to press Jackson further on the shrewd strategy and significance of the Rainbow Coalition as an alternative space that might not fit within the traditional Democratic Party or union politics:

> **SH:** But isn't it the case that those different elements in the Coalition have been traditionally organized – either within the Democratic Party or within unions, or within ethnic groupings – in such a way as to sharpen rather than reduce their sense of difference, of different interests from each other? Politically your strategy seems to be based on attempt to cut across existing traditional divisions and alignments in American politics to redraw those lines of connection in a different way, around a new programme.

> **JJ:** Alignments are changing. Some of your old liberals are now your new conservatives. Many of them are intimidated by Reagan. With his success in being elected and re-elected, they are trying to pattern and style. And, what they are doing, in this radical shift to the right, is leaving, or creating, a new majority. There are more people to the center and left of center. There are more people locked out than locked in. The polarising economic shift in this country in terms of wealth concentration in the top 5% and the poverty concentration in the bottom 25%. There's no sense of planning in the economy. And that gap between the haves and have-nots is becoming very pronounced. There is no sense of planning in the economy. There's not enough central leadership to keep the labour, management and business forces in a proper relationship. The radical shift in taxation is a pretty good indicator of it. In 1932, 68% of taxes were paid by corporations, and, 32% by individuals. That's extreme, that's revolutionary. [Clarification of speakers mine] (Hall, 1986, p. 6)

Hall pursued vigorously Jackson's positions on the strengths of the Rainbow Party and its differences from traditional political party thinking and politics, as well as Jackson's stances on Civil Rights leadership, economic and foreign policy under Reagan, Apartheid in South Africa, and a range of diverse transnational issues – from the Middle East to the political future of Afro-Caribbean migrants living in Britain versus the positions faced by

African-Americans in the USA. He asked Jackson to elaborate on Reagan's destructive effects on the social progress of the Civil Rights movement and other progressive gains prior to Reagan. Hall pressed further, asking Jackson to elaborate how he could realize Rainbow Coalition vision which seemed to exceed what was possible through using the Democratic Party as his 'vehicle' for the 'alternative' Jackson 'envisaged' (Hall, 1986, p. 7). Jackson shared a number of significant insights, particularly on how Reagan had made 'political hay by reviving the fears of many poor and threatened white people' (Hall, 1986, p. 7), observing how white leadership had abandoned the urban centers of American cities just as African-Americans became mayors for the first time historically. With these concessions from Jackson, Hall then shifted from the voice of a critical journalist with a populist discourse as public pedagogue to one invoking a critical Left materialist scholarly vocabulary. He challenged the limits of the Democratic Party to embrace an anti-capitalist and anti-imperialist alternative. Hall waded into the fray:

> **SH:** To observers in Europe the platforms you have been advancing on the economic and industrial front seem to have a strong anti-capitalist and anti-corporate content. They aim to bring corporations into a framework of social responsibility. Your policies also have a strong anti-imperialist thrust on the world scene, centering on Third World questions, and a powerful anti-racist thrust not just in terms of domestic politics but on a global scale … Is that how you would characterize your position? [Clarification of speakers mine] (Hall, 1986, p. 11)

With Hall's pointed question, tension mounted. Both Dennis and I recall Jackson's posture stiffening. He sat up in his chair and straightened his tie. Then, he cleared his throat, answering evasively, with feigned naiveté and 'naturalistic' logic:

> **JJ:** Well, I am not sophisticated enough to understand all the labels you just made up. I just try to use the natural reasoning process … [I]t just makes good sense to feed the flower you rob. Many American industries rob the flower that feeds them. That's not good sense. The honey bee – it doesn't have a brain, it's just a bug. It only has instinct. But whatever it's got, it's got enough sense to drop pollen when it picks up nectar. These corporations get their nectar from America – their bank loans, their education, their labour and consumer base. But they're maintaining slave labour markets abroad. When the honey bee comes back, if it didn't leave any pollen, the flower will die. And, if the flower dies, the honey bee will die … Their obligation [as corporations who have benefited from tax breaks] is to reinvest, reindustrialize and retrain. That's just a natural process. [Clarification of speakers mine] (Hall, 1986, p. 11)

Given his status as a politician, Jackson could not or dare not declare explicitly any understanding, much less embrace of a full-blown anti-imperialist critique, making clear the limits on alternatives framed within US party politics and capitalist global imperatives. He was shrewd in his presentation of a socially responsible industrial policy, but also clear that he believed industry and labour could work comfortably together. Hall could not press through to a more critical position in the context of US discourses of populism and global capitalism. This was the first time I had ever heard Stuart Hall get responses that sometimes evaded his deep reflexive probes, hailing but not altogether registering as a counter-public.

It was novel to hear how Hall's diasporic ideas shaped his interview questions – a definite refreshing change from mind-numbing US nationalism. As the interview wound down, Hall asked Jackson to reflect on the current situation of African and Caribbean people who were now living in England. Jackson's reflections had both a paternalistic and prophetic ring, given recent events in the USA with police shootings of unarmed Black youth. Hall queried Jackson, referring to Jackson's speech in 1985 at the Anti-Apartheid protest in Trafalgar Square, asking him whether he thought the conception of a Rainbow Coalition might be applicable to Britain:

> **JJ:** Sure. You have a significant Afro-Caribbean population that has known the legacy of colonialism and racial rejection. And, you have a Conservative government that has expressed no plan or policy to make them first-class citizens. There's a tremendous sense of alienation within the Afro-Caribbean people on the ground. They are a very disappointed people because a lot of them left the Caribbean and other places with a sense of going home to the ultimate democratic experience. But they have been reduced to living in the maid's quarters of the Crown. They have come to accept that they were somehow inauthentic, somehow not the beneficiaries of the royal blood. Of course, our religion teaches us that we have all have royal blood. The alienation was expressed in the riots. [Clarification of speakers mine] (Hall, 1986, p. 22)

Jackson's prophetic discourse had and still has a deep resonance in the USA with African-Americans, who during Slavery and the Civil Rights' Movement have used it to speak the language of resistance and freedom through songs. He also made it clear to Hall that he believed it was an incorrect strategy in Britain for anti-racists to work against racial integrating the mostly White police force. Clearly aware of the riots in Britain in the 1980s, Jackson spoke of them as representing the 'pain and frustration of [black] people who speak but can never be heard' (Hall, 1986, p. 22). Then, he argued for a policy of racial integration of the police force, working from the assumption that 'if black and white police are riding together in the same car, it alters the behaviour of both' (Hall, 1986, p. 22):

> **JJ:** You've got 18% blacks in London – something like that. You've got 26,000 police in Britain, only 300 of whom are blacks. That is symptomatic of a lockout. There should be at least 5000 black policeman … I tried to convince them when I was last there, that the idea of fighting for the right not to have your own share of police is a very unwise strategy … The Afro-Caribbean people have got to deal with the identity question. They are *not* going back to the Islands or Africa … That means fighting for your share of everything that's available, vertically and horizontally. So blacks and Afro-Caribbean people in Britain must begin to fight for equity and parity – in the labour movement, in the government, in property ownership. They must break up the red lining from disinvestment in Brixton and investment in South Africa. [Clarification of speakers mine] (Hall, 1986, p. 11)

Stuart Hall would then go on in 1987 to write one of his most profoundly personal and political essays on his own diasporic experiences and the 'identity question' for diasporic migrants, particularly Afro-Caribbean Black youth in Britain in his essay, 'Minimal Selves' for the Institute for Contemporary Arts in London (Hall, 1987) and a number of now well-known pieces on diasporic identities (Hall, 1990a, 1990b; 1995; 1996a, 1996b, 1996c; 2005). 'Minimal Selves', a title he was given, was deeply reflexive in tackling the 'identity question' Jackson so famously suggested in his closing words of the interview. Hall repositioned questions of diasporic identity in his critique of postmodern assumptions about 'minimal identities' being unstable and yet remarkably re-centering of colonial narratives of culture, history and subjugation. Who can forget these words: 'Identity is formed at the unstable point when the unspeakable stories of subjectivity, meet the narratives of history, of a culture?' (Hall, 1987, p. 1). Public thinking extends the life-world of one context into other contexts, rather than containing ideas and debates to a private or single sphere.

The interview concluded around 11 pm, about two–and-a-half hours after it began. We left sensing that history was made. Yet, in the moment, its deeper significance was still elusive to us. To get a better handle on what transpired, we headed to the Tiki Restaurant for Polynesian food at the wee hours – where again it was clear in our debriefing that Jackson had evaded many crucial questions or appeared condescending to diasporic British Black experience, observations which, like us, readers would independently share in the Letters to the Editor of *Marxism Today* published after the interview came out (Bloomfield, 1986; Whittier, 1986).[11]

Poetic world-making: being *part of* public and counter-public thinking

An overlooked and underestimated aspect of publics and counter-publics is what Warner (2002) calls 'poetic world-making' (pp. 113–114), the capacity to mobilize and even stage other imagined worlds which counter-pose what could be with what is. I would extend this to both the fact of and the quality of people's participation in social movements. By participation, I mean the capacity to be *part of* rather than *apart from* social movement praxis, and by sharing space with others as who would dare to act in ways that challenge the limits of past and current social inequalities, to become maximal selves. Maximal selves, I posit, step outside privatized or possessive individualism to participate in an ethic of belonging and collective quest for social justice and social well-being. It is crucial to know how to be *part of* the hard and often un-glamourous work of simply being one of a many-peopled counter-public's 'attempts to realize the world it stages' and 'characterizes through address' (Warner, 2002, pp. 113–114). Such was the experience we would share together on the occasion of visit of Bishop Desmond Mpilo Tutu, human rights and anti-Apartheid activist and Nobel Peace Prize winner's speech to the congregants of and visitors to the American Liberty Baptist Church on the occasion of his visit to Chicago, the day after Hall's interview with Jackson.

On 26 January 1986, an almost record-breaking bitterly cold day, we went to hear Bishop Tutu speak at American Liberty Baptist Church, following an electrifying chain of speeches he had been giving in the week prior. Tutu had been speaking at Cathedral St Jane, Daley Plaza near the federal government buildings,[12] The Chicago Hilton, The Rockefeller Memorial Chapel and preceding his last event at the Midway Airport for his send-off by the Martin Luther King high school band, among others. South Africa's Apartheid was reported in Chicago's only African-American newspaper, *The Defender* (Crockett, 1986a, p. 22), as being on the brink of toppling in the midst of the movement worldwide to disinvest in it and its terrible regime of exploitation and inferiority for Black South Africans. Tutu had come on this fundraising mission supported by Chicago's Free South Africa Movement, a coalition of labour, community organizations and professional groups to fundraise to support the 20,000 Black South African miners who had been fired for striking against unfair working conditions and low wages, as well as for victims of Apartheid. The funds raised were to contribute to educational scholarships, provide housing and food for displaced families and families of political prisoners (*Chicago Tribune*, 1986). His speech at Liberty would be a momentous counter-public covered by local and national media but more than that, deeply symbolic as example of hopeful cultural politics in the midst of much historical exploitation and degradation of Black South Africans. This was understood at all of the venues but perhaps most resonant with the huge audience at the American Liberty Baptist Church steeped in Civil Rights history and whose congregants were predominantly African-American. Public high school marching bands from mostly African-American and Latino schools performed at each of the public venues of Tutu's speeches.

It is only now that I can truly appreciate the magnitude of this wider social movement and diaspora history in light of investigating the news coverage of all of these events and the poetic-world-making they inspired and properly understand what Stuart Hall's contributions mean. Jackson and Mayor Harold Washington, Chicago's first African-American mayor, took turns introducing Bishop Tutu at each of the events. In tracing the different venues and audiences for Tutu's stops in mainstream as well as African-American media, one can see that Tutu, Jackson – and Hall, and Martin Luther King Jr. before them – arguably among the greatest diasporic African, African-American and Caribbean British public pedagogues and human rights activists of the twenty-first century, participated together in a linked chain of mass public gatherings to end Apartheid. Hall's intellectual and moral force was among these greats – making, moving and bearing witness to publics and counter-publics to topple Apartheid and fight for civil and human rights of Black people. Jackson, himself the former Lieutenant of Martin Luther King's Civil Rights' campaign, asserted to the audience numbering 6000 at the Daley Plaza 'If you missed Martin Luther King Jr. in this life, his spirit still lives on and is embodied in Bishop Tutu' (Strausberg, 1986, p. 22). Mayor Washington too had been living a witness to Martin Luther King Jr. Thirty years prior, like Tutu, Martin Luther King Jr. was conferred an honorary theological degree from the Chicago Theological Seminary. So much history travelled diasporically across national spaces and time, what Brah (1996) calls the 'diasporic migration of ideas'. This was the unstoppable freedom train, which the *Chicago Defender* headlines blared, 'Freedom Messenger Leaves Spiritual Imprint on Chicago' (Strausberg, 1986, p. 22). No community in Chicago better understood Tutu as a 'freedom messenger' than the counter-public we would with Stuart Hall be privileged to experience the next day at American Liberty Baptist Church (herein called Liberty as it is known locally).[13]

Bearing witness: diaspora 'freedom messenger' at Liberty

In order to get floor space, we arrived two hours early to a packed gospel service with standing room only and 'onslaught of reporters' at Liberty on 4849 South King Dr for a service scheduled to run from 12.30 pm to 2.00 pm (Jamison, 1986, p. 22).[14] The Church was filled with under- and working-class African-Americans and middle-class notables and, influential community leaders who supported Tutu's drive to achieve racial equality by ending Apartheid and disinvesting in White South Africa. For the educational record, several local high schools (Martin Luther King Jr., and Rosa Parks, Wendell Phillips, among others) sent their students to Liberty for this momentous occasion. *The Defender's* reporter, Sandra Crockett wrote: 'Unlike Tutu's previous stops, where crowds were enthusiastic but relatively sedate, folks at American Liberty Baptist Church proudly displayed their joy at hosting this small but dynamic individual' (1986, p. 22). The place went up with shouts of praise and Gospel singing when Tutu, a mighty moral force dressed in white robes appeared, declaring, 'We're not waiting for the white man's bread! Apartheid and Christianity are totally incompatible'. The room swayed with palpable emotion. Tutu continued sometimes barely audible over the thrill, offering these words later quoted in the *Chicago Tribune* and recounted in Naomi Tutu's (2006) memoirs of

Tutu's words: 'This is what our Church and others are saying when they declare Apartheid is heresy'. *The Defender* (Strausberg, 1986, p. 22) quoted Tutu beyond these rousing words, adding that Tutu left his 'spiritual imprint' on Chicago, 'You and I both know that we are going to be free not because we are going to go to Whites and say politely, "Please let us be free". We have been given that mandate from God.' Then, speaking from the pulpit, Tutu affirmed, 'We don't want freedom when we've died. What good is it then? Blacks in South Africa want freedom. And, they want it now!' High schools students from Chicago and Harvey, Illinois energized the audience with a thrilling pageantry of excited energy. It was as if the students of the high schools, named after Martin Luther King Jr, Wendell Phillips and Rosa Parks, were proclaiming to the congregants and world Martin Luther King's eloquent words from his speech in Atlanta, Georgia (King, 1967):

> I am somebody! I have a rich and noble history. How painful and exploited that history has been. Yes, I was a slave through my fore-parents and I am not ashamed of that. I'm ashamed of the people who were so sinful to make me a slave. Yes, we must stand up and say, 'I'm black and I'm beautiful'. (Martin Luther King, Jr, 1967)

Some students chanted 'Freedom now, Freedom yes, Apartheid no, Justice yes!' Just then Tutu raised his arms in praise, signifying back, and joyously proclaiming, 'You really are beautiful.' Tutu in his amazing lilting voice led the Church in a rousing anthem of 'Lift Every Voice and Sing', also sung during Martin Luther King's visit to American Liberty Baptist Church in the years prior. Tutu renewed his fervent call to President Reagan that 'constructive engagement' with the white-ruled South African regime was futile, contending that the moment such a policy is jettisoned 'will be the day that Apartheid crumbles!' As the voices of ordinary people swelled, so did our tears. At that moment, we all felt moved, privileged to be making history, to forge a body politic and justice.

I looked over to Stuart who was sitting on the cramped floor beside me wiping tears from his eyes. Stuart Hall never saw himself as a grand-stander. He was morally courageous and yet, just as comfortable moving in a community as he was mobilizing communities. Both Dennis and I 'felt privileged to be part of these extraordinary moments, steeped in diasporic social justice history among ordinary people *and* some of the most significant African diaspora figures of the twenty-first century. What made these individuals great was that they moved ordinary people to become extraordinary counter-publics. We learned from them that vulnerability to our mistakes sometimes produces venerability. 'So much of Black diasporic experience was coming together – South Africa, Jamaica, London, UK, Chicago, the USA. We felt a small part of a larger history', (Dworkin, personal communication, 2014a), dare I say a maximal public?

Hardly retreating from public life, it is very clear that the diverse constituencies Stuart Hall helped to mobilize came to him and worked with him even when he was becoming gravely ill and incapacitated. Making and moving publics from the arts to politics, scholarship to popular cultural media and identities always as part of an 'unfinished conversation' as not in the past to be found but in the future to be constructed (Hall, 1995, p. 113). Hall articulated futures we then dared to imagine with him. His co-authored *Kilburn Manifesto* (Hall, Massey, & Rustin, 2013) and numerous works (Hall, 2011) critiquing neoliberalism moved onto the terrain with which we now reckon. The tribute I offer here, I am quite confident is only one part of collective memory-making and one of many histories in which multiple intellectual generations of people in different locales globally and politically were moved and will continue to be shaped by the life and work of Stuart Hall to educate and engage diverse publics.

A meditation: 'the last conjuncture' or 'absolute beginnings'?

Stuart Hall's public intellectual moving and making of publics was borne of political commitments to think and act as an educator, public pedagogue, and to treat his cultural politics as teaching publicly, and not as mere accidents of birth, class privilege, travel or intellectual tourism. The scholar who could write about 'minimal selves' (Hall, 1987) also taught us about constituting 'maximal selves' as extraordinary ways of creating, educating and becoming worldly and most importantly, poetic counter- publics. What can we learn from Hall's example? My thesis has been simple but the practice of it is complex and contradictory: pedagogy becomes public when it is taught dialogically, openly and receptively and when its critical-mindedness hails or calls a public or counter-public into being through the affective, the rational and sometimes, the ineffable, circuiting at once through hearts, heads, spirits and bodies. This nod to honour Hall's post-structural and Gramscian materialist articulation of public-making has not been merely honourific. It is to say instead that, constituting publics involves more than rational (and yes) socially realist plans, strategies and objectives. If Hall's legacy is to be a living one as public pedagogue, and not merely memorializing, then this means listening to his voice in his texts (from BBC broadcasts to scholarly articles and books, from films associated with the Black Arts' Movement to news editorials, etc.) as we would to a moose in our classrooms, with colleagues and ordinary activists. Such extraordinary ways of educating, teaching and learning move beyond or may even start from sites outside the formal schooling or the academy, most particularly being grounded in social movements and with people often marginalized or alienated from social and educational institutions. It means queering as does Warner (2002) our understandings publics and counter-publics, recognizing that not all calls to join or hails of recognition register: Hall's registered repeatedly both affectively and effectively by galvanizing artistic, scholarly, intellectually and politically engaged constituencies, which then became counter-publics. He not only made and moved publics; he was humble enough to bear witness to them – angry enough to feel the call to action and never prone to preach. Stuart Hall's extraordinary educational achievement is our inheritance.

Moving publics for moving times is no easy feat. It requires a lingua franca and proposes no easy either-or solutions or guarantees for the future. There may be little glory in this; after all as Michael Apple (2015) says of critical education, one of the tasks is to be the secretary of social movements and another is to bear witness. Hall was more than secretary for the Left; he shared his moral vision and leadership with others in the process of building progressive publics and counter-publics, willing to participate, not just lead. 'To be of use', writes Canadian poet, Marge Piercy is analogous to 'swimming' and submerging in the tasks that need to be done to move things forward, to being neither 'parlor generals' nor 'field deserters' when 'the fields need to be harvested' (Piercy, 1982, p. 106). To create public pedagogies that move against the grain and speak in different registers which both hail or call publics to come into being *and* get their positive responses in specific contexts was Hall's repeated educational accomplishment and a living legacy we are only beginning to grasp. What made Stuart Hall an extraordinary educator is precisely that he understood how to reach and articulate broader audiences and move them as particular publics – perhaps we might say, from being a particular categorical public (such as the Black Power movement) to becoming a broader public which is counter-hegemonic and works with the Black Art's Movement and linked across their differences (e.g. antiracist coalitions in London that united with working class whites, Blacks, and Asian and Caribbean groups to struggle against police violence in Britain). To put it bluntly, Stuart Hall's public pedagogies (as both publics and pedagogies) were maximal, that is, they covered a large terrain and swatch of political and intellectual interests, collaborators, constituencies and audiences. Yet because his interventions built broader oppositional constituencies which were visible through the arts, scholarship and cultural politics, identities were transformed from singular and categorical identity politics to relational humanities.

Hence, the teachable moments became broader publics, moving people from their sense of being 'out of place' to work with struggles for justice in particular places:

Stuart,

I am so grateful that you 'got hold' of, reached, and taught me. At a time in the USA, land of patriots, bombs, secrecy, militarism, and Reaganism, when the din of 'white noise' had all but blown out the lungs of the country, you, with your resonant and resoundingly articulate voice, lifted all who heard you. In retrospect, a book titled Noise could not have been more apropos. I learned from your example as an extraordinary educator that activist scholarship could actually make some noise.

Bear with me, Stuart, while I continue our conversations — ones we've been having for years. Derek Walcott, St Lucian poet, playwright and Nobel Laureate, laid down these words as if to spirit your final diasporic passage and give you peace:

After the storm

There are so many islands!
As many islands as the stars at night
on that branched tree from which meteors are shaken
like falling fruit around the schooner flight.
But things must fall, and so it always was,
on one hand Venus, on the other Mars;
fall, and are one, just as this earth is one
island in archipelagoes of stars.
My first friend was the sea. Now, is my last.

I stop talking now. I work, then I read,

cotching under a lantern hooked to the mast.
I try to forget what happiness was,
and when that don't work, I study the stars.
Sometimes is just me, and the soft-scissored foam
as the deck turn white and the moon open
a cloud like a door, and the light over me
is a road in white moonlight taking me home
(Walcott, 1990)

In peace,
Leslie

Should we call Hall's departure from this earth 'the last conjuncture' – as Jamaican-born David Scott (2014, vii–x) writes beautifully in his posthumous letter to Hall? Should we simply absorb the finality and finitude Scott observes to mark his loss and at once mourn our collective loss? Or, should we think of ourselves as educators, much as Hall does in his recollections on his own teaching in an un-named secondary modern school in which he casts the experience of learning how to teach and joining the ranks of educators as one of 'Absolute Beginnings' (Hall, 1959)? Let us meditate on Hall's title as a worthwhile refrain: 'Absolute Beginnings'.

Acknowledgements

My deep appreciation goes to Avtar Brah, Les Back, John Clarke, Jessica Evans, Annette Henry, Bob Lingard, Peter McLaren and André Mazawi for their insightful comments and/or enriching conversations. I thank Avtar for the example of a spiritual and meditative approach to scholarship, Les for the epistolary encouragement, John for pointing me to Warner's work and Dennis for all our shared history with Stuart Hall. Dawn Butler of *Discourse* made all of us look good. The Rainbow PUSH office in Chicago helped me rediscover Lillian Lohman's name. Becky O' Connell deserves appreciation for her archival work on my behalf to locate 'hidden treasures' of African-American and mainstream press coverage on Tutu in Chicago. I thank Catherine, Becki, Jess and Stuart's extended family for sharing Stuart with all of us. This paper was made possible by all the extraordinary educators with whom I have had the privilege of working – among them Michael Apple, Fazal Rizvi, Dorothy E. Smith and Stuart Hall.

Notes

1. See Brah (1999) for an example of such a meditative approach.
2. Hall discloses his experiences playing jazz with Caribbean bus drivers and at Oxford in an interview with writer, Caryl Phillips (1997).
3. I have capitalized here because Hall himself uses this name of 'Secondary Modern' to discuss his recollections of teaching in this specific school, standing for a pseudonym. (Hall, 1959, pp. 17–25.)
4. See Davis' (2004) discussion of Hall's speech to the National Committee for the Common-wealth on 'Young Englanders' and its references to his teaching in the Secondary Modern School.
5. Hall (1958) commits to what we now call a critical public pedagogy and a living conception of life and culture in plays, poems and films which offer both readers and writers ways to engage meanings relevant to their lives.

6. See Linder (2000) who argues that 'Absolute Beginnings' is a 'blueprint' for Hall's work at the CCCS.
7. See Dworkin (2014b).
8. See Dworkin (1990, 1997) – the latter, the book it would become.
9. See Lohr (1985).
10. Both photos in Figures 1 and 2 have been granted permission to be published here alone by Dennis Dworkin. The Figure 2 photo was not selected to be published by *Marxism Today* and remains in the personal archival collection of Dennis Dworkin. *Marxism Today* no longer exists but in its day it was a most influential left British magazine.
11. Judy Bloomfield (1986, p. 33) expressed discomfort with what she saw as Hall's fascination with Jackson's star figure status, stating, 'It is only too easy to be dazzled by the stardom and avoid posing the sticky and difficult questions'. Her letter writer asked why Jackson was not pressed harder on the racial division in the labour movement, Louis Farakan's anti-Semitism, the re-emergence of anti-Semitism in the black community, the role of black businesses or issues where race and class intersect. John Whittier (1986, p. 33) commented that it unfair of Jackson to say 'British black people do not have a voice in our society', advising 'us to pursue representation in various institutions'. Astutely, his letter mentioned that African-Americans have one fundamental advantage over Black British peoples in developing a Civil Rights movement – the fact of being the ninth or tenth generation to work out what representation means in business, politics, labour, etc., whereas British Blacks were only the second generation at this time.
12. See Sandra Crockett's (1986b, p. 3) coverage of Tutu in Daley Plaza in which she quotes Robert Spark's speech as the Co-Chair of Chicago's Free South Africa Movement on how symbolic Daley Plaza was to mainstream Chicago's anti-Apartheid lineup of engagements by Bishop Tutu. Free South African protesters had just been acquitted due to arrested related to their sit-in protest against Apartheid. Daley Plaza was located in near the Federal buildings where the protests had taken place.
13. Upon his return to South Africa, Tutu would face tremendous White anger over his increasingly vocal criticism of Apartheid. See *Chicago Defender* (1986/January 28), 'Fear mars Tutu's Return'. http://www.lbcofchicago.org/History.html
14. Dennis Dworkin (personal communication, 2014a) recalls that he sat next to Mayor Washington with Stuart Hall between the two of us.

References

Apple, M. W. (2015). Understanding and interrupting hegemonic projects in education: Learning from Stuart Hall. *Discourse: Studies in the Cultural Politics of Education, 36*(2), 171–184.
Attali, J. (1985). *Noise: The political economy of music*. (Brian Massumi, Trans., Foreword by Frederic Jameson. Afterward by Susan McClary). Minneapolis: The University of Minnesota Press.
Back, L. (2014). *Personal communication/Skype interview from Goldsmith's University*. London: UK.
Bloomfield, J. (1986, May). Letters to the editor: Stuart Hall interviews Jesse Jackson. *Marxism Today*, p. 33.
Brah, A. (1996). *Cartographies of diaspora: Contesting identities*. New York, NY: Routledge.
Brah, A. (1999). The scent of memory: Our own, strangers and others. *Feminist Review, 61*(1), 4–26. doi:10.1080/014177899339261
Chen, K. (2010). The formation of a diasporic intellectual: An interview with Stuart Hall. In D. Morley & K. Chen (Eds.), *Critical dialogues in cultural studies* (pp. 476–483). New York, NY: Routledge.
Chicago Defender. (1986, January 28). United Press International News. 'Fear mars Tutu's return.' *Chicago Defender*, Chicago, IL, p. 5.
Chicago Tribune. (1986, January 11). Tutu's visit will include service, honorary degree. Chicago, IL. Retrieved from http://articles.chicagotribune.com/1986-01-11/news/8601030585_1_bishop-tutu-mayor-harold-washington-council-of-religious-leaders
Clarke, J. (2014). *Personal communication*. Milton Keynes: Open University.
Clarke, J. (2015). Stuart Hall and the theory and practice of articulation. *Discourse: Studies in the Cultural Politics of Education, 36*(2), 272–283.

Crockett, S. (1986a, January 25). Martin warns of Armageddon. *Chicago Defender*, Chicago, IL, p. 40.

Crockett, S. (1986b, January 25). Tutu visits to raise funds. *Chicago Defender*, Chicago, IL, p. 3.

Davis, H. (2004). *Understanding Stuart Hall*. London: SAGE.

Dworkin, D. (1990). *The politics of culture: Historical and critical theory in Great Britain, 1946– 79* (Unpublished PhD doctoral dissertation). University of Chicago, Chicago, IL.

Dworkin, D. (1997). *Cultural Marxism and post-war Britain, in Postwar Britain: History, the New Left, and the origins of cultural studies*. Durham, NC: Duke University Press.

Dworkin, D. (2014a). *Personal communication by email and phone*. Reno: University of Nevada.

Dworkin, D. (2014b, June 24). *The lost world of cultural studies*. An invited paper presented for the conference, The Centre for Contemporary Cultural Studies 50 Years On, University of Birmingham, Birmingham, UK.

Evans, J. (2014a). Stuart Hall: An Open University perspective. Milton Keynes: Open University. Open University web page http://www.open.edu/openlearn/society/politics-policy-people/stuart-hall-ou-perspective.

Evans, J. (2014b). *Personal communication by e-mail from Open University*. Milton Keynes: UK.

Hall, S. (1958). Inside the whale again. *Universities and Left Review, 4*, 14–20.

Hall, S. (1959). Absolute beginnings: Reflections on the secondary modern generation. *Universities and New Left Review, 7*(4), 16–25.

Hall, S. (1979, January). The great moving right show. *Marxism Today*, pp. 14–20.

Hall, S. (1983). Teaching race. *Early Child Development and Care, 10*, 259–274. doi:10.1080/0300443830100402

Hall, S. (1985a). Is there a materialist theory of ideology? Invited Distinguished Keynote. Unpublished paper. Eugene V. Haven's Lecture Series (September, 9, 1985, 8417 Social Sciences Building). Madison, WI: University of Wisconsin-Madison.

Hall, S. (1985b). The structuralist critique. Invited Distinguished Keynote. Unpublished paper. Eugene V. Haven's Lecture Series (September, 13, 1985, 8417 Social Sciences Building). Madison, WI: University of Wisconsin-Madison.

Hall, S. (1985c). Is there a theory of ideology in Gramsci? Invited Distinguished Keynote. Unpublished paper. Eugene V. Haven's Lecture Series Eugene V. Haven's Lecture Series (September 16, 1985, State Historical Society). Madison, WI: University of Wisconsin-Madison.

Hall, S. (1985d). Towards a theory of articulation. Invited Distinguished Keynote. Unpublished paper. Eugene V. Haven's Lecture Series Eugene V. Havens' Lecture Series. (September, 23, 1985, 8417 Social Sciences Building). Madison, WI: University of Wisconsin-Madison.

Hall, S. (1985e). *Graduate Seminar, Sociology 994. Syllabus, Havens Lecture Series List*. Madison, WI: University of Wisconsin-Madison.

Hall, S. (1985f). *Graduate Seminar, Sociology 994. Roster*. Madison, WI: University of Wisconsin-Madison.

Hall, S. (1986, March). Jesse Jackson interviewed by Stuart Hall. *Marxism Today*, pp. 6–11.

Hall, S. (1987). Minimal selves. *London Institute for Contemporary Arts Documents, 6*, 44–46.

Hall, S. (1990a). Cultural identity and diaspora. In J. Rutherford (Ed.), *Identity, community, culture, difference* (pp. 222–237). London: Lawrence & Wishart.

Hall, S. (1990b). The emergence of cultural studies and the crisis of the humanities. *Cultural Studies, 53*, 11–23.

Hall, S. (1995). Negotiating Caribbean identities. *New Left Review, 209*, 3–14.

Hall, S. (1996a). Gramsci's relevance for the study of race and ethnicity. In D. Morley & K. Chen (Eds.), *Stuart Hall: Critical dialogues in cultural studies* (pp. 411–441). London: Routledge.

Hall, S. (1996b). New ethnicities. In D. Morley & K. Chen (Eds.), *Stuart Hall: Critical dialogues in cultural studies* (pp. 442–451). London: Routledge.

Hall, S. (1996c). Who needs identity? In S. Hall & P. Du Gay (Eds.), *Questions of cultural identity* (pp. 1–17). Thousand Oaks, CA: SAGE.

Hall, S. (2005). Thinking diaspora: Home thoughts from abroad. In G. Desai & S. Nair (Eds.), *Postcolonialisms: An anthology of cultural theory and criticism* (pp. 543–560). New Brunswick, NJ: Rutgers University Press.

Hall, S. (2011). The neo-liberal revolution. *Cultural Studies, 25*, 705–728. doi:10.1080/09502386.2011.619886

Hall, S., & Back, L. (2009). Stuart Hall and Les Back in conversation: At home and not at home. *Cultural Studies, 23,* 658–687. doi:10.1080/09502380902950963

Hall, S., Massey, D., & Rustin, M. (Eds.). (2013). After neoliberalism: Analysing the present (Framing statement). In S. Hall, D. Massey, & M. Rustin (Eds.), *After neoliberalism? The Kilburn Manifesto.* London: Lawrence and Wishart. Retrieved from http://www.lwbooks.co.uk/journals/soundings/pdfs/manifestoframingstatement.pdf

Hall, S., & Whannell, P. (1964). *The popular arts.* London: Hutchinson Educational.

Henry, A. (2015). Nostalgia for what cannot be: An interpretive and social biography of Stuart Hall's early years in Jamaica and England, 1932–1959. *Discourse: Studies in the Cultural Politics of Education, 36*(2), 225–240.

Jamison, P. (1986, January 27). Tutu welcomed by Rockefeller crowd. *Chicago Defender.* (News section, Monday, January 27, 1986). Chicago, IL, p. 22.

King, M. L., Jr. (1967). Where do we go from here? Speech given to the Southern Christian Leadership Conference, August 16, 1967. Atlanta, GA. Retrieved from http://www.famous-speeches-and-speech-topics.info/martin-luther-king-speeches/martin-luther-king-speech-where-do-we-go-from-here.htm

Linder, R. (2000). Absolute beginnings: In search of a lost time. In P. Gilroy, L. Grossberg, & A. McRobbie (Eds.), *Without guarantees: In honor of Stuart Hall* (pp. 203–211). London: Verso.

Lohr, S. (1985, November 3). Special to the *New York Times.* Jackson leads Britons. Retrieved from http://www.nytimes.com/1985/11/03/world/jackson-leads-britons-in-denouncing-pretoria.html

Marxism and the Interpretation of Culture Conference. (1983, July 8–12). Sponsored by the Unit for criticism and interpretive theory. University of Illinois-Champagne, Urbana, IL.

Piercy, M. (1982). 'To be of use.' *Circles on the water: The collected poems of Marge Piercy.* New York, NY: Alfred A. Knopf.

Phillips, C. (1997, Winter). Interview: Stuart Hall. *Bomb 58,* Retrieved from http://bombmagazine.org/article/2030/stuart-hall, n.p.

Roman, L. G. (1985). Class notes for Sociology 994, Professor Stuart Hall and Hall Lectures. Eugene V. Havens Invited Distinguished Keynotes. Unpublished papers. University of Wisconsin-Madison. (Numerous handwritten pages, identified by topic, lecture, and date).

Roman, L. G. (1987). *Punk femininity: The formation of young women's gender and class identities in the extramural curriculum within a contemporary subculture* (Unpublished PhD dissertation). University of Wisconsin-Madison.

Roman, L. G. (1988). Intimacy, labor, and class. In L. G. Roman, L. Christian-Smith, & L. Ellsworth (Eds.), *Becoming feminine: The politics of popular culture* (pp. 143–184). New York/London: Falmer Press of Taylor & Francis.

Scott, D. (2014). The last conjuncture. *Small Axe, 18*(2), vii–x.

Strausberg, C. (1986, January 27/Monday). Freedom messenger leaves spiritual imprint on Chicago. *The Chicago Defender*, p. 22.

Tutu, N. (2006). *The words of Desmond Tutu.* New York, NY: New Market Press.

Walcott, D. (1990). After the storm. In D. Walcott (Ed.), *The collected poems of Derek Walcott, 1948–1984.* New York, NY: Farrar, Strauss & Giroux. Retrieved from www.fsgbooks.com

Warner, M. (2002). *Publics and counterpublics.* New York, NY: Zone Press.

Whittier, J. (1986, May). Letters to the editor: Stuart Hall interviews Jesse Jackson. *Marxism Today,* p. 33.

'Nostalgia for what cannot be': an interpretive and social biography of Stuart Hall's early years in Jamaica and England, 1932–1959

Annette Henry

Department of Language and Literacy Education, University of British Columbia, Vancouver, Canada

Much has been written about Stuart Hall's intellectual and theoretical contributions especially after the mid-1960s. This interpretive and social biography places Stuart Hall's life from 1932 to 1959 in a socio-historical context, beginning with his childhood in Jamaica and his early years in England. I draw on Hall's own biographical reflections during the last years of his life and his writings about secondary schools and working-class youth from his insights as a teacher in South London, as well as his writings on identity and diaspora, as he reflects on the early years later in his life. By examining this less celebrated time, I hope to bring insights about pedagogy, identity, exile and nostalgia, and make connections between the early experiences and the more celebrated years of Stuart Hall as an outstanding educator and public intellectual.

Stuart Hall was one of the leading cultural theorists of our time, as well as a remarkable teacher, public intellectual and an advocate for justice, peace and equity. He is celebrated worldwide as the founding editor of *New Left Review* (*NLR*), Director of the Birmingham Centre for Cultural Studies, professor of sociology at Open University, an activist in antiracist struggles, a catalyst and mentor for Black artists and photographers, a Fellow of the British Academy, a member of various advisory boards and committees and someone who could relate to a range of publics.

Stuart Hall is most celebrated for his accomplishments after 1960. In this discussion, I am interested in the early years of Hall's childhood in Jamaica (1932–1951) and the early years in England (1952–1959) as well as his relationship to Jamaica during the first nine years after immigrating to England. By focusing on this time period, I hope to contribute insights about pedagogy, identity, displacement, diaspora and 'the nostalgia for what cannot be' through an exploration of aspects of the life and activism of Stuart Hall.

Methodologically, I am drawing from social biography and interpretive biography. Social biography is a form of historical writing that explores both the individual and the broader social context (Salvatore, 2004); interpretive biography involves the collection and interpretation of essays, documentary artefacts, stories, and accounts which describe significant moments in the individual's life. Meaning is created through the interaction of texts, writers and readers (Denzin, 1989). In this discussion, I rely most heavily on Hall's own biographical reflections and his writings about secondary schools and the education system from his insights as a school teacher in South London. I also draw upon his writings on identity and diaspora. Secondary sources include biographical and journalistic accounts, Hall's colleagues' writings as well as documentation of significant socio-political events of the time periods in question. In this discussion, then, I am interested in insights about Stuart Hall's life at the intersections of race, class, gender, cultures, identities and diaspora and how they informed his creative imaginings, political and intellectual ideas and activism.

History and remembering involve interpretation. They may rely on personal accounts, but they are also collective accounts (Passerini, 1996). Remembering the past, then, is not only personal, but also social and political (Smith, 1999). In my recounting and interpreting of Hall's early years, I attempt to explore the collective through a range of historical, social and political texts, including the work of Jamaican poets.

I was moved to explore the less documented years in the life of Stuart Hall after viewing the moving film, *The Stuart Hall Project* (2013) by brilliant film-maker John Akomfrah,[1] with its rich archival footage, and reading the following remark by David Scott, founding editor of the journal of Caribbean criticism, *Small Axe*. In a letter to Stuart Hall on his 80th birthday, Scott (2012) noted that the early years in Jamaica have been 'less searchingly told than the stories of other parts of your life' (p. viii). By examining this relatively overlooked period (1932–1959), I hope to explore not only how Hall's politics and theories were shaped by the events in these early years but also to contribute to understandings about pedagogy, identity, exile and diaspora through the life of this renowned educator and public intellectual.

Early years in Jamaica: 1932–1951

She tried to step across the border of who she was and who she might be. They wouldn't let her. (Dionne Brand, 2005, *What We Long for*)

Stuart Hall was born in 1932, the youngest of three children. He was preened for an elite life. He attended Cardiff preparatory school and Jamaica College, a school that graduated former Jamaican Prime Ministers Michael Manley and Bruce Golding, as well as chief minister and Premier Norman Washington Manley. A bright and curious youth, he was interested in all that was taking place in Jamaican politics – the decline of Garveyism, the rise of Rastafarianism, the formation of Jamaican political parties, the trade unions labour movements after 1938 and Jamaica's posture towards decolonization and independence after the Second World War.

Hall received a rigorous classical education, albeit one that promoted Anglo-supremacy. Even today, Jamaican education bears the stamp of British colonialism, despite efforts to reform and indigenise the system. Hall recalled to Kuan-Hsing Chen, 'Only in my last two years did I learn anything about Caribbean history and geography' (Chen, 2010, p. 500). During this époque, one had to travel abroad to attend university. To be eligible for a scholarship, one had to be over 18 years of age. Hall spent three years in the sixth form because he was too young for a scholarship (Chen, 2010). During this time he profited from the opportunity to read widely – T.S. Eliot, James Joyce, Marx, Lenin and literature and poetry. He explained, 'I got a wider reading than the usual, narrowly academic British-oriented education. But I was very much formed like a member of a colonial intelligentsia' (Chen, 2010, p. 488).

Hall grew up in a 'respectable upwardly mobile brown family' (Jaggi, 2000) that espoused the very idea of Britishness and as will become clear in the following discussion, the structures of class, colour and colonialism were at play in the family dynamics. His parents came from different middle-class backgrounds. Hall's father, Herman Hall, grew up in a lower-middle-class family that was ethnically mixed, in ways that most Jamaicans would be familiar.[2] His ancestry was African, East Indian, Portuguese and Jewish (Morley & Chen, 2010). Mr Hall worked at the United Fruit Company (UFC, now Chiquita). This multinational corporation underpaid its workers throughout the Caribbean and Central America, thwarted economies and increased poverty (Chapman, 2007; Putnam, 2002). On the other hand, it promoted the idea of Jamaica as a White person's paradise. In the spirit of its profit-driven agenda, the UFC doubly used their steamships for cargo and cruises from the early 1900s until the Second World War. The advertisement below gives a sense of the colonialist attitude of the company and its profit-driven agenda. This advertisement is one of many, most of which erase the visibility of Jamaican bodies (Figure 1).[3]

Herman Hall was promoted in every position that he held and moved up through the ranks to become the UFC's chief accountant – the first non-White person to be promoted to a senior position (Mendez, Cueto, & Deynes, 2003), yet he did not belong. He tried to join the appropriate circles, but as Stuart Hall recalled, 'He was negotiating his way into this world. He was accepted on sufferance by the English ... they patronized him' (Chen, (2010, p. 487).

Stuart Hall's mother, Jessie Hall, was born into a poor family but was adopted by affluent relatives of whom the uncle was a prominent lawyer (Mendez et al., 2003). She took pride in her British ancestors whom she traced back two generations. She preferred

Figure 1.   Invisibility of Jamaican bodies in a white paradise.

the identifications, social and cultural practices of the English to those of Jamaica, especially those customs associated with people of African descent (Hall, 1990b) and attempted to instil British values in her son Stuart. She also felt that her status was above that of her husband's (in terms of class, colour and background) and it created tensions in the marriage (Jaggi, 2000). Hall described his mother as 'overwhelmingly dominant' (Chen, 2010, p. 491). She had particular expectations for him above and beyond his two siblings; his older brother was dependent on the parents; not much was expected of his sister, whom his mother despised 'because she was a girl'. Hall recalls in his interview with Chen that, according to Mrs Hall, 'women were not interesting' (Chen, 2010, p. 491).

As a child, Hall rejected the class/colour politics playing out in his family, and his parents' espousal of 'Englishness': 'my parents [were] not only brown but thought the world would disappear with the departure of the British' (Hall & Back, 2009, p. 662). He described his family life as 'horrendous'. They were playing out 'a huge colonial drama':

> I came to understand that my family were [*sic*] living out in the interstices of the family, the most private domestic space, this huge colonial drama. That is what it was about. So the meaning of colonization was internalized into the intimate and the emotionally charged theatre of the family. (Hall & Back, 2009, p. 662)

Stuart Hall lived in Jamaica at a time when there would have been a well-defined correspondence between race, colour and class in Jamaica – a 'tripartite racial hierarchy with socio-economic correlates' (Alleyne, 2005, p. 203). Orlando Patterson (see Scott, 2013) reinterpreted the tripartite relationship between White, Brown and Black in Jamaica during the pre-independence period. Patterson explained: 'I saw brown and white as very much *one*, what I called Anglo-Jamaica' (p. 155). In other words the Brown and White classes were in some ways in collusion against the (often poorer) Blacks. Patterson's thesis gives a context to Hall's parents' preoccupation with colour, class and status as well as their interpersonal tensions and expectations for Stuart's career.

Black was not beautiful in the Hall family nor in most 'brown' Jamaican families of that era. Stuart Hall was reminded that he was the darkest Hall – another indication of the family's investment in aspirations to Britishness: 'I was always the blackest member of my family and I knew it from the moment I was born' (Chen, 2010, p. 487). Hall's sister apparently looked at him in his crib and asked, derogatively, 'Where did you get this coolie baby from? Not black baby, you will note, but low-class Indian' (Chen, 2010, p. 487). Hall was forbidden from bringing home dark-skinned friends. Thus, Hall withdrew emotionally from his parents and kept his friendships out of their sight. He recalled to Chen, 'My adolescence was spent continuously negotiating these cultural spaces' (p. 487).

As a youth in Jamaica, Hall was able to analyse the family tensions at a sophisticated level, that is, he explained, they were 'playing out the conflict between the local and the imperial in a colonial context' (Chen, 2010, p. 486), importantly amidst the backdrop of the majority – the poor Black Jamaicans. The very family member who commented on her 'coolie-looking' brother also encountered the perniciousness of colour, class, gender and race and in colonial Jamaica when she started dating a middle-class *Black* medical student originally from Barbados. Her parents forbade it. Hall's sister sunk into a deep depression and later underwent electroconvulsive therapy – a treatment predominantly administered to women (Bloch et al., 2005; Weale, 1999). According to Hall, his sister 'never properly recovered. She never left home after that' (Chen, 2010, p. 502). She remained in her parents' home, caring for her and Stuart Hall's older brother who later became blind, and her parents, until all three died. Although Hall does not analyse his sister's situation in gendered terms in this interview, one can argue that the familial expectations for her life and his own were indeed gendered.

Witnessing these events brought clarity to Hall's analysis of the structures of colonialism: 'I was suddenly aware of the contradiction of a colonial culture, of how one lives out the colour-class-colonial dependency experience and of how it could destroy you, subjectively' (Chen, 2010, p. 490). His sister's misfortune was a turning point in Hall's consciousness. He explained:

> It broke down forever, for me, the distinction between the public and the private self. I learned about culture, first, as something which is deeply subjective and personal, and at the same moment, as a structure you live ... I don't just mean they are personal ... they are also institutional, they have real structural properties, they break you, destroy you.

Hall realised that it was imperative to leave Jamaica or he, too, would be 'destroyed'. Breaking from Jamaican codes of speakability, he was brutishly honest about the dysfunction in his family:

> I was not going to stay there. I was not going to be destroyed by it. I had to get out. I felt that I must never put myself back into it, because I would be destroyed. When I look at the snapshots of myself in childhood and early adolescence, I see a picture of a depressed person. I don't want to be who they want me to be, but I don't know how to be somebody else. And I am depressed by that. All of that is the background to explain why I eventually migrated. (Chen, 2010, p. 490)

In 1950, Hall won a Jamaica Scholarship. He also won a Rhodes scholarship.

The early years in England: 1951–1959

Wat a joyful news, Miss Mattie, I feel like me heart gwine burs
Jamaica people colonizin Englan in reverse (Louise Bennett, 1966, *Jamaica Labrish*)

In 1951, Hall won a Rhodes scholarship to Merton College at Oxford, an institution that he described as 'the pinnacle of Englishness' (Chen, 2010, p. 493). He was the second student from Jamaica College to win a Rhodes scholarship. He admitted to Les Back, 'Ok so I was in flight' (Hall & Back, 2009, p. 662) and to Kuan-Shing Chen, 'My decision to emigrate was to save myself' (Chen, 2010, p. 491). He fled the colour-consciousness of Jamaican society and his dysfunctional family dynamics, accompanied by his mother on a steamship to England. Upon arrival, Mrs Hall said to the college scout, 'This is my son, his trunks, his belongings. Look after him' (Chen, 2010, p. 491). Jamaican cultural studies and literary theorist Carolyn Cooper (2013) notes, ironically, 'the bearers of Caribbean popular cultural forms took their hybridised culture to Mother England and reasserted their humanity at the very seat of Empire' (p. 11).

Hall was part of the massive influx of Caribbean, African and South Asian immigrants, most of who went to Britain to fulfil the post-war labour needs and in the hope of a better life.[4] Unlike Hall destined for an elite education, the majority were 'quite prepared to undertake the dirty, dangerous, and poorly paid jobs that white workers no longer wanted' (Mishra, 2013, p. 3). Howard Winant (2009, p. 38) explains:

> The influx of substantial numbers of nonwhites during the postcolonial period has deeply altered a dynamic in which the racial system and the imperial order had been one, and the '*other*' by and large was kept outside the walls of the 'mother country'.

Caribbean immigration to Britain before 1951 never exceeded 1000 annually (Foner, 1979). The Caribbean population grew from approximately 15,300 in 1951 to 171,800 in 1961. The immigration policy was tightened in 1962 and 'West Indians' no longer had the right of free entry to Britain (Foner, 1979).[5] More precisely, the Tory government ensured a halt to non-White migration by establishing a voucher system that allowed entry only to those who had secured a job beforehand with strict penalties for South Asians, Africans and West Indians. Claudia Jones (2000) writes, 'the main blow fell as intended on coloured commonwealth citizens' (p. 52; Figure 2).

En route to Oxford, at Paddington train station, Hall discovered his life-long subject of study:

> or rather it discovered me. My subject was coming out of the station at Paddington. It was Caribbeans but over here, it was the Windrush journey to here. That has been my subject, ever since: the diaspora. (Hall & Back, 2009, p. 662)

Hall understood the Caribbean as already the diaspora of Africa, Europe, China, Asia, India and this diaspora, 're-diasporized' itself in the UK. Before emigrating from the

Figure 2.   Hopes and dreams of Jamaican immigrants in England (London, 1952).[6]

Caribbean, one was in a diasporic situation that he considered 'the first, the original and the purest diaspora' (Hall, 1995, p. 6). In this Jamaican diaspora issues of race, class and gender were ubiquitous as reflected in the social commentary of many Jamaican writers and artists.

Performance poet Jean Binta Breeze (2000) notes the gendered and familial costs of transcultural, transnational, diasporic relationships for Jamaicans in her poem, 'The arrival of Brighteye' through the voice of a young girl whose mother has gone to England to work and has promised to 'send back' for her: 'My mommy gone over de ocean/My mommy gone over de sea/she gawn dere to work for some money/an den she gawn sen back for me'. After several years, she fears forgetting what her mother looks like, 'granny seh it don't matter but supposin I forget' (2000, p. 7).

Trotz and Mullings (2013) remind us that diaspora cuts across the territorial borders of nation-states in gendered ways. Jamaican women and men experience and participate in cross-border networks differentially 'in a region with a high proportion of female-headed households and a sturdy tradition of women emigrating in numbers equivalent to, and at times exceeding, those of men' (p. 155).

Louise Bennett's poem is a social and political commentary on post-war immigration for Jamaicans. 'Man an woman, ole an young /tun history upside dung!' Eldon Birthwright (2011) argues that Bennett's poem not only highlights the 'reverse colonisation' but also foreshadows the consequences of, and implications for the 'Empire striking back', in a Britain in which Whites became intolerant of the increase in Caribbean immigrants, as Hall discusses later. The famous political poem of Linton Kwesi Johnson (1980) 'Inglan is a bitch' is a social commentary of the plight of some of these very Jamaicans. He tells the story of a working-class Jamaican man who works several menial and back-breaking jobs, sometimes more than one job at a time, so much that he cannot sleep at night. He falls out of favour at his jobs, gets laid off, eventually becomes redundant and is on the dole at 55 years of age. The refrain reminds the reader of the unrealized dream: 'Inglan is bitch/Deres no escaping it/Inglan is a bitch/no badda try fi hide fram it'.[7] [England is a bitch/There's no escaping it/England is bitch/Don't bother trying to hide from it.]

Now in England and creating some distance from his family and his country, Hall was able to be circumspect, putting both countries and issues of class in a larger socio-historical and political context as well as deconstructing his own 'Jamaicanness'. During these early Oxford days, he was exposed to expatriates from various parts of the Caribbean as well as Africa – all grappling with, and debating the possibilities of anti-colonialism and postcoloniality. He recalled, 'My "reconnection" with the Caribbean happened because of the formation of a Black diasporic population here' (Chen, 2010, p. 503). Hall found a sense of belonging and rediscovered his Caribbean identity: 'So it was … a rediscovery of my thinking about culture, and a rediscovery of the black subject' (Hall & Back, 2009, p. 662). This 'rediscovery' is a common theme in the work of Caribbean émigrés (Cooper, 2013). Hall collaborated with Lamming, V.S. Naipaul another notable Caribbean writers in BBC broadcasts. His social and political activities with people from various ethnicities, racial backgrounds and socio-economic back-grounds expanded his thinking and gave him pleasure. For example, he played jazz with a group of Caribbean bus drivers. 'When you're out of place, the Left becomes a kind of home', Hall explained (Hall & Back, 2009, p. 673). This emerging 'New Left' consisted of people from colonial backgrounds, intellectuals, working-class people and people 'moving between classes' (Chen, 2010, p. 496).

Most of Hall's anticolonial student compatriots returned to the Caribbean after completion of their studies. In fact, many of his schoolmates took on positions of political prominence in post-independence Jamaica. Hall found his voice as an activist, intellectual and political thinker at the same time that Jamaica found its voice towards independence in 1962. Hall pondered returning and teaching at the University of West Indies (UWI) or getting involved with Federation politics. This ambivalence was life-long and might be considered part of the diasporic condition of displacement. In other words, as Paul Zeleza (2008) writes that 'diaspora identities are always suspended in anxious flight: never [quite] arriving or returning, a navigation of multiple belongings' (p. 7).

Hall changed his mind about a return to Jamaica. He won a second scholarship and started graduate work at Oxford. He found himself increasingly using his research time to read anthropological literature about African 'survivals' in the Caribbean and New World Culture. It would seem that he was thirsting for knowledge and understandings that were not provided in his official education. He forsook his doctoral studies on Henry James at Oxford in 1956. 'I didn't feel it was right for me to go on thinking cultural questions in "pure" literary terms' (Chen, 2010, p. 499).

During this time, Hall became acquainted with people on the Left, mainly from the Communist Party and the Labour Party, meeting like-minded people such as Alan Hall, Peter Sedgewick, Charles Taylor and Raymond Williams. The 1950s was an intellectually and politically rich time for Hall (Stratton & Ang, 2010) and a time for radically rethinking culture through his New Left activities. Much was happening globally – the Soviet invasion of Hungary, the British invasion of Suez, the class hierarchy was becoming less rigid, and Britain was losing its status to America, a new superpower. In 1956, in response to these events, Raphael Samuels established the *Universities and Left Review* (*ULR*). The *ULR* became the *New Left Review* (*NLR*) in 1960. Hall was one its four editors (along with other Oxford graduates, Charles Taylor, Gabriel Pearson and Raphael Samuels).

In 1957, Hall left Oxford and moved to South London where he found a job as a supply teacher. He continued to edit *ULR* in the evenings in an office in Soho, whilst working at a secondary modern school in South London during the day (Chen, 2010). Hall was an educator, whether working pedagogically through the *ULR/NLR* journal or teaching in various classrooms throughout his illustrious career – whether at the secondary modern school in South London, Chelsea college of Art and Design, the Director of the Birmingham Centre for Cultural Studies or Professor at Open University. (see Roman, 2015.)

It is noteworthy that Hall taught youth in a predominantly white working-class secondary modern school in Kennington Oval area. Many of the students were Irish and Scottish working-class students (Roman, 2015). Hall's interest in working-class cultures was influenced by his intellectual friendships with Richard Hoggart and Raymond Williams. It is also noteworthy that he remained at this school until 1960, a secondary modern school in which other supply teachers and even permanent teachers would not stay for long (Hall & Back, 2009). He wrote in *ULR* that secondary modern schools (now mostly comprehensive schools) were considered lower-status schools, and that supply teachers were often non-White foreigners, a source of contention for many permanent (White) teachers (Hall, 1959a). Provocatively, Hall asked, 'How much of this is due to professional jealousy, how much to the fact that supply teachers are often foreigners – Australians, West Indians, Indians, Pakistanis, etc. – is difficult to judge' (Hall, 1959a, p. 17). Taking on a supply teacher position, Hall now shared a commonality with many of the working-class Jamaicans whom he encountered at Paddington Station. That is, they were a 'reserve army' (Hall, 1983, p. 267) addressing the British shortage of labour in particular jobs. Black workers can be considered a dark-skinned underclass that suffer race, gender and class-specific oppression (Sarup, 1982).

Out of need to support himself, Hall had naively decided that he could teach: 'So I thought well, what can you do? Practically, nothing! I couldn't then drive, so I couldn't drive a milk float. You can teach' (Hall & Back, 2009, p. 671). Reflecting upon the experience years later, he admitted that he was unprepared:

> I'd never been taught to teach so I just walked in. I was given a class, which was 4FX. This was a Secondary Modern school so everybody in it had already failed their 11 Plus … So this is kids right at the bottom of the pile.

From this teaching experience, Hall became interested in mobilising and motivating secondary modern teachers to reflect on their work. He spoke to educators and wrote about how the educational system positioned particular children for failure (Hall, 1959a, 1959b, 1983; Hall & Back, 2009). These kids 'at the bottom of the pile' saw no purpose in education and were destined to leave school at the first opportunity. A few of his secondary students aspired to work in the local print shop like their fathers. In *ULR*, Hall critiqued the stratification of the British educational system: 'these children have very little sense of how much their future is likely to be affected by having failed at the first jump of the social barrier' (1959a, p. 18). In other words, 'at the bottom of the pile' they could never succeed academically; they spiraled down into a sense of despair. The curriculum did not draw upon their interests. Rather, they were squeezed 'into pre-digested categories' (Hall, 1959a, p. 20). Why bother try to learn? By 13 or 14 years of age, they began to draw upon friendships and 'subterranean relationships' outside of home and school and lose interest. Hall held teachers and schools accountable for instilling a sense of failure in working-class students at modern schools. He recognised that there were dedicated teachers in these settings, but for the most part, 'the philosophy of the secondary modern school is that what's left over after the Grammar and Public schools have had a bite, *will do*. The system is clogged, like a sealed tube' (1959b, p. 4).

Although Hall played down his success at teaching the students a range of subjects from swimming to Shakespeare, it is clear that the South London years provided a powerful pedagogical experience for students and teacher alike. First, the students experienced the rare opportunity of consistency in a setting of high teacher attrition. Second, Hall listened to them and learned from them in and out of the school. He valued youth and youth subcultures; he was curious about their 'out of school curriculum' (Schubert, 2010), which helped him understand their community, culture and identities. Hall was incorporating what Gutiérrez, Hunter, and Arzubiaga (2009) conceptualise as 'horizontal forms of expertise'. These include the 'everyday practices of individuals and their communities' (p. 3). For example, one evening on the train from the school to the *ULR* office in Soho, Hall noticed that some of the boys were also on the train, claiming to go for some 'argy-bargy' in *Notting Hill* (Hall & Back, 2009, p. 671). Curious about their lives and interested in *Notting Hill*, a neighbourhood of some *ULR* club members, Hall followed the boys and became exposed to another world – one in which White British racism was literally on the streets in the form of harassment of Black women.

This excursion occurred before the famous *Notting Hill* riots in 1958. The experience provided Hall with valuable knowledge about his pupils' lives and provided a culturally relevant curriculum that is, both teacher and students were able to critically discuss and reflect on the *Notting Hill* experience (Hall & Back, 2009) and discuss questions of identifications and allegiances. In so doing, classroom learning was not divorced from real-world issues. Perhaps Hall was ill-prepared for the job, but he began to cultivate a critical pedagogy with, and because of, the students.

Notting Hill was not the fashionable district portrayed in the film *Notting Hill* (Kenworthy & Michell, 1999) with Julia Roberts and Hugh Grant. It was a catchment for Caribbean immigrants who were exploited in housing and unemployment and encountered racist name-calling while going to and fro from work on the streets. Hall explained:

> I used to go down there to see where on earth these kids were, and they were on the street corners and the adults were in the pubs behind them shouting through the doors; and they were harassing black women who were walking home from work, going in to the multi-occupation flats in Powys Terrace and the terraces behind. (Hall & Back, 2009, p. 672)

Nationality, race, gender and class were flagrantly at work in this setting in which immigrant working-class Black women were denied their humanity. Black immigrants settled in this area because of inexpensive housing and were exploited by landlords such as the notorious Peter Rachmann who packed them into multi-occupational flats.

Poet Louise Bennett (1966) asked the question in her poem, 'But me wonderin how dem gwine stan/Colonizin in reverse'. [But I'm wondering how they will endure reverse colonisation (if there is really such a thing).] Not well at all. *Notting Hill* racial violence which started in late August and ended in early September 1958 represented a historical moment in which, as Hall explained to Les Back, 'a great deal of racism which has been simmering underneath finally gets spoken; finally erupts in the straightforward open aggression and violence' (Hall & Back, 2009, p. 672). The riots are thought to have been started when a crowd of white men attacked a white Swedish woman who was married to a Caribbean man and had been seen arguing with him the day before (BBC News, 2001). However, the growing sense that England was becoming 'flooded' with coloured people of low moral standing who were supposedly taking away jobs (Banton, 1983; Jones, 2000), and the racism simmering below the surface (Hall & Back, 2009) were all contributing factors. After all, Churchill wanted to keep England White (Hennessy, 2001).

The New Left became politically active during the *Notting Hill* 1958 riots, as Hall told Chen (2010) 'organising on the ground' (p. 496), organising with tenants who were being exploited and thrown out of their buildings by Michael X, a strongman who worked for Rachmann, and organising defence groups for Black people. Hall and colleagues set up *ULR* and *NLR* clubs in these communities. At one time there were 26 clubs.

Diaspora and Stuart Hall's relationship with Jamaica

> [D]iaspora is about globalisation and dispersal, but at the same time it's also about location and 'staying put'. (Avtar Brah, 1996, *Cartographies of Diaspora*)

In this final section, I want to explore Hall's relationship with Jamaica. Our relationships with our countries of origin can be complicated and fraught. My own parents had completely different relationships with Jamaica. My mother left for England to study nursing in 1949. She returned frequently from wherever she lived (England and Canada) to Jamaica and to the USA to visit her siblings and mother and continued to do so until her death at 83. They were a letter-writing family. Between her 13 family members, on a weekly basis I remember at least one blue aerogramme letter being received or sent in this familial diaspora during most of my childhood. My father, however, left Jamaica as a teenager, signed up for the Royal Air Force, fought in WWII, lived in England and moved us to Canada in 1965. He rarely spoke of his family in Jamaica and never visited them. He kept putting off a visit, saying, 'Next year, next year', despite his mother's letters and her annual gift. She would send a large 'love box' of items hardly attainable in England in the 1960s – ackee carefully preserved in coconut oil, tamarind sweets, coconut drops, toto, bulla, a Christmas cake drenched in rum, and a large juicy mango tenderly wrapped in newspaper that the five of us could not wait to dissect into five and savour around the kitchen table.

Stuart Hall did not have strong familial ties and acknowledged that he lived most of his adult life in the shadow of the Black diaspora, 'in the belly of the beast' (Hall, 1990a, p. 223). Cultural Studies and literary professor Carolyn Cooper (2014) wrote an obituary to Hall in two forms of Jamaican Creole in the *Jamaica Gleaner*, the national newspaper. She posed the question, 'So wa mek Stuart Hall never come back a yard? Im did visit. But im live out im life a Inglan'.[8] [So what made Stuart Hall never come back to the country? He did visit. But, he lived out his life in England.] Why did he not go back? Perhaps a follow-up question might be: Why should he have gone back? 'Staying put' does not necessarily mean a lack of desire to return to one's country. A return may be fraught with ambivalence, fear, doubt, displacement or responsibilities. What are the spiritual and emotional costs of return or staying put? (see Brah, 1996, for a discussion of 'staying put' and diaspora.) Crossing borders and crossing oceans can be a kind of psychic Middle Passage.

There is a cultural or familial expectation that Jamaican expatriates should 'bring back' (goods) or 'give back' (time, effort or money). Even those Jamaicans who may be financially strapped abroad often feel the necessity (and desire) to send or bring goods for relatives. (Think of the famous 'barrel' of everyday items shipped 'home'.) There is an additional expectation for Jamaicans who have achieved financial success or great educational achievement: They should 'give back' to institutions and in fact many institutions rely on diasporic economic and human capital, such as the Old Boys and Old Girls Associations of Jamaica. These are high school alumni associations whose diasporic members are critical to the survival of the alma mater in Jamaica. This ubiquitous tension is part of Jamaican diaspora discourse and is encouraged in the business world.[9]

Hall experienced the dilemma of the immigrant experience – one cannot return home and one cannot find home in new country. He shared the following with Zoe Williams of *The Guardian:*

> Three months at Oxford persuaded me that it was not my home. I'm not English and I never will be. The life I have lived is one of partial displacement. I came to England as a means of escape, and it was a failure. (*Guardian Online*, 2012)

The notion of failure evokes the kinds of hopes and dreams expressed in the poems of Louise Bennett, Jean Binta Breeze and Linton Kwesi Johnson. That is, the idea of going to the 'mother country' and making a life for oneself is shattered by the intersectional realities of gendered racism, classism and tenuous economic situations, as well as other forms of marginalisation and displacement.

Despite the 'failure' of an escape in England (from racism, colourism, classism and British colonialist attitudes), throughout the years, Hall found community and solidarity across classes and races through his political and cultural activities in educational institutions, his writing and lectures and in his mentorship of scholars and artists, as well as his involvement with the Black Arts. Through these activities he helped transform British society. Farred (2014, *The Con Online*) argues that England did not fail Stuart Hall at all. He writes in his tribute that 'the logic of the partial brings things, paradoxically, full circle' and that Hall 'made of his partial displacement a full-time commitment to a radical politics and as irony would have it, England was also perhaps the most fertile site for Hall's thinking'.

The longer that Hall stayed in England, the less realistic a return to Jamaica became. Even after the death of his parents when he no longer needed to negotiate Jamaica through them, he did not return (Chen, 2010). His marriage to Catherine Barrett, English social historian and feminist and the birth of their two children helped anchor him in the UK. As mentioned earlier during the 1950s, he kept in touch with his former schoolmates but their experiences and identifications differed. 'Now that gap cannot be filled. You can't "go home"' (Chen, 2010, p. 492), Hall confessed to Chen. 'That dream [to return] was over at the moment in the 1950s when I decided to stay, and to open a "conversation" with what became the New Left ... I found a new kind of political space here' (p. 503).

As a public intellectual, Hall visited Jamaica regularly and contributed for several years on a Jamaican radio programme, *The Breakfast Club*, a forum for global affairs (*Jamaica Gleaner*, 2014), in which he brought his sharp understandings of the local and the global, the periphery and the centre (Jaggi, *Guardian Online*, 2000).

The life and death of Stuart Hall have been marked by many tributes worldwide, especially in academic circles, including Jamaica. For example, UWI, Mona campus in Kingston, re-mounted an exhibition previously shown in 2004 in honour of Stuart Hall,[10] and several academic units have published short obituaries. An anonymous tribute in the *Jamaica Gleaner* likens Stuart Hall to athlete Usain Bolt and to acclaimed Jamaican scholar, critic and artistic director Rex Nettleford (whom Stuart Hall knew well), celebrities whom most Jamaicans would recognise. The author laments, 'our ignorance of Stuart Hall, at all levels of society, perhaps says more of national inattention to ideas and the people who generate them – especially the big ones'.

In her reflection on the life of Stuart Hall in the *Jamaica Gleaner*, Carolyn Cooper suggested that Jamaica's race, class and colour stratification and his own positionality in it played a role in Hall's staying in Britain. Cooper cites Hall's recounting of being the Blackest member of his family and a 'coolie-baby'. She writes, 'Plenty colour did mix up inna it [...] Seet deh now! Good ting Stuart Hall never bodder come back ya so. Im might as well tan a England'. [Colour played a big part in it. ... There you have it! Good thing Stuart Hall never bothered come back here. He might as well stay in England.] In a personal communication, Cooper explained that both countries have their share of racism and classism, in different ways, so Hall might as well have remained in England (Cooper, personal communication, September 23, 2014).

Hall admitted that Jamaica was not a country that he recognised after some years in England. He had changed; the country had changed. The rise of Pan Africanism, Rastafarianism, the civil rights movement in the USA, increasing Black consciousness, the global shift in race relations, and Jamaican independence all contributed to a Jamaica unfamiliar to Hall. He described this cultural transformation as 'profound' (Hall, 1990b,

p. 12), although economically the country was poorer than when he left in the 1950s. He admitted, 'It's partly because the break in the politics there – the cultural revolution that made Jamaica a "black" society for the first time in the 1970s – coincided with a break in my own life' (Chen, 2010, p. 503). He was a stranger to the culture *and* the language. He expressed 'shock' at the language that he heard on the Jamaican radio and television: 'I couldn't believe my ears that anybody would be quite so bold as to speak patois, to read the news in that accent' (Hall, 1995, p. 12). Hall was forbidden to speak Creole (patois) at home, yet in the Jamaica that evolved after he left, Creole had become more acceptable and even celebrated in certain milieux as a viable spoken and written language. In this Jamaica, probably unimaginable to Hall, a cultural studies professor would write his obituary in the very language that he was forbidden to speak! (Cooper, 2014, *Gleaner Online*).

Hall felt out of place before he had even emigrated from Jamaica:

> In relation to black culture and the life of ordinary black people, I really didn't know what it was about in any depth and I couldn't get to it. I was a middle-class brown schoolboy with middle-class parents, I couldn't reach it [the culture]. (Hall & Back, 2009, p. 669)

Later in life Hall realised that 'Migration is a one-way trip. There's no home to go back to. There never was' (Hall, 1987/1996, p. 44). 'Displacement as a place of "identity" is a concept you learn to live with' (p. 45). Throughout *Home and Not Home* (Hall & Back, 2009), Stuart Hall emphasised that he did not have the luxury of feeling at home in his country of origin nor in the country where he settled. This neither/nor positionality, this double marginalisation, this 'in-betweenness', this 'nostalgia for what cannot be' gave Hall, a brilliant thinker, a particular intellectual acuity, and contributed to his theoretical, creative, and political ideas and activism.

The years between 1932 and 1959 represent a significant time in the life of Stuart Hall and worthy of examination. Not only does this overlooked time-period offer accounts of politically important life moments in Hall's personal trajectory but also, more collectively, it highlights the broader social, economic and historical context for his work amid the influx of diasporic Caribbean immigrants to England during the post-war years. Hall's early formation in Jamaica allowed him to raise poignant questions about colonialism, racism and classism with a particular relationality to Britain. Migration to England turned that relationship on its head. Through his frank reflections, he shared some of the ways in which diasporic bodies carry loss, grief, nostalgia and displacement. Yet, once on British soil, he continually expanded his intellectual, political and pedagogical development towards justice.

During his first nine years in England, Hall found his political voice amongst his student colleagues who shared his anti-colonialist desires and amongst the broader and Caribbean and Left communities across social classes. These were the beginning years of his pedagogical work: editing and writing in ULR, working for justice at a grass-roots level with communities through the ULR clubs, as well as teaching at the secondary modern school in South London. These pedagogical activities can be articulated as significantly positioning Hall towards his life-long path as a brilliant thinker on the Left, a public intellectual and an outstanding educator at many institutions – Chelsea College (1961–1964), Birmingham Centre for Cultural Studies where he started as a research fellow and became its director (1964–1979), Open University where he held a professorship and Headship (1979–1997), Goldsmiths college as a visiting professor and 14 visiting professorships during retirement (University of West Indies, 2004).

As this interpretive and social biography of Hall's early years has shown, 'diaspora' is not divorced from the formative experiences of family, class, race, ethnicity, culture, colour, gender and language, and the specificities of how they are interwoven in particular contexts. Diasporic migrations are socially textured as at once interwoven and inseparable private and public narratives. By exploring Hall's early years, we can more fully appreciate the complexities and contradictions of his displacements and dispositions, and the ways in which they informed his political and intellectual contributions as well as his activism, and consequently changed the ways in which we understand and theorise cultures and diasporas.

Acknowledgement

A special thank you to Guest Editor Leslie Roman for the opportunity for rich discussion and helpful insights while writing this essay.

Notes

1. In John Akomfrah's film, the Stuart Hall Project (2012), the music of Miles Davis is as much a feature of the film as Hall's life history. In the film, Hall remarks, 'Nostalgia for what cannot be is in the sound of Miles Davis's trumpet'. 'The nostalgia for what cannot be' exemplifies Stuart Hall's relationship with Jamaica and perhaps the immigrant's diasporic consciousness; thus, it was chosen as the title of this essay.
2. See chapter 8 in Mervyn Alleyne's (2005) *Construction and Representation of Race and Ethnicity in the Caribbean World* for a discussion of these various waves of immigrant groups, and the interrelationships between race, colour, ethnicity and class.
3. Permission for use of this image was granted by Patrick Montgomery, Caribbean Photo Archives, Jamaica https://www.flickr.com/photos/caribbeanphotoarchive/3025515206/in/set-72157608965430475/lightbox/
4. This influx feeds the erroneous notion that Africans and Caribbeans did not live in the UK before the Second World War. See Green, 2000, 'Before the Windrush'.
5. I have used the term 'West Indian' to mark this particular era of migration history and when citing authors who used the term when writing about this time period. While still prevalently used, 'West Indian' reminds us of the erroneous naming attributed to Christopher Columbus and needs to be problematized.
6. Photograph from author's personal collection. Photographer: Ernest Smith, 37, the Main Way, Chorleywood.
7. Listen to poets Bennett and Johnson perform their poetry on Youtube to appreciate the beauty of the Jamaican language.
8. Cooper writes her tribute to Hall in two separate forms of Creole orthography that she calls 'chaka-chaka' (irregular) and 'prapa-prapa' (proper). I used the former above because of its proximity to English orthography for the sake of the reader. Prapa-prapa is based upon a phonetic system devised by Jamaican linguist Frederic Cassidy and updated by the Jamaica Language Unit at UWI. The sentence above would be written more phonetically as follows: 'So wa mek Stuart Hall neva kom bak a yaad; Im did visit, yes. Bot im liv out im laif a Inglan' (Cooper, 2014).
9. In The magic of diaspora (2011), the author argues for the growing economic importance of diasporas and the contribution they make to a country's economic growth. The Economist.com, online. See Trotz and Mullings (2013) for a critique of this 'diaspora option'.
10. http://www.mona.uwi.edu/library/sites/default/files/library/uploads/Stuart%20Hall.pdf

References

Akomfrah, J. (2013). Director. *The Stuart Hall project*. Produced by The British Film Institute, BBC, Arts Council England, Creation Rebel Films, Open University and Smoking Dog Films.

Alleyne, M. C. (2005). *Construction and representation of race and ethnicity in the Caribbean and the world*. Kingston: University of West Indies Press.

Banton, M. (1983). The influence of colonial status upon Black-White relations in England 1948–1958. *Sociology, 17*, 546–559. doi:10.1177/0038038583017004005

BBC News. (2001, May 28). *Long history of race rioting*. Retrieved from http://news.bbc.co.uk/2/hi/uk_news/1355718.stm

Bennett, L. (1966). *Jamaica Labrish*. Kingston: Sangster Books.

Birthwright, E. (2011, March 16). *Perspectives from back 'home': Rethinking Louise Bennett's 'Colonization in reverse' 1966*. Paper presented at the annual meeting of the 35th Annual National Council for Black Studies, Cincinnati, OH. Retrieved from http://citation.allacademic.com/meta/p493121_index.html

Bloch, Y., Ratzoni, G., Sobol, D., Mendlovic, S., Gal, G., & Levkovitz, Y. (2005). Gender difference in electroconvulsive therapy: A retrospective chart review. *Journal of Affective Disorders, 84*(1), 99–102. doi:10.1016/j.jad.2004.10.002

Brah, A. (1996). *Cartographies of diaspora: Contesting identities*. New York, NY: Routledge.

Brand, D. (2005). *What we long for*. Toronto: Vintage Canada.

Breeze, J. B. (2000). *The arrival of Brighteye*. Newcastle: Bloodaxe.

Chapman, P. (2007). *Bananas: How the United Fruit Company shaped the world*. New York, NY: Cannongate.

Chen, K. H. (2010). The formation of a diasporic intellectual. In D. Morley & K. H. Chen (Eds.), *Critical dialogues in cultural studies* (pp. 486–505). New York, NY: Routledge.

Cooper, C. (2013). Islands beyond envy: Finding our tongue in the Creole Anglo-Caribbean. The sixth Edward Baugh distinguished lecture. *Caribbean Quarterly, 59*(1), 1–19.

Cooper, C. (2014, February 16). Stuart Hall roots and legacy. *Jamaica Gleaner*. Retrieved from http://jamaica-gleaner.com/gleaner/20140216/cleisure/cleisure3.html

Denzin, N. (1989). *Interpretive biography*. Newbury Park: SAGE.

Farred, G. (2014, February 21). The failure of partial displacement: In honour of Stuart Hall. *The Con*. Retrieved from http://www.theconmag.co.za/2014/02/21/the-failure-of-partial-displacement-in-honour-of-stuart-hall/

Foner, N. (1979). West Indians in New York City and London: A comparative analysis. *International Migration Review, 13*, 284–297. doi:10.2307/2545033

Green, J. (2000). Before the Windrush. *History Today, 50*, 29.

Gutiérrez, K., Hunter, J., & Arzubiaga, A. (2009). Remediating the university: Learning through sociocritical literacies. *Pedagogies: An International Journal, 4*(1), 1–23.

Hall, S. (1959a). Absolute beginnings: Reflections on the secondary modern generation. *Universities and New Left Review, 7*(4), 16–25.

Hall, S. (1959b). Politics of adolescence? *Universities and New Left Review, 6*(3), 2–4.

Hall, S. (1983). Teaching race. *Early Child Development and Care, 10*, 259–274. doi:10.1080/0300443830100402

Hall, S. (1987/1996). Minimal selves. In H. A. Baker, M. Diawara, & R. H. Lindeborg (Eds.), *Black British cultural studies: A reader* (pp. 44–46). Chicago, IL: University of Chicago Press.

Hall, S. (1990a). Cultural identity and diaspora. In J. Rutherford (Ed.), *Identity, community, culture, difference* (pp. 222–237). London: Lawrence & Whishart.

Hall, S. (1990b). The emergence of cultural studies and the crisis of the humanities. *October, 53*, 11–23. doi:10.2307/778912

Hall, S. (1995). Negotiating Caribbean identities. *New Left Review, 209*, 3–14.

Hall, S., & Back, L. (2009). Stuart Hall and Les Back in conversation: At home and not at home. *Cultural Studies, 23*, 658–687. doi:10.1080/09502380902950963

Hennessy, P. (2001). *The prime minister: The office and its holders since 1945*. New York, NY: Palgrave.

Jaggi, M. (2000, July 8). Prophet at the margins. *The Guardian*. Retrieved from http://www.theguardian.com/books/2000/jul/08/society

The Jamaica *Gleaner* (anonymous). (n.d.). Rediscovering Stuart Hall. Retrieved from the Jamaica Gleaner, http://jamaica-gleaner.com/gleaner/20140212/cleisure/cleisure1.html

Johnson, L. K. (1980). *Inglan is a bitch*. Retrieved from http://www.webalice.it/t.christiansen/Inglan %20Is%20A%20Bitch.htm. See also, https://www.youtube.com/watch?v=qqmVvQuzGO4

Jones, C. (2000). The Caribbean community in Britain. In K. Owusu (Ed.), *Black British culture and society: A text reader* (pp. 52–60). New York, NY: Routledge.

Kenworthy, D. (Producer), & Michell, R. (Director). (1999). *Notting Hill*. United Kingdom: Universal Studios.

The magic of diaspora. (2011, November 18). *The Economist*. Retrieved from http://www.economist.com/node/21538742

Mendez, S. M., Cueto, G., & Deynes, E. R. (2003). *Notable Caribbeans and Caribbean Americans: A biographical dictionary*. Westport, CT: Greenwood.

Mishra, V. (2013). Multiculturalism, 2010–2011. The year's work in critical and cultural theory, 21,1–21. @The English association (2013). Retrieved January 22, 2014, from http://ywcct.oxfordjournals.org/ at The University of British Colombia Library.

Morley, D., & Chen, K. H. (Eds.). (2010). *Critical dialogues in cultural studies*. New York, NY: Routledge.

Passerini, L. (1996). *Autobiography of a generation: Italy, 1968*. Hanover, NH: University Press of New England [for] Wesleyan University Press.

Putnam, L. (2002). *The company they kept: Migrants and politics of gender in Caribbean Costa Rica, 1870–1960*. Chapel Hill, NC: University of North Carolina Press.

Roman, L. (2015). Making and moving publics: Stuart Hall's projects, maximal selves and education. *Discourse: Studies in the Cultural Politics of Education, 36*(2), 199–224.

Salvatore, N. (2004). Biography and social history: An intimate relationship. *Labour History, 87*, 187–192. doi:10.2307/27516005

Sarup, M. (1982). *Education, state and crisis: A Marxist perspective*. Boston, MA: Routledge & Kegan Paul.

Schubert, W. (2010). Outside pedagogy and public pedagogy. In J. Sandlin, B. Schultz, & J. Burdick, (Eds.), *Handbook of public pedagogy: Education and learning beyond schooling* (pp. 2–16). New York, NY: Routledge.

Scott, D. (2012, July). Stuart Hall at eighty. *Small Axe, 16*(2), 38, vii–x.

Scott, D. (2013, March). The paradox of freedom: An interview with Orlando Patterson. *Small Axe, 17*(1) (40), 96–242. doi:10.1215/07990537-1665461

Smith, S. (1999). Memory, narrative and the discourses of identity. In A. Hornung & E. Ruhe (Eds.), *Postcolonialism and autobiography* (pp. 37–60). Amsterdam: Rodopi.

Stratton, J., & Ang, I. (2010). On the impossibility of a global cultural studies: 'British' cultural studies in an 'international' frame. In D. Morley & K. H. Chen (Eds.), *Critical dialogues in cultural studies* (pp. 360–392). New York, NY: Routledge.

Trotz, D. A., & Mullings, B. (2013). Transnational migration, the state, and development: Reflecting on the 'diaspora option'. *Small Axe, 17*, 154–171. doi:10.1215/07990537-2323373

University of West Indies. (2004, June 17–August 31). *Culture, politics, race and diaspora: The thought of Stuart Hall*. Exhibition at University of West Indies, Mona Library. Retrieved from http://www.mona.uwi.edu/library/sites/default/files/library/uploads/Stuart%20Hall.pdf

Weale, S. (1999, November 18). Shock tactics. *The Guardian*. Retrieved from http://www.ect.org/news/women.html

Winant, H. (2009). Race in the 21st century. *Tikkun, 17*(1), 33–40.

Zeleza, P. T. (2008). The challenges of studying the African Diasporas. *African Sociological Review, 12*(2), 4–21.

Diasporic reasoning, affect, memory and cultural politics: An interview with Avtar Brah

Leslie G. Roman and Annette Henry

Educational Studies, Faculty of Education, University of British Columbia, Vancouver, Canada

This interview explores the intellectual contours of Stuart Hall's work through the insights of Professor Avtar Brah[1], Emerita, Birkbeck College, whose feminist post-colonial voice has shaped generations of scholarship on diaspora thinking, achieving public intellectual status. Her *Cartographies of Diaspora* (1996) received international acclaim, challenging nationalist feminisms to engage diasporic cultural politics. The longest standing member of the *Feminist Review* editorial collective, Brah's intertwining of feminist theorisation with transformative pedagogies is well known. It is rare that feminists of colour or diasporic feminists are celebrated as 'public intellectuals', even when they are exceptionally accomplished in multiple spheres of intellectual life. Thus, we have chosen to interview Professor Avtar Brah, whose transnationally recognised work both owes a debt to and extends Hall's work in some surprising directions. Our interview explores some questions together as a 'we' and others individually to respect and highlight our own respective theoretical, socio-political and transnational experiences. This approach to interviewing acknowledges our different voices, as well as our affinities through this collaboration.

Notations for interview transcript

AH:	Questions asked by Annette Henry
LGR:	Questions asked by Leslie G. Roman
AH & LGR:	Grouped questions in which one of us sparked the other to ask additional related questions
AB:	Responses and reflections of Avtar Brah
T:	Questions asked together from a shared perspective

Relational genealogies

LGR: Would you start by telling us about how you first came to know Stuart Hall as a graduate student, and later, becoming privileged to know him as a colleague and friend, and in what contexts and over what period of time did you know him? I ask because this helps situate the contours and shifts in his thinking and yours over time.

AB: I met Stuart Hall as a graduate student in the mid-1970s. Three of us students went to see him at the Centre for Contemporary Cultural Studies in Birmingham. We were totally in awe of him and wondered when or indeed whether, we would succeed in getting an appointment with him. We need not have worried, for he made time in his very busy schedule for an early appointment with us. Our meeting with him was memorable. Apart from the excitement of meeting such a renowned figure, we were deeply touched by the warmth with which he greeted us and the encouragement he gave to our fledgling ideas. His generosity was immense. This was one of his endearing qualities. He genuinely valued and respected each and every person for her or his uniqueness even if he seriously disagreed with them intellectually or politically. And he was generous to a fault. I admired him for this as much as for his towering intellect.

During the early 1980s, I was appointed as a lecturer in the Faculty of Education at the Open University. Stuart Hall was then a Professor in the Faculty of Social Sciences at the Open University. This was when I began to know him better. I was chair of a course on race and ethnicity which was threatened by cuts in the Faculty budget. We had to mobilise support within the university, not least because it was the only course specifically concerned with these topics in the university's curriculum. Hall's helping hand, as a respected, renowned full professor, was crucial in extending the life of the course. But my own job as contract staff could not be saved, and I left academia behind for a while and took up post as head of resources within the Women's Committee Support Unit at the Greater London Council (GLC). The GLC, under Ken Livingstone, was a left project, sometimes dubbed as an experiment in 'municipal socialism'. It attracted extreme opposition from the then Prime Minister Margret Thatcher, a major global icon of neoliberalism. Eventually her government succeeded in abolishing the GLC.

For me personally, the transfer to the GLC worked out to be a good move. It gave me the opportunity to intervene in the funding of women's groups across London. We tried to put into practice what I believed in – to develop the funding policy within, what today we call, the 'intersectionality' frame. At the time, we did not use this term. Rather, we firmly believed that 'woman' was not a homogeneous category. Our needs, wants and practices are differentiated by power dimensions embedded within and across axes of class, gender, racism, disability, sexuality and so on. We tried to develop policies which took into account these different facets of our social world. We involved women's groups and activists in developing these policies. There were sometimes heated but on the whole creative discussions and debates within the Women's Unit, within the GLC, and with diverse communities of affiliation. In 1985, during the last days of the GLC, I returned to an academic post in the Faculty of Adult and Continuing Education at Birkbeck College.

During these years, I got to know Stuart Hall well and had the privilege to call him a friend. My own work has drawn inspiration from his incisive theoretical and political thought over nearly three decades. I have tried to use his insights in order to analyse the problematics I was engaged with, which have dealt with the interactions of class, race, gender, ethnicity, diaspora, sexuality and nationalism. During the 1970s and 1980s, I was researching issues associated with youth – unemployment, cultural predicaments, identity – and some of the work undertaken at the Centre for Contemporary Cultural Studies at Birmingham on youth subcultures was influential, although much of it was about young men while I was working with both young men and women. One of the major exceptions was of course the brilliant text, *Empire Strikes Back* (Centre for Contemporary Cultural Studies, 1982). During the 1990s and the first decade of this century, I was far more focused on theorising culture, identity and diaspora, and this work engaged with Hall's expositions on these themes, although I had my own takes on them. Feminist politics and intellectual resources have been critical in the development of my work. So my conversations with Stuart Hall's thought have been refracted through this prism of feminism.

LGR: In thinking about those contours, for example, the reworking of Foucault, Laclau and Gramsci in Hall, where have you departed along the way from the some of the directions Stuart Hall took?

AB: My intellectual and political work has been informed by 'intersectional' perspectives informed by socialist, anti-colonial and anti-imperialist agendas. In this, Hall and I have shared much ground. Our diasporic positioning in Britain also made for certain affinities. During the early stages of my academic career, I, like Stuart Hall, was influenced by Marxist perspectives but he was a scholar of Marxism which I have not been. I have used Marxist insights whenever I could but my focus on issues of race, gender and ethnicity made me sensitive to the limitations of class-centric paradigms where phenomena such as racism, sexism and heteronormativity were at best secondary to the primacy of class. Was it at all possible to bring these axes of differentiation within the explanatory orbit of Marxism? How could one undertake non-reductive understanding of these relational phenomena? There were also, of course, internal critiques within Marxism itself leading to many neo-Marxist revisions but they rarely questioned the primacy of class. Within this context, some of Gramsci's concepts offered resources of hope. Gramsci's work is class-centric too, but some of his concepts had the potential to be used in the analysis of broader parameters some of us were exploring. For me, the notion of 'hegemony' and 'commonsense' were particularly attractive. Hall has, of course been, on the forefront of developing these two Gramscian concepts. In *Selections from the Prison Notebooks* Gramsci distinguishes 'hegemony' from 'direct domination' (1971, p. 12). Hegemony is about the complex ways in which social 'consent' is secured in non-coercive ways, at the level of the state and civil society. Hall and his colleagues put this distinction to excellent use in the book *Policing the Crisis* (Hall, Critcher, Jefferson, & Clarke, 1978). Hall's exposition of non-reductionism and economism, relationality and hegemony in the essay 'Gramsci's relevance for the study of race and ethnicity' (1996a) remains distinctively suggestive. Hegemony is exercised not only in the economic and administrative fields, Hall reminds us but 'encompasses the critical domains of cultural, moral, ethical and intellectual leadership' (1996a, p. 426). In relation to race or gender, for instance, an important question is how discourses and practices of race or gender figure in the attempts at securing hegemony. The importance of 'commonsense' in the play of hegemony is a crucial point. Commonsense is our practical, everyday pool of knowledge and consciousness, with which we make sense of the world. It does not work just on the intellectual terrain, but touches and mobilises our deepest emotions and affectivities:

> 'Commonsense' is not coherent: it is usually 'disjointed and episodic', fragmentary and contradictory. Into it the traces and 'stratified deposits' of more coherent philosophical systems have sedimented over time without leaving any clear inventory. It represents itself as the 'traditional wisdom or truth of the ages', but in fact, it is deeply a product of history. (Hall, 1996c, p. 431 as cited in Morley & Chen, 2010).

In the *Kilburn Manifesto* (2013), Stuart Hall and colleagues further elaborate on the concept of commonsense and demonstrate how neoliberal ideas and perspective are becoming part of our commonsense.

Hall's use of Foucault was part of his turn to post-structuralism. I too found Foucault's conception of power as not just coercive but also productive a helpful innovation. The notion of discursive constitution of the subject was enabling in thinking through formation of the subject via intersectional articulations. I have used Foucault's concept of genealogy to theorise diaspora. Hall also pointed to the importance of psychoanalysis in understanding constitution of the subject. I agree with Hall on this. Racism, for instance, could hardly be understood without addressing the role of unconscious processes in the genealogy of racialised formations. I have tried to hold on to the strengths of the theorisations of class within neo-Marxist and other sociological works such as the work of Bourdieu, alongside post-structuralist thought in analysing subject, subjectivity and identity. The importance of 'creolised theory' underpins my own theorisation of 'difference' along four axes: difference understood as social relation, as subjectivity, as identity and as experience. Hall, in a somewhat different way, seems also to have deployed 'creolised' theoretical formations. In the *Kilburn Manifesto*, the influence of Gramsci is palpable.

LGR: The incisive tribute you wrote to Stuart Hall which appeared in the online magazine, *Open Democracy* in 18 February 2014 (Brah, 2014, n.p.) went beyond the commemoration of his personal qualities to point out the ways in which Hall's ideas on 'race', ethnicity and identity were at the heart of understanding British society and post-imperial identity and society. You note that Hall did so at a time when 'race' was considered as 'something to do with people of colour' rather than simultaneously being at the basis of formations of whiteness. Can you elaborate on this more specifically to show the potency and relevance of his ideas?

AB: I first encountered the potency of Hall's ideas in a BBC television lecture as part of series of five lectures by influential intellectuals on 'multiracial Britain' in 1978. In his very own erudite fashion, he defined the centrality of 'race' in understanding the history of colonial and post-colonial Britain. He examined both the racialised class composition of Britain as well as the ideological terrain in which racialised groups are constructed as the Other (Hall, 1980). Race, he argued, was not an external but internal dynamic of the British social formation. The book *Policing the Crisis* (Hall et al., 1978) also undertakes this task. Although it is primarily about discursive construction of 'criminality', the analysis is that of 'mugging' which is recognised in Britain as a racialised crime. Similarly, his theorisation of Thatcherism placed race at the heart of his analysis alongside class and gender. This mode of analysis was a great boost to those of us post-graduate students who were grappling with the problem of how to avoid treating 'race' as defined in those days in terms of 'something to do with coloured people'. The implication of Hall's analysis was that racialised discourses are simultaneously about white groups, although the discourse of whiteness itself was not much on the horizon in the late 1970s and early 1980s. It was scholars such as the late Ruth Frankenberg (1993) and yourself (Roman, 1993) who placed theories of whiteness and white defensiveness on the agenda. Simultaneously, the problematic of how to theorise the interconnections between race, class and gender were debated in Britain in the pages of the feminist journal, *Feminist Review.*

In the later stages of the debate, whiteness as a relational regime of knowledge and practice came to be widely accepted. At a practical level, women's groups such as

Organisation of Women of Asian and African Descent (OWAAD) and Southall Black Sisters were organising on the basis of how to build solidarity among differentially racialised categories of people such as South Asian and African heritage groups. Coalitions with white groups were secured on the acknowledgement of the specificity of experience of differently positioned racialised groups in the power hierarchies of Britain and the globe. I learnt a great deal from working in these groups and these insights fed into my intellectual work. There has been a tendency to dismiss such work as merely engaging in 'identity politics', but I believe that we would not have made much progress without the solidarity activism of the oppressed groups themselves.

Neoliberalism

LGR: Your co-authored article with A. Gill (Brah & Gill, 2014), 'Interrogating cultural narratives about honour-based violence' argues that if gender is analysed along with other axes of power, non-Western cultures need not be treated in an essentialist manner as 'uncivilised'. This article makes use of the concept of 'neoliberalism' to unpack 'intersectional' axes of power. Hall also argued that despite the over-use and penumbra of vagueness of certain uses of neoliberalism, it was still an important concept for understanding current economic conditions. In what ways have you found the concept useful in showing multiple and constitutive axes of power?

AB: The politics of intersectional equality, justice and solidarity do not sit comfortably with neoliberal agendas with profitability for capital as their major priority. Neoliberalism is not a new phenomenon. As Hall has argued in his essay, 'Neoliberal Revolution' (2011), that neoliberalism has been in the making for 200 years, and represents many variants and crises, but takes a specific form in our own times. From 1970s onwards, its tentacles have spread around the globe, enmeshed with new regimes of late capitalism. Its emphasis on the importance of the 'free possessive individual' and its extreme disdain, even enmity of the interventionist state has meant a degradation of the life chances of the poor, the dispossessed, the deprived and the discriminated against. Free market is its cornerstone, and any efforts to address the inequities and inequalities it generates are anathema. Of course, neoliberalism needs the state to perform all the tasks which are needed for the lubrication of the capitalist wheel. Rather, it is the state welfarism that it is poised against. In Britain it found its most prominent proponent in Margaret Thatcher, who became Prime Minister in 1979.

Hall is said to have coined the concept of 'Thatcherism', the neoliberal phenomenon of which he was an astute analyst. Hall understood Thatcherism as a singularly significant and successful economic, political and ideological project promoting what he called 'authoritarian populism' that was accompanied by a massive swing to the Right. It spawned discourses of mugging, law and order, permissive society and social anarchy. It conjured up fears of racial dilution of national character through the presence of People of Colour. On the economic front, Thatcherism was characterised by monetarism, deregulation, privatisation of key national industries and a commitment to flexible labour markets. It mounted an onslaught on trade unions and argued for a minimal national and local state. This was a political agenda for free markets, cuts in state funding and cuts in taxes. It produced a nationalism which harked back to imperial glories and spoke of social threats from 'enemies within'. In a consolidated form, neoliberalism continued through the Blair period and is thriving in contemporary Britain. But since the financial crisis of 2008, it speaks the 'reasonable sounding' language of 'austerity': 'we must all tighten our belts,' 'accept cutbacks for the greater good of society' and so on. The financial deregulation which Thatcher instituted is somewhat curbed because the crisis demanded it but the cutbacks in state funding are unstoppable, and the gap between the rich and the poor grows. The policies carried out under the banner of austerity do not impact equally on all groups. Women, minority ethnic groups and young people are the worst affected. An understanding of this differential impact is important in order to challenge the intersectional inequalities wrought by neoliberalism.

LGR: Scholars who use 'neoliberalism' often have not thought of relationality between East and West, and Global South and Global North. Your theorisation has drawn upon your diasporic experiences to address some of the neoliberal contexts and consequences of racism. How might diasporic formations be better illuminated through the concept of neoliberalism and vice versa?

AB: Neoliberalism is a global phenomenon. Globally, the international organisations such as the International Monetary Fund (IMF) have instituted structural adjustment programmes on the South which are conceptualised in the mould of neoliberalism with devastating consequences. There is privatisation of social economic structures with cuts in state-funded programmes in education, health and employment. If the poor in the global North suffer, those in the South do not even have the bare necessities of life. In the Western countries, racism often serves to secure consent of the population for neoliberal projects. I mentioned above how discourses of race operated in forming the commonsense of people during Thatcherite Britain. Today, it is the 'migrants' who are the subject of demonisation. It is not only the Far Right parties such as the Britain First, which deploy this discourse, but also more 'mainstream parties such as the Independence Party which are strongly against Britain staying in the European Union, partly because it opens the doors to migrants from Eastern Europe. Racialised discourses about the refugees and asylum seekers play a similar role in fomenting fear. Ironically, in some discourses, the long-standing diasporic groups are represented as more acceptable compared to the Eastern European migrants, but on the colour axis of differentiation, People of Colour remain inferiorised.

New ethnicities and diasporas

LGR: Hall's important essays, 'New Ethnicities' (1996b) and 'Who Needs Identity?' (Hall, 1996a; Hall & DuGay, 1996), bring into view the work of then young Black British film-makers such as Isaac Julien and musicians about which he wrote that the new cultural politics of their art forms expressed:

> a real shift in the point of contestation …What is involved is the splitting of the notion of ethnicity between, on the one hand, the dominant notion which connects it to nation and 'race', and what the other is the beginning of a positive conception of ethnicity on the margins, of the periphery. (Hall, 1996c, p. 447 cited in Morley & Chan, 1996)

Now that much of this work has moved from the margins to the centre, what is the ground for 'new ethnicities' and 'contestation'? Walk us through the process of moving from margin to centre and the politics of contestation for renewal and social justice. Is incorporation into the 'culture industries' the necessary result of success in the mainstream?

AB: Hall has consistently argued that cultural settlements are rarely achieved once and for always. The gains are not made in a linear fashion and can easily be overturned under new circumstances. There is a continuous tension between different groups around arts and culture. Both the 'centre' and the 'periphery' are heterogeneous categories and the gains for different segments of the population are not the same. Some individuals and certain fragments of the population have indeed done well in the arena of creative industries, but others still experience exclusion and marginalisation. Indeed as recently as 17 March 2014, the famous Black comedian, actor and writer Lenny Henry discussed in the annual television Lecture of BAFTA (British Academy of Film and Television Arts) that, according to the latest census conducted by the Creative Skillset, there was a 30.95% decline in the number of Black, Asian and Minority Ethnic (BAME) people working in the UK television industries between 2006 and 2012. He argues for monitoring and proactive steps towards encouraging more productions to use BAME actors and production staff. 'The evolution of BAME involvement in British TV seems to lurch one step forward and two steps backward', he said. He pointed to the fact that many BAME actors seem to find more work in America than in the UK. In the 1980s, there were major campaigns to improve the representation of BAME groups in the creative industries. The GLC funded a number of individuals and film collectives to improve the situation. Those initiatives have shifted the terrain significantly but nothing can be taken for granted, especially in the face of financial cuts introduced under the ideology of austerity (Henry, 2014). Research shows that women, BAME groups, young people and the working class poor in general are far more seriously affected by the cuts (Brah, Gedalof, Szeman, 2015). So, overall, the entry into the 'centre' is partial and sporadic.

Hall's arguments about 'New Ethnicities' would seem to be about at least three aspects: intergenerational change, shifts in how to conceptualise cultural politics, and a move in theoretical perspective from structuralist/materialist to post-structuralist perspectives. It is an extremely complex and innovative analysis which retains its critical relevance today. The valorisation of a concept of ethnicity that challenged racism, a thoroughly non-essentialist notion of the Black subject, and recognition of a difference – 'which is positional, conditional and conjunctural, closer to Derrida's notion of difference, though if we are concerned to maintain a politics, it cannot be defined exclusively in terms of an infinite sliding of the signifier' (Hall, 1996c in Morely & Chan, 1996, p. 447) – are some of its major insights. The politics of representation have shifted in the present times of new social media, and films such as *Twelve Years a Slave* and *Belle* are fully recognised as American and British films respectively, but to my mind they combine what Hall characterises as 'a struggle over relations of representations' and 'a politics of representation itself'.

In the context of the present politics of 'War on Terror' and rampant Islamophobia, there is much struggle over 'relations of representation' even as conceptually, it is 'the politics of representation' that are at stake. The question is how best to hold on to both at the same time.

AH & LGR: The introduction to *Cartographies* (1996) asks, 'What does it mean to think about the politics of diaspora in the present historical moment?' You speak of moving from Uganda as part of a forced migration. How has your own experience of forced migration informed and grounded your theorisation of cartographies of diaspora?

AB: I was on my way back to Uganda after completing my studies in the USA and stopped in Britain for a short period. Suddenly, out of the blue, the then President of Uganda passed an edict that all Asians living in Uganda had to leave the country. This was 1972. Since, I held a Ugandan passport, his edict made me a stateless person, and I was so for five years until I was able to take up British citizenship. So, although I was not a part of the direct exodus from Uganda, I remain haunted by the fact that my home was taken away from me. I could not return home. This experience has made me acutely sensitive to the plight of refugees and asylum seekers. *Cartographies* is, in part, about different experiences of migrancy. It articulates a theory of 'politics of difference'. How, on the one hand, 'difference' can be a component of Othering, and on the other hand, it can be the basis for coalition politics. I have experienced both aspects. Idi Amin constructed the putative difference of Asians as a threat. Whereas in Britain in the 1970s and 1980s, Asians and African descent Blacks mobilised together under the sign of political colour 'Black', against racism and class exploitation. So, yes, my experiences have informed my theoretical and political projects.

AH: You mention how wonderful it was to have had time to think, write and work with US colleagues when you went to California. How did that period help you rethink notions of race and solidarity, notions of blackness 'diasporically'?

AB: My sojourn in California was indeed wonderful, made rather special by collegiality and friendship of persons such as Angela Davis, James Clifford and Donna Haraway. These encounters were intellectually and politically tremendous. After the extremely hectic pace of my job in London, I now had the time and space to think and write. The distance from London also gave a different vantage point. One issue that comes immediately to mind is that not all concepts travel well. I became aware that the British version of the political colour Black to include Asians was not viable in the USA. Black referred to the specificity of African-American experience. Other racialised categories – Asians, Latinos, Native Americans and so on – could not be grouped under the signifier 'Black'. The term that galvanised all these groups together was People of Colour. Indeed, since then, I too have adopted this terminology. The political colour 'Black' fractured and fragmented in the 1990s, as did the figure of 'Asian', after the Rushdie Affair. Religion has since become much more important as a ground for organising. Although, having said that, I know of a number of young women of colour who have started organising again under the label 'Black'. A group named Black Feminists with branches in Manchester and Liverpool, currently organises under the sign of 'Black'. On their website they describe their membership as those women who are Black in the political sense that is to say that:

> all women descended (through one or both parents) from Africa, Asia (i.e., the Middle East to China, including the Pacific nations), Latin America and those descended from the original inhabitants of Australasia, North America and the Islands of the Atlantic and Indian Ocean. (Black Feminists, 2010, http://blackfeminists.blogspot.ca/p/about.html, accessed 2014)

They have set themselves up 'to provide a safe space to discuss issues that affect us'. They address intersectionality by mounting a collective fight 'against racism, sexism, disablism and homophobia'. This is undertaken in the context of 'legacies of oppression' such as 'slavery, colonialism, neocolonialism, imperialism and militarisation'. They expect of their members, religious, cultural and ethnic sensitivity. OWAAD was predominantly a coalition of African, Caribbean and South Asian origin women. But the New Black Feminists self-consciously include a wider group of women.

You are right in saying that in *Cartographies* my concern with issues of racism and gender became embedded in an intersectional framing of diasporacity. This was part of a focus in which the local and the global articulate.

AH & LGR: In fact, how has your own autobiography and living on several continents contributed to your thinking about citizenship, diaspora, dispersal, displacement and belonging? As you reflect on these influences in the current economic, global and political crises, what are your thoughts? What are your thoughts on uneven globalisation and its implications for transnational feminist solidarity or alliances? What transnational feminist projects have inspired the Southall Black Sisters?

AB: Living in four continents makes you acutely sensitive to the historically specific power dynamics that impinge differently in different contexts. One is positioned differently across axes of class, race, gender, caste and so on. In Punjab, India, I belong to a dominant caste and this has a major impact on social ranking. In Uganda, I was a part of the so-called middle layer of the colonial sandwich with Europeans at the top, Asians in the middle and Africans at the bottom. This makes you look at life from different positions of privilege/non-privilege. Europeans inferiorised both Asians and the Africans, and Asians, in turn inferiorised Africans. In the USA, I was a student who was orientalised but quite differently from my experience in Britain. Questions of belonging are always fraught, deeply invested as they are in affect and emotionality and marked thoroughly by power. I felt I belonged to Uganda, but Idi Amin thought differently. After living in Britain since the 1970s, I feel I belong here and many accept it so, but racist groups question my right to Britishness. Immigration and Nationality Law continually contests the borders of citizenship in terms of who belongs and who does not belong. Uneven globalisation, neoimperial wars, neocolonial occupations, ethnic and religious conflicts, genocides, droughts and famine, neoliberal politics, all make for a dire situation. Global inequalities and inequities have deepened over the years (Brah, Hickman, & Mac an Ghaill, 1999a, 1999b; Brah & Coombes, 2000) (Cf. Baksh & Harcourt, 2014; Rawwida & Harcourt, 2015). Within nation states, there are all manner of social divisions made worse by economic and social neoliberal policies.

There is indeed a great need for transnational feminist solidarity alliances. The plight of the poor and those living in or fleeing war-torn conditions demands urgent attention. Mobilisation against inequalities of class, gender, race, caste and so on, in the global South and the North is crucial. The economic and political dominance of a global political class at the helm of global capitalism implementing neoliberal strategies warrants continual challenge. Precise strategies for struggle are of course dependent on the specific context of a region. But there should not be a top down approach. We, feminists in the North need to be cognizant of our relative privileged position in relation to those in the South (Brah et al., 1999a, 1999b). Our politics have to emerge from sensitivity to the power dynamic inherent in our relationally differential positionalities. On a more positive note, it is worth bearing in mind that a great deal of such work is already underway such as in the Oxford Handbook of Transnational Feminist Movements (cf. Baksh & Harcourt, 2014/2015; Rawwida & Harcourt, 2015; Brah & Coombs, 2000).

AH & LGR: By 2015 (time of this publication), 19 years have gone by since you wrote *Cartographies*, how do you now think about diaspora, diasporic space (borders, politics of location) in the present conjuncture? For example, how have the 'gendering' and racialisation of diasporas changed since *Cartographies* in the wake of 9/11 and 5/5 and their new 'security regimes'? How have economic cuts to health care and childcare changed the ways cartographies of diaspora should be analysed, theorised and engaged politically?

AB: I tried to think of the concept of diaspora as mapping the changing circumstances of a given diaspora:

> These journeys must be historicized if the concept of diaspora has to serve as a useful heuristic devise. The question is not simply who travels, but when, how and under what circumstances? What socio-economic, political and cultural conditions mark the trajectories of these diasporas? What regimes of power inscribe the formation of a specific diaspora? (*Cartographies*, 1996, p. 182)

Diaspora and diaspora space as concepts are investigative technologies that could be brought to bear on the present conjuncture. The world has changed significantly since 9/11 and 5/5. The 'War on Terror' has spawned rabid Islamophobia. The after-effects of the 2003 war in Iraq are there for all to see with the unleashing of sectarianism with a vengeance, the erosion of state welfare and the mushrooming of more extremist elements in the political culture. Violent conflict also rages in other places such as Afghanistan, Gaza, Syria and Ukraine, all enmeshed in the power machinations of the dominant countries of the world. These political conflicts have ripple effects in the diasporic communities. In Britain, for instance, the impact of Islamophobia is palpable. There are attacks on Muslim persons and places of worship. The discourse of the 'terrorist' or 'extremist' impinges overwhelmingly on Muslim populations who are represented as the Other par excellence. The word 'immigrant' is once again a term of abuse which now includes East Europeans. Refugee and asylum seekers are constantly demonised. Since the financial crisis of 2008, the austerity policies of western governments impact far more on women, youth and minority ethnic groups. On the other hand, there are a substantial numbers of multi-millionaires, even a few billionaires that can be counted among diasporic communities. There are thus internal class hierarchies emerging among diasporic groups. I would like to reiterate that diaspora is a heterogeneous category. It is differentiated internally, as well as in its relationship to the social divisions in broader society. The concept of intersectionality is critical in engaging with the complexity of such differentiations and divisions.

Public intellectual work: public pedagogies, working theory

LGR: I was very touched and struck by the tribute to Stuart Hall put out by the Media Diversified 'Collective' and curated by Yasmin Gunatratam in *Open Democracy* with feminist post-colonial and diasporic scholars of note including Sara Ahmed, Ann Phoenix, Nirmala Puwar and Pratibha Parmar, among others (Media Diversified in *Open Democracy*, 2014, n.p.) It began with 'We are here because you were there' – a moment when diasporic feminist scholars of colour raised their voices together in homage to Stuart Hall. It is all too rare that a 'towering intellectual mind' and male figure also embraced feminist practice, activism and scholarship and had 'street credibility' in numerous conjoined anti-oppression movements and scholarship. Similarly, your work also has had wide public intellectual impact, articulating ideas across and within multiple sites of the academy, feminist movements and diasporic communities from the Southall Black Sisters to campaigns educating about violence against women in India, as well as against racism and racist incidents in London (Campaign against racism and fascism/ Southall Rights, 1981). What makes such affinities possible for you and what has sustained you during all these years?

AB: I think one does not set out to become a public intellectual, but our involvement in curricular, pedagogical and grass roots level politics of equality and freedom from exploitation and oppression renders our work relevant to different publics. As I said when I was interviewed by Les Back for *Feminist Review* 100 in 2012, I became politicised during my teenage years when I read feminist works by two Punjabi authors, namely, Nanak Singh and Amrita Pritam. This work critiqued various social hierarchies, divisions and oppressive practices in Punjabi society. As an undergraduate in the USA, I was further influenced by radical politics of the late 1960s including the Civil Rights movement and the Black Power movement. In Britain, I became involved in the women's movement, especially the Black women's groups, as well as in anti-racist, socialist politics. *Feminist Review*, with which I have had an association since the 1980s, used to define itself as a socialist feminist journal. Perhaps it is this association with diverse projects that accounts for affinities within and across different publics. In all this, I have been sustained by the support of people I have worked with, some of whom have become lifelong friends.

AH: I have written a feminist critique of Hall's work in cultural studies for failing to attend to the issues of intersectionality of gender and race in his work. I found it 'dangerous' to take on Hall in this regard in terms of the double-binds diasporic women of colour feel in relation to authority and voice (Henry, in Weiler, 2001, p. 166). I undertook my critique with significant reservations, worrying that writing about Hall might fuel expectations that Black women fit their work to existing theoretical frameworks and further reinforce the 'hegemonic and elite "grand narrative" of the Britishness of British cultural studies'? (p. 166). What is your take on this? Do you share my trepidation?

AB: Your analysis is astute. Yet, Hall's body of work is heterogeneous – theoretically, politically and substantively. It is in part made up of sets of engagements/arguments with mainly male, western, theoretical canon of the period. His own immensely creative innovations upon this canon have been singularly productive and seminal. He did write on gender, but on male gender – *Policing the Crisis* (Hall et al., 1978); *Resistance through Rituals: Youth Subcultures in Post-War Britain* (Hall & Jefferson, 1975) work on sexuality – although not from within women/gender studies analytics. I think he was a feminist though. And, in the British context, his theorisation of race as a key feature and dynamic of how society works has been singularly suggestive and enabling for further work by others. His theorisation of identity is simply brilliant, especially the essay in the book *Questions of Identity* (Hall, 1996a). His exposition of how Black identity enables one to analyse the concept of 'identity politics', for instance, in ways that does not just dismiss it, as sometimes its detractors do. Sometimes the self-organising activities of women of colour are dismissed as such. Of course, for me, his analysis of diaspora and 'new ethnicities' opens up a whole new vista for conceptualising feminist diasporic lives.

AH: What is your conception of pedagogy? Teaching and pedagogies are important to both of us. Leslie and I teach in a Faculty of Education at UBC. Would you speak about the joy you have experienced teaching at Birkbeck with its particular students?

AB: Pedagogy for me is a form of co-learning activity that is sensitive to the power relations embedded in the intersectional background of the learner and the teacher. For my entire teaching career, I have worked with adult students. In the faculty of continuing education, I had responsibility for a variety of courses in Urban Community Studies which were taught by part-time lecturers and some by myself. These were mostly certificate and diploma level courses, although we did also offer a masters level course in Race and Ethnicity on which I taught. Courses ranged from those in Asian, Caribbean, Irish, Jewish, Palestinian studies through Childcare to Development studies to Lesbian Studies. Our students as well as lecturers came from diverse backgrounds. All this made for exciting times. A large proportion of our students were returners to studying after leaving school, and so the pedagogic strategies had to be relevant to their specific needs. They were mostly working class with a substantial proportion being Black in the sense of Black as a political colour. I loved this work, and it did indeed bring a great deal of joy.

LGR: What are the constraints and possibilities for untenured scholars in today's neoliberal academy to practise public intellectual scholarship, bridging communities outside and within the academy? Many of my 'junior' (I detest that word) colleagues bemoan the fact that expectations for publication have intensified such that they cannot safely and securely do public intellectual or community-engaged work. What advice would you give to them?

AB: We do not have a tenure system in Britain so that makes it comparatively easier. But the pressure to publish in order to gain promotion has intensified over the years. Neoliberal cuts in university funding results in the availability of fewer academic positions. Academic jobs are thus much harder to obtain. But on a positive note, I know many junior lecturers who are practising sterling public intellectual scholarship, despite the pressures.

LGR: I resonated with your interpretation in the *Open Democracy* (Brah, 2014, n.p.) tribute to Hall with your analysis that his theoretical perspective was 'usefully eclectic', eschewing high theory as gross abstraction, while not getting drawn back into productivist Marxism or relativistic uses of post-structuralism. You comment in your tribute that his uses of theory depended on the context and political conjuncture being explained. What might others learn from Hall's approach to often conflicting theoretical traditions and ways of teaching them?

AB: I learnt from Hall that it is not helpful to make a fetish out of theory. Scholars become hugely invested in particular theoretical paradigms so that drawing from a different paradigm comes to be seen almost as an act of disloyalty. Whereas, Hall used theoretical concepts as and when they were best suited to the analysis of a specific context and problematic. Within feminism, for instance, scholars have taken entrenched positions in terms of materialist vs. post-structuralist perspectives, as if they are wholly antagonistic. To my mind, there are many productive conversations to be had between and across seemingly disparate theoretical perspectives, although of course one also must know the limit to how far diverging perspectives may be reconciled. Hall showed us that it was possible to use Marxism as well as post-structuralism, incisively depending upon the nature of the analytic questions that needed to be addressed.

T: We sense from your political activism and scholarly work that theory is a work in progress, not something to be taken up as given, fixed or held on high. Can you speak to the uses of theory in creating publics and thinking publicly – whether with the Southall Black Sisters or in the context of the *Feminist Review* Editorial Collective or elsewhere.

AB: Like Audrey Lorde and Foucault, I think theory is a tool for analysis. Just as not all tools are effective in all situations, not all theories are effective in all contexts. Theory is not independent of the empirical or the experiential but is closely enmeshed with it. Theory which attempts to eliminate politics is not useful in my view. In my work, theory permeates intellectual and political projects, rather than standing apart from them. Empirical and the political inform the development of theoretical constructs, and the latter help illuminate the social and political issues and problem which are under scrutiny. My theoretical work owes much to grass roots level activism, although of course theory operates at a different level of generality and abstraction.

'Scent of memory: strangers, our own and others': empire and diasporic futures

AH: In *Cartographies* (1996), you acknowledge an intellectual debt to Stuart Hall, and in the Afterword of *Feminist Review's* 100th edition (2012), he reappears as a kind of catalyst whose keynote on 'Scent of Memory' inspired the *Feminist Review* to celebrate your retirement and contributions with a 'Scent of Memory' special issue. Could you talk a little about how Hall's ideas have helped your own theorising?

AB: This is a difficult question to answer although in part, I have already answered it – Hall's reworking of Gramsci, and his particular take on post-structuralist authors such as Foucault, Derrida and Butler have been influential. One may also answer this question in another way – by invoking the 'theoretical/intellectual moments' which formed us both. Hall himself points to this in his contribution to my festschrift in *Feminist Review* 100 (2012). He speaks of how we shared the 'moment of the diasporic' and the 'moment of the problematic of the subject'. The theoretical and political debates of the time both formed us and we speak and write about it. Thinking through related though by no means identical concerns, we turned to some common theoretical resources. My own theorising of the concept of diaspora was inspired by Hall's work, although the concept of diaspora space owes a great deal to the work of women feminist writers and activists.

LGR: For example, in your tour de force and much celebrated *Feminist Review* essay, 'Scent of Memory: Strangers, Our Own and Others' (Brah, 1999) your use of Hall's reworking of Gramsci and Althusser in the relation to the concepts of 'articulation' and popular 'commonsense' are clear. Would you elaborate on your uses of Hall in this context? Where do you depart from him in this essay?

AB: I was interested in the Althusser's (1971) concept of interpellation, the concept, which as I said in 'The Scent of Memory', 'struggles with what I am trying to grapple with here, namely the making sense of being situated and "hailed" socially, culturally, symbolically, and psychically, all at once' (Brah, 1999). I was also thinking about his notion of 'articulation' and Gramsci's view of ideology and commonsense. Hall has been a very lucid exponent of both Althusser and Gramsci's theoretical framework. These conceptual concepts were a point of departure in the 'Scent of Memory'.

AH: Your research in Southall produced telling data. Moreover, your creation of a dialogue between those interviews and 'Jean' (*Scent of Dried Roses: Our family and the end of English suburbia* (Lott, 1996)) was brilliant, speaking to the importance of 'other contexts' as you 'write back' with your own autobiographical experiences, knowledge and questions. I love the idea that the 100th issue of *Feminist Review* (2012) festschrift was conceptualised as an opportunity for you, the longest standing member of the collective, to 'write back' to the article in a journal that you call your 'intellectual home' and have your esteemed colleagues, including Stuart Hall also write back. How did that come about?

AB: My faculty at Birkbeck College, through the hard work of my then colleague Yasmin Narayan, held a colloquium to mark my retirement. The speakers included Stuart Hall, whose contribution concluded the day. Some members of the *Feminist Review* Collective present there thought that it would be a good idea if collective members jointly worked on a special issue of the journal around the 'Scent of Memory' and related themes. In the event, not all members were able to contribute, but the idea for the special issue sprouted on the day. We were delighted that we could include Stuart Hall's contribution in it.

LGR: Hall pays deserved tribute to your work overall, singling out 'Scent of Memory' for its wide resonance. He underscores what makes it a tour de force:

> Brah confronts the necessarily complex and contradictory specificities of differentiated subjectivities in the diasporic frame within a distinct 'methodology' – analytic and interpretive. The very structures 'out there', which have so often been thought of as determining, are understood as themselves providing frameworks of meaning, as having an internal psychic and discursive dimension. Avtar Brah is one of the few who have begun to capture such a double inscription through ongoing research. Such is particularly evident in 'The Scent of Memory', and it is through a reading of that essay that Brah's distinct 'methodology' is presented – an approach which is sensitive to the always already contradictory condition of 'reality'. What I suggest of Brah's 'methodology' is that it is a practice that has significant consequences for the meaning and value placed on social

contexts, for the 'presence' and 'absence' of information and knowledge in interpretation and analysis, a practice that we might call diasporic reasoning. (Hall, 2012, pp. 32–33)

'Scent of Memory' is just a marvellous way of thinking through 'difference' as the 'double inscriptions of contradictory conditions of reality'. Since it is such meditative way of thinking, would say it is a methodology that can be reproduced? What would you recommend to critically minded scholars who wish to embrace its methodology and pedagogy, drawing upon contrasting memories and amnesia of the same historical events?

AH: Stuart Hall is very generous with his tribute. As you say, 'Scent of Memory' is about thinking through 'difference'. In *Cartographies*, as I note above, I have suggested that 'difference' could be analysed and understood simultaneously across four axes: as structural/social relation, as subjectivity, as experience and as identity. In a way, 'Scent of Memory' attempts to practise this mode of analysis. It operates at the level of social relation as well as addressing thought and affect in working through experience, subjectivity and identity. This essay is also underpinned by the concept of diaspora space, although I did not consciously set out to do this, and the term diaspora space is not evident anywhere. It is an attempt at a non-reductive, non-essentialist lens on lived lives. Hall is right in saying that it is not a 'method' in the conventional sense but is nonetheless a distinctive 'methodology' in the sense of a particular kind of 'reading'. As a 'reading' I suppose it might be reproduced, through exploring memories and amnesias, contrasting and contesting narratives, sociological/historical/cultural analysis, avowals and dis-avowals, by examining conscious and unconscious processes, rational, non-rational subjectivities and analysing the play of experience and identity.

LGR: How did you become so moved to write back to Tim Lott's account of his mother's suicide, reaching across genres, first and third person writing, affect and analysis, identification and dis-identification, memory and amnesia, or racist denial. Walk us through your 'methodology' of double inscription which captures an internal psychic and discursive dimension to memory – what Hall calls 'diasporic reasoning', for example, the choice to juxtapose Toni Morrison's *Beloved* (1987) with Tim Lott's *Scent of Dried Roses: Our family and the end of English suburbia* (1996)?

AH: Why was I so moved by Tim Lott's account of his mother's suicide is a question I have raised myself but without a satisfactory 'rationalistic' explanation. It was almost a 'spiritual' connection invoking poetics of affect and thought. Toni Morrison's *Beloved* too has a spiritual quality to itself and I was deeply moved by its politics which did not evacuate those mystical dimensions of human existence which are difficult to put into words. As for the 'methodology' of double inscription which captures an internal and discursive dimension to memory, I think Hall's essay is a better guide to that than one which I could provide. I was trying to interrogate 'origin stories', exploring both material and non-material aspects of human life, exploring how sympathy and empathy might be used to make affective and political connections. It features hate, love, death – things that divide us and those which bring us together.

AH: You say in a conversation with Les Back (Back & Brah, 2012), professor and sociologist at Goldsmiths for the *Feminist Review* commemorative 100th issue, that 'spirituality attracts me'. And in that sense, 'Scent of Memory' is a very spiritually informed essay. Back does not pick up on that statement, and you do not elaborate. Would you like to expand on this?

AB: As a feminist I have had a troubled relationship with organised religion. I am critical of the patriarchal discourses and practices which undergird most religions. But I believe that there is also a spiritual dimension to life which is opposed to exploitation and oppression and is not antithetical to secular politics, but rather, complements it.

LGR: Your tribute to Hall briefly mentions that his Open University texts were as avidly read by lecturers as by the students. Can you shed some light or give some examples of this in the context of how such a scholarly pedagogical approach to writing may indeed expand critical publics by thinking and acting with larger publics in mind, reflecting on examples from your writing, as well as his in relation to drawing in and appealing to larger audiences?

AB: Open University courses normally attracted large audiences, as they were in part broadcast. They were also accompanied by Course Readers with essays specially written for the course by specialists from all over the UK. These courses had some of the most up-to-date curricular material on a subject. These books were usually read by both by students and lecturers. The courses for which Hall co-wrote, edited Course Readers, produced television programmes and which he chaired were singularly popular courses, and these materials were widely used by lecturers in other universities for teaching purposes. I certainly used material from the course 'The Formations of Modernity' in my own teaching.

LGR: Your presentation featured on YouTube (Brah, 2013) at the University of Muenster, Germany discusses some of the limitations and possibilities of the concept of intersectionality. Hall steadfastly refused categorical identity politics and claims or any idea that differences were simply secondary appendages to class. What you see as the vices and problems with the concept of 'intersectionality' which has been used quite understandably to put race and women of colour on the largely white feminist agenda (Crenshaw, 1989)? More recently, though, intersectionality has been hailed by Leslie McCall (2005) as a methodology in and of itself. Would you concur with McCall?

AB: I believe that intersectionality is an important feminist concept. I lean towards what McCall calls an anti-categorical approach in that categories are not assumed as given. The task is to examine the processes – historical, economic, cultural, political – in and through which these categories are produced and come to assume meaning in the first place. I also do not use a 'road crossing' metaphor to think about intersections, rather I conceptualise intersection as 'articulation'. As I noted in the 'Scent of Memory' (Brah, 1999), articulation is a metaphor used to:

> indicate relations of linkages and their effects across different levels of the socio-cultural formation such that, as Stuart Hall notes, 'things are related as much through their differences as through their similarities. (Hall, quoted in Brah, 1999, p. 8)

I do not think that intersectionality is a 'methodology in and of itself', as McCall (2005) suggests. Intersectionality is first and foremost an inter/trans-disciplinary concept and therefore relies on various subject-based methodologies. My understanding is closer to what she later describes in Cho, Crenshaw, and McCall (2013) as 'an analytic sensibility':

> Rather, what makes an analysis intersectional – whatever term it deploys, whatever its iteration, whatever its field of discipline – is its adoption of an intersectional way of thinking, about the problem of sameness and difference and its relation to power. This framing – conceiving of categories not as distinct but as always permeated by other categories, fluid and changing, always in the process of creating and being created by dynamics of power – emphasizes what intersectionality does rather than what intersectionality is. (2013, p. 795)

That is how the concept features in *Cartographies*, although, regrettably, I was not at the time familiar with Crenshaw's earlier formulations.

LGR: Feminist post-colonial disability scholars such as Fiona Kumari Campbell, Helen Meekosha and Nirmala Erevelles have provided accounts of post-coloniality through the lens of disability and feminist disability studies. What elements of your work and thinking might you revisit in light of the insights from post-colonial disability studies about 'citizenship', diaspora and displacement in the context of global capitalism? For example, you give a nod to acknowledging possible impairments Jean faced and certainly her medicalisation when you write that Jean hid her alopecia from her family and its consequent prescribed medication relying on drugs 'normally used in serious cases of epilepsy' and later those associated with schizophrenia. About Jean, you say:

> From then on, she wore a wig and never let anyone, including her husband and her children, see her without the wig. She even slept with a head scarf knotted tight in 'gypsy style'. What must it have felt like to live in fear of the 'wig' coming off? What constructions of female 'beauty' did Jean's mind occupy that she lived in terror of her 'camouflage' being discovered? It is only after her death that her son discovers how, as part of the treatment for alopecia, Jean had been prescribed a tranquilizer that was powerful enough to be used in serious cases of epilepsy. Later, for years, she was put on drugs normally used in cases of schizophrenia. The doctor's note speaks of 'emotional factors playing a part' in the condition that resulted in her hair loss. (Brah, 1999, p. 22)

Yet, possible impairment and disability are not part of your analysis or lenses in the same ways 'race' and racism, gender, sexism, and class and classism play constitutive parts in your analysis of Jean's 'interpellation'. By the way, Hall did not take into account disability either. What would you change in your reading of Jean, bearing in mind feminist post-colonial disability studies? How might you reflect on your nod above in light of the resources feminist post-colonial disability scholars have given to us in terms of theoretical tools and activist rights struggles? So often, disability is the disappearing signifier or the 'etc.' in our analytics of intersectionality.

AB: I do not know how I would rethink Jean's life through a disability/debility lens. But the lack of a focus on issues of disability/debility in my academic work is not a reflection of indifference to the political importance I attach to addressing this axis of differenti-ation. At the GLC, disability was one of the major criteria used in relation to issues associated with equality. There is however a large body of academic literature in this field, and it is an academic field where I cannot claim any significant expertise. Helen Meekosha (2006) writes that disability is a social relationship rather than a characteristic of individuals with impairment. As with 'race' and class, disablement has been the subject of eugenics, population control, and processes of discrimination and exclusion. I would suggest that these processes operate at the level of structure, subjectivity, experience and identity.

Meekosha (2006) makes a helpful distinction between 'impairment' as a functional limitation of the individual and 'disability' as a socio-cultural, economic and political system of discrimination. She also highlights that different 'disablements' are differently culturally coded and she subscribes to a 'human variation' model as compared to a 'minority group model'. In a paper originally given to the regional conference of Women with Disabilities, Australia, and then later published, Carolyn Frohmader and Helen Meekosha (2012) show how 80% of people with disabilities live in the resource-poor global South, with all the associated consequences flowing from inequality between North and South.

Writing from a quite a different analytical perspective, Jasbir Puar (2012) foregrounds what she calls an 'interdependent' relationship between bodily capacity and debility. She points to 'bioinformatics frames which interrogate analytics in which bodies figure not as identities but as data' (p. 153). She proposes a 'methodology that inhabits the intersections of disability studies, the affective turn, and theories of posthumanism' (p. 154), whereby 'affect entails not only a dissolution of the subject, but more significantly, a dissolution of the stable contours of the organic body, as forces of energy are transmitted, shared, circulated' (p. 155). She adds that 'there is a shift underway, from Althusserain interpellation to an array of diverse switchpoints of the activation of the body' (p. 155). Clearly, there is a rich debate between the disability rights movement and what Puar calls the disability justice movement in terms of how to theorise debility. The 'affective turn' is quite fascinating in its conceptual repertoire. Yet the 'subject', in my view, does not disappear but needs to be rethought through the affective lens. To be a subject of Althusserian interpellation was not inevitably to be an able-bodied figure. There is much food for thought in these intricate debates. My work, and I believe that of Hall, has been influenced by the 'linguistic turn' and by the 'politics of the subject'. The 'affective turn' poses interesting questions to be explored.

T: Looking forward, what does it mean for feminist scholars to be 'public intellectuals' in their politics, pedagogies and lives? How do feminists remain hopeful amidst in context of so many different political and humanitarian crises, from Palestine and Israel in the Middle East to the current situation in Iraq, among other serious crises?

AB: The role of 'public intellectuals' is critical today. I have just read the excellent 'Statement in Solidarity with the Palestinian People of Gaza and with Seekers of Freedom and Justice World-wide', issued by a number of 'public intellectuals' within the US academy such as Judith Butler, Angela Davis, Zillah Eisenstein, Chandra Talpade Mohanty and many others (2014). Given the dominant role of the USA in geopolitics, it is important that the statement comes from there. Many of us have been on protests marches against wars such as the Iraq war and what is happening in Gaza There is a tendency in the media to demonise 'Muslims' while paying little attention to the role of the Western and other global powers in sustaining power dynamics which underpin the crisis in the Middle East, for instance.

We in academia produce regimes of knowledge, which have a bearing on understanding the conditions that have produced current problems and issues. We can utilise critical, situated knowledge produced in the academy in our activism to throw light on appropriate political contexts. Within the academy too, critical knowledge discourses could inform the choices we make about curriculum and pedagogies. We need to remain optimistic despite the dire economic and political conditions that we face today. We remain hopeful through our political commitments, analysis and activism.

Disclosure statement

No potential conflict of interest was reported by the authors.

Note

1. Avtar Brah is Professor Emerita at Birkbeck College, University of London. She is a member of the Academy of Social Sciences, UK and the Editorial Collective of *Feminist Review*. She was born in India but grew up in Uganda. Since then, she has lived and worked in Britain and the USA. She is committed to intersectional politics of equality and justice. She is the author of *Cartographies of Diaspora, Contesting Identities* (1996), and co-author of *Thinking Identities: Ethnicity, Racism and Culture* (1999); *Global Futures: Migration, Environment, and Globalization* (1999); and *Hybridity and Its Discontents: Politics and Science and Culture* (2000). Her most recent article co-authored with Aisha Gill, "Interrogating cultural narratives" about 'honour'-based violence' is published in the *European Journal of Women's Studies* 21(1), May 2014.

References

Althusser, L. (1971). *Lenin and philosophy and other essays*. London: New Left Books.

Back, L., & Brah, A. (2012). Activism, imagination and writing: Avtar Brah reflects on her life and work with Les Beck. *Feminist Review, 100*(1), 39–51. doi:10.1057/fr.2011.66

Baksh, R., & Harcourt, W. (2014/2015). *The Oxford handbook of transnational feminist movements*. Oxford. Online publication date, 2014. Forthcoming hardback publication, 2015.

Black Feminists. (2010). Black feminists blogspots.org. Retrieved from http://blackfeminists. blogspot.ca/p/about.html

Brah, A. (1996). *Cartographies of diaspora: Contesting identities*. New York, NY: Routledge.

Brah, A. (1999). The scent of memory: Our own, strangers and others. *Feminist Review, 61*(1), 4–26. doi:10.1080/014177899339261

Brah, A. (2013, September 22–24). *Diasporic constructions of home and belonging*. A paper given on a panel for the Diaspora Studies in the 21st Century Conference, University of Muenster, Germany. Retrieved May 7, 2014, from https://www.youtube.com/watch?v=DZcmnSJbNjM

Brah, A. (2014, February 18). Stuart Hall: Endearing theoretician of note. *Open Democracy*. Retrieved from https://www.opendemocracy.net/avtar-brah/stuart-hall-endearing-theoretician-of-note

Brah, A., & Coombes, A. (Eds.). (2000). *Hybridity and its discontents: Politics, science and culture*. London: Routledge.

Brah, A., Gedalof, I., & Szeman, I. (Eds.). (2015). Politics of austerity. *Feminist Review, 109*.

Brah, A., & Gill, A. (2014). Interrogating cultural narratives about 'honour'-based violence. *European Journal of Women's Studies, 21*(1), 72–86.

Brah, A., Hickman, M., & Mac an Ghaill, M. (1999a). *Global futures: Migration, environment, and globalization*. New York, NY: St Martin's Press.

Brah, A., Hickman, M., & Mac an Ghaill, M. (1999b). *Thinking identities: Ethnicity, racism and culture*. New York, NY: St Martin's Press.

Butler, J., Davis, A., Eisenstein, Z., & Mohanty, C. T. (2014, August). Statement in solidarity with Palestinian people of Gaza and with seekers of freedom and justice world-wide. Facebook. Retrieved from http://mondoweiss.net|2014|08|coalition-feminists-massacre.html

Campaign against racism and fascism/Southall Rights. (1981). *Southall: Birth of a Black community*. London: Institute of Race Relations and Southall Rights.

Centre for Contemporary Cultural Studies. (1982). *Empire strikes back: Race and racism in 70's Britain*. Birmingham: Hutchinson.

Cho, S., Crenshaw, K. W., & McCall, L. (2013). Toward a field of intersectionality studies: Theory, applications, praxis. *Signs, 38*, 941–965. doi:10.1086/669608

Crenshaw, K. W. (1989). *Demarginalizing the intersection of race and sex: A Black feminist critique of antidiscrimination doctrine*. Feminist Theory and Antiracist Politics, University of Chicago Legal Forum 1989, 139–167.

Frankenberg, R. (1993). *White women race matters: The social construction of whiteness*. Minneapolis, MN: University of Minnesota Press.

Frohmader, C., & Meekosha, H. (2012). Recognition, respect and rights: Disabled women in a globalized world. In D. Goodley, B. Hughes, & L. Davis (Eds.), *Disability and social theory: New developments and directions* (pp. 287–307). New York, NY: Palgrave Macmillan.

Gramsci, A. (1971). *Selections from the prison notebooks of Antonio Gramsci* (N. Geoffrey, G. Smith, & Q. Hoare, Trans.). London: Lawrence & Wishart.

Hall, S. (1980). Race, articulation and societies structured in dominance. In UNESCO (Ed.), *Sociological theories: Race and colonialism* (pp. 305–345). Paris: UNESCO.

Hall, S. (1996a). Gramsci's relevance for the study of race and ethnicity. In D. Morley & K. Chen (Eds.), *Stuart Hall: Critical dialogues in cultural studies* (pp. 411–441). London: Routledge.

Hall, S. (1996b). New ethnicities. In D. Morley & K. Chen (Eds.), *Stuart Hall: Critical dialogues in cultural studies* (pp. 442–451). London: Routledge.

Hall, S. (1996c). Who needs identity? In S. Hall & P. Du Gay (Eds.), *Questions of cultural identity* (pp. 1–17). Thousand Oaks, CA: SAGE.

Hall, S. (2011). The neo-liberal revolution. *Cultural Studies, 25*, 705–728. Retrieved from http://dx.doi.org/10.1080/09502386.2011.619886

Hall, S. (2012). Avtar Brah's cartographies: Moment, method, meaning. *Feminist Review, 100*, 27–38.

Hall, S., Critcher, C., Jefferson, T., & Clarke, J. (1978). *Policing the crisis: Mugging, the state, and law and order*. London: Macmillan.

Hall, S., & Dugay, P. (Eds.). (1996). *Questions of cultural identity* (pp. 1–17). Thousand Oaks: SAGE.

Hall, S., & Jefferson, T. (1975). *Resistance through rituals: Youth subcultures in post-war Britain*. London: Hutchinson.

Hall, S., Massey, D., & Rustin, M. (Eds.). (2013). After neoliberalism: Analysing the present (Framing statement). In S. Hall, D. Massey, & M. Rustin (Eds.), *After neoliberalism? The Kilburn Manifesto*. London: Lawrence & Wishart. Retrieved from http://www.lwbooks.co.uk/journals/soundings/pdfs/manifestoframingstatement.pdf

Henry, A. (2001). Stuart Hall and cultural studies: Theory letting you off the hook? In L. Stone & K. Weiler (Eds.), *Feminist engagements: Revisioning educational and cultural theory* (pp. 165–182). New York, NY: Routledge.

Henry, L. (2014, March 17). *Minority representation now. Annual Lecture of the British Academy of Television and Film Artists*. London. Retrieved from http://www.bafta.org/press/transcripts/bafta-television-lecture-lenny-henry-cbe

Lott, T. (1996). *The scent of dried roses: Our family and the end of English suburbia*. London: Viking.

McCall, L. (2005). The complexity of intersectionality. *Signs, 33*, 1771–1800.

Media Diversified [Sara Ahmed, Gargi Bhattacharyya, Yasmin Gunaratnam, Vera Jocelyn, Patricia Noxolo, Pratibha Parmar, Ann Phoenix, Nirmal Puwar, Suzanne Scafe] (2014, February 20). Meeting Stuart Hall. Retrieved from http://www.opendemocracy.net/ourkingdom/media-diversified/meeting-stuart-hall.

Meekosha, H. (2006). What the hell are you? An intercategorical analysis of race, ethnicity, gender and disability in the Australian body politic. *Scandanavian Journal of Disability Research, 8*, 161–176.

Morley, D., & Chen, K. H. (2010). *Critical dialogues in cultural studies*. New York, NY: Routledge.

Morrison, T. (1987). *Beloved*. New York, NY: Vintage.

Puar, J. K. (2012). Coda: The cost of getting better: Suicide, sensation, switchpoints. *GLQ: A Journal of Lesbian and Gay Studies, 18*(1), 149–158.

Rawwida, B., & Harcourt, W. (2015). *Oxford handbook of transnational feminist movements: Knowledge, power and social change*. Oxford: Oxford University Press.

Roman, L. G. (1993). White is a color! White defensiveness, postmodernism, and antiracist pedagogy. In C. McCarthy & W. Chrichlow (Eds.), *Race, identity, and representation in education* (pp. 279–378). New York, NY: Routledge.

Stuart Hall on racism and the importance of diasporic thinking

Fazal Rizvi

Melbourne Graduate School of Education, The University of Melbourne, Melbourne, Australia

In this article, I want to show how my initial encounter with the work of Stuart Hall was grounded in my reading of the later philosophy of Ludwig Wittgenstein, and was shaped by my interest in understanding the nature of racism across the three countries in which I had lived. Over the years, Hall's various writings have helped me to make sense of the shifting logics of racism, especially his insistence that racism cannot be understood in its own terms, but requires a conjunctural analysis of the contested processes of historical and political formation. I argue moreover that Hall does not so much as write about racism in or from diaspora, but rather he thinks diasporically, a notion that has significant implications for public pedagogy.

I first encountered the work of Stuart Hall in 1981 through a short article that Hall had written a few years earlier on the politics of racism and reaction in Britain. I had been thinking tentatively about issues of race and racism for a number of years, though never in any sustained and systematic way. Born in India, I was conscious of the diverse and complex ways in which minorities were subjected to racism while negotiating their lives and, also in Australia, a country to which my family had immigrated while I was still a teenager. However, it was as a graduate student in England that I first confronted racism in its more explicit forms, forcing me to think more seriously about its various configurations, its origins, and its social consequences. I read widely on the then popular theories of racism, most of which seemed located within the empiricist traditions of social psychology. These theories viewed racism as an expression of prejudice that some individuals harbored toward those they regarded as culturally different and inferior. While there were clearly many elements of truth in these theories, I found them inadequate, incapable of accounting for the complexities of racial formation and racism that I had experienced and which were clearly evident in British society.

Stuart Hall's article (1978) therefore 'spoke' to me instantly and in a manner that was most profound at so many different levels. To begin with, in Stuart Hall, I found a theorist who wrote about some of the most difficult issues of race and racism in a manner that was not only astute, but also accessible. In the tradition of Raymond Williams (1958), he focused on the ordinariness of cultural practices, and the ways in which they were shaped by the complex configurations of social, political, and economic formation, constantly contested and evolving. He used language in ways that were driven by pedagogic and political motivations – not to impress the Oxford Senior Common Room, but to provide theoretical resources to those activists in England and elsewhere, for whom the struggle against racism had become a matter of everyday life. I deeply admired his commitment to public sociology, long before the idea was popularized by Michael Burawoy (2004). So, over the past three decades, Stuart Hall has become a constant inspiration to me, although I had an opportunity to meet him only once.

In the 1980s, Hall showed how the brutality of Thatcherism was giving rise to new forms of racism. Couched in a language of 'authoritarian populism' (Hall, 1988), it often masked its destructive effects on the black communities in Britain. This was a very different form of racism to those associated with the crude biological theories of racial differentiation and hierarchy. It was also different to the racism that I had encountered in white Australia based on a fear of Asian immigrants, and in India, where it was associated with a caste politics, often justified in religious terms. So, at a more personal level, Hall's analysis led to me to appreciate how the logics of racism in India, Australia, and England – the three countries in which I had, by that time, lived – were in some ways similar, but also significantly different. I was persuaded by Hall's insistence that local histories and political struggles mattered, even if forms of racism in these three locations were connected through a common cultural history of the British colonial project.

Hall and Wittgenstein

At a theoretical level, my entry into Hall's writings was through the research I was doing in the 1980s toward my doctoral degree on the later philosophy of Ludwig Wittgenstein. Perhaps, inevitably, this influenced the ways in which I interpreted Hall's work on culture and politics. I saw many theoretical similarities between Wittgenstein and Hall. In particular, they both rejected an empiricist view of the relationship between language and reality, and instead viewed language in terms of its performativity. With words, argued Wittgenstein (1974), we do things. In this way, Wittgenstein rejected the empiricist conception of language in which words stood for, or referred to, a phenomenon in the world. He denied that the task of language was to 'picture' reality, a view that he had himself once enunciated in his earlier work. Instead, Wittgenstein now saw language as activity. In a variety of ways and on many levels, Wittgenstein argued that language consisted in the act of speaking and responding to speech, and that these were things we did in a collective manner. "The speaking of language is part of an activity, or of a form of life," Wittgenstein (1974, p. 23) noted. Thus, understanding a language, for Wittgenstein, was not a matter of grasping some inner essence of meaning, but of knowing how to do certain things with words. His notion of language-game was designed to capture this insight.

Wittgenstein highlighted the importance of examining the context in which particular linguistic utterances are made. His theory of meaning suggested that words did not mean in *just one way*, but could be articulated and rearticulated in a wide variety of ways. He argued that a "craving for generality" lay at the heart of most philosophical problems and confusions. He thus asked us to "moderate our contemptuous attitude towards the particular case" (Wittgenstein, 1969, p. 18). He called into question the whole business of reaching conclusions about reality in an abstract manner, by identifying some formal rules of linguistic structure. Meaning, he suggested, resided within a wider system of conventions and social practices, and that it was impossible to provide general accounts of linguistic rules, for the rules themselves could not be divorced from the contexts in which words were used to engage in particular human actions, within the broader systems of social activities. In this sense, Wittgenstein underlined the importance of human creativity and imagination in linguistic and social formations.

Wittgenstein's later work thus pointed to the difficulties associated with attempts by theorists to stand apart from the processes of analysis, for the analysts' own perspectives could not be divorced from the theoretical work they did. Wittgenstein thus encouraged philosophers – and for that matter social theorists – to see themselves as actors and not as spectators. By the time I first read Hall, I had already come to conclude that the distinction between philosophy and social theory was not as clear-cut as many philosophers had often presupposed. Once we recognize that all uses of language are ultimately practical, we come to see how we were deeply implicated in our theoretical constructs and their political consequences. Freed from the assumptions of essentialism, Wittgenstein's work had further implied that there were no necessary restrictions on radical conceptual and social change. In any organic grouping of people it was always possible to use our existing conceptual resources to imagine how things might be different, and what might be required to make them different. In this way, while Wittgenstein accorded an essential role to historical continuity in linguistic practices, he did not rule out dissent, criticism, and speculation about norms that were opposed to existing modes of practice. In other words, his arguments implied that the possibilities of politics were inherent in all linguistic practices, no matter how abstract. So I wondered why it was that Wittgenstein did not address issues of politics.

To the best of my knowledge, Stuart Hall never wrote about Wittgenstein, though I doubt that Hall would not have engaged with Wittgensteinian ideas, since these were widely canvassed during the 1970s and 1980s, both in Britain and elsewhere. At the Open University in particular, where interdisciplinary scholarship was encouraged, Hall could not have avoided considering Wittgenstein's views on meaning and truth, especially as they stressed the relationship between language and human forms of life. Whatever the nature of Hall's encounters with Wittgensteinian scholarship, my own understanding of Hall's work was clearly filtered through my reading of Wittgenstein. In particular, I appreciated Hall's anti-foundationalism and antiessentialism against the backdrop of Wittgenstein's philosophical insights. Also significant to me was the importance Hall attached to the practical (and political) nature of language, and the ways he used the notion of discourse to refer to a range of interconnected ideas, concepts, and generalizations. He viewed theoretical concepts as tools with which we engaged the world. Indeed, well before Hall and more recently Deleuze, it was Wittgenstein who had used the toolbox analogy to describe the dynamic, contested, and creative uses of words in our ordinary social practices. Also remarkable to me were the ways in which Hall's insights about "conjunctural analysis" resonated with Wittgenstein's notion of a grammar of concepts and ideas, which only made sense in relation to each other.

Yet, for my purposes, as someone interested in understanding forms of racism, what was missing from Wittgenstein was any serious engagement with the issues of history and politics, and in particular an analysis of the ways power shaped the modalities of conceptual and political change. A number of philosophers have pointed out that Wittgenstein's writings on language do indeed have major implications for understanding politics, and while this work was not carried out by Wittgenstein himself his philosophical insights are deeply normative. Hanna Pitkin (1972), for example, provides a most comprehensive account of how Wittgenstein's work can be employed to develop a theory of justice. Such a theory, she argues, "emphasizes politics as a continuing practice over the body of propositions it produces," involving "the plurality of particular cases and their conflicting implications" (Pitkin, 1972, p. 325). Danford (1978, p. 205) has similarly suggested that a Wittgenstein "focus on particularities and differences would also mean paying more attention to the perspective of the members of the political community themselves." More recently, in a book edited by Heyes (2003), a number of philosophers have noted that while Wittgenstein was largely indifferent to many of the political challenges of his own times, his approach to language is deeply political, suggesting ways of interpreting and negotiating the dilemmas and challenges of political life.

Conjuncture and new times

Hall's methods of analysis were driven by a similar impulse, present in his idea of disjuncture. His methods brought together insights from sociology, philosophy, ideology critique, media studies, semiotics, and social theory to observe various cultural phenomena from multiple perspectives, showing their dominant form to be historically constituted and politically contested. Stuart Hall's (2010) concept of "conjunture" was drawn from Gramsci, especially the importance Gramsci attached to locating thinking within a particular historical moment or set of conditions. A conjuncture, Hall suggested, "is a period during which the different social, political, economic and ideological contradictions that are at work in society come together to give it a specific and distinctive shape" (p. 1). For example, he regarded the postwar period, dominated by the welfare state, public ownership, and wealth redistribution through taxation as one conjuncture, and suggested that the neoliberal era had unleashed another. A conjuncture, he noted, "is not defined by time or by simple things like a change of regime, but by the complex, historical meeting point of forces and institutions where things change, where new connections are wrought, in more or less coherent fashion" (p. 1). A conjunctural analysis, he argued, helps us to understand how "relatively autonomous" sites, such as schools, which have different origins and are driven by different contradictions, nevertheless fuse or are condensed in the same moment. This suggested that racism could not be adequately described without paying attention to the complex relationship its various forms had with the always dynamic cultural, political, and economic formations.

Deeply suspicious of abstractions, Hall used his concept of conjuncture to understand the nature of these "new times," insisting that the key issue for this understanding was the issue of power in everyday practices. In his analytical work, he often began with a simple example, such as the discernible contrast between a media-driven "moral panic" about the supposed epidemic of street robberies perpetuated by black young men on white citizens, and the statistics that pointed to no such rise. In *Policing the Crisis* (1978), Hall, Critcher, Jeffferson, Clarke, and Robert sought to explain how this phenomenon represented a political tendency – a conjuncture – which was in the process of becoming crystallized into the New Right. He described the emergence of the right wing "authoritarian populism" that he foresaw becoming embedded in British cultural politics. His account of "authoritarian populism" inspired not only generations of critical scholars, but artists and filmmakers as well. Informed by his conjunctural analysis, these scholars and filmmakers sought to counter the Thatcherite project and thus brought into existence a broad-based popular politics (Rojek, 2003).

For Hall, this democratic politics was closely linked to the projects of multiculturalism and antiracism. Indeed, his participation in it led many to refer to him as the godfather of British multiculturalism (Blackburn, 2014), a characterization with which

Hall was never very happy, though he always insisted that issues of race, ethnicity, and postcoloniality lay at the heart of the struggle over British identity. His interrogations underlined the importance of the constructed categories of race, class, and gender as key parameters in the always-contested processes of identity formation. Like Wittgenstein, Hall rejected any attempts at any teleology, and believed that political endeavor was always "without guarantees" (Hall, 1983). (A phrase that Gilroy, Grossberg and McRobbie (2000) used in their edited collection to honor the work of Stuart Hall.) Indeed, Hall insisted that Britain never had an essential national character, and that it was always influenced by its engagement with others. This observation was underpinned by the relational character of his thinking, perhaps most visible in his understanding of the concept of articulation, which he defined as "a unity of two different elements, under certain conditions. It is a linkage that is not necessary, determined, absolute and essential for all time" (Hall, 1986, p. 53). In another place, he suggested that "articulation involves a complex structure in which things are related, as much through their similarities and as through their differences" (Hall, 1980, p. 325).

Race and racism

It is in terms of this theoretical analysis that Hall's account of the logic of race and racism is best understood. Hall insisted that racism did not have some essential form; it was continually changing, being challenged, interrupted, modified, and reconstructed, in actual everyday practices in which people participated. While he acknowledged that there were no doubt some general features to racism, it was more significant to recognize the ways in which general features were modified, and transformed by the historical specificity of the contexts in which they became active (Hall, 1986, p. 23). Hall implored us, in a manner that is reminiscent of Wittgenstein, to look not for racism in general, but 'racisms,' in order to study its particular formations in actual practices in specific sites. Racist meaning, Hall insisted, was constructed in and through ideology. Following Gramsci (1971), Hall argued that ideology organizes the everyday activities in which human beings engaged, thought about their options, explained their predicaments, and conjectured their sense of struggle. Ideologies, Gramsci maintained, were organic because they were embedded in people's sense of common sense, but in ways that were disjointed, episodic, fragmentary, and often contradictory: they were continually changing as people encountered and forged new ways of engaging with the world around them. Following Gramsci, Hall thus rejected the idea of a pre-given, unified ideological subject, with a consistent set of attributes. Like Wittgenstein, consciousness, Hall insisted, was not an individual, but rather a collective relational phenomenon, located in cultural and political practices. Hence, he coined the phrase, "cultural politics," showing how the two were inseparable. As an aside, I might note that it was Hall's account of cultural politics that the editors of *Discourse* used to define the scope of the work they wished to promote when relaunching the journal in 1992.

Hall's insights led me to see how at any historical juncture racism had a popular ideological form, and that it described a kind of collective thinking about social relations. It was historically constituted, and like all ideological practices, it described a way of engaging with others, through a conjuncture of ideas, concepts, and generalizations that defined a distinctive mode of reasoning about society. Its forms were always subject to change and rearticulation. So, for example, while in the past, racism might have involved physical violence, political repression, and psychological abuse, its more contemporary forms in most western countries were no longer so overt, but involved cultural expressions such as paternalism, inequality of access and treatment, and various other forms of ideological practices. Hall's methods of analysis helped me to realize that while many overt forms of marginalization and exclusion were no longer tolerated in advanced industrial societies, they were nonetheless replaced by a set of new ideological expressions, which often escaped recognition as racism because they were masked by various discourses of social cohesion, nationalism, and patriotism. Contemporary forms of racism often established a discursive distance from the crude ideas of biological and cultural inferiority and superiority, but worked instead with an equally exclusive logic associated with a normative image of a nation that marginalized particular groups of people. It was because popular racism represented a contextually specific ideology, rooted in everyday practices, that its expressions were highly contested, and that therefore they were not always easily recognizable, even by those who are subjected to them. This was particularly so with people who were transnationally mobile, whose points of reference were constantly shifting.

Diaspora and cultural identity

Indeed, this was clearly the case with Stuart Hall himself. In a number of interviews (for example, Hall, 1996), Hall discussed the confusions he experienced upon his arrival in England from Jamaica. In Jamaica, Hall was brought up in a middle class family, with a mother proud of her cultural links to England. With fairer complexion, she was widely regarded as "local white," with English attitudes and sensibilities. As a young boy, Hall had a somewhat antagonistic relationship with his mother, refusing to accept her personal and cultural aspirations for him. Just the same, he had acquired a form of colonial education that had given him an opportunity to go to Oxford on a Rhodes scholarship. Upon his arrival, he found, however, that while he had greater familiarity with English cultural values, mores, language, and literature, he was not accepted as English, despite the fact that he was always encouraged in Jamaica to view himself as a British citizen. Invariably, Hall was perceived as an outsider, marginalized within the community to which he, like most colonial subjects, had assumed he had belonged. While Hall was not unfamiliar with expressions of colonial racism in Jamaica, in England he encountered a very different form of racism. He now had to negotiate a different kind of relationship to colonialism, in the heart of the imperial center itself. In Jamaica, he had become sympathetic to the anti-imperialist independence movement, but, in diaspora, he had to develop a new understanding of that struggle, connected to diasporic colonial formations in Britain but also distinctively local.

Hall did not address the issues of diasporic identities in any direct manner until the mid-1980s. In his earlier writings, he did not explicitly confront the question of how his Jamaican background and colonial education had shaped his intellectual and political development in England. Proctor (2004, p. 5) finds this puzzling, since Hall's Caribbean childhood, especially his troubled experiences of colonial color hierarchies, arguably formed the basis of his "intellectual preoccupation with class, race and identity politics." Kobena Mercer (2000, p. 233), in contrast, rejects this reading of Hall's relationship between his scholarship and background, arguing that such a view overlooks the complex movements back and forth between the Caribbean and England, as well as Hall's continuing identification with and development through Caribbean organizations in Britain. Mercer (2000, p. 233) admits however that Hall's earlier approach to the subject of diaspora is indirect and even circuitous, rather than programmatic or goal-directed. Indeed, while in such widely read and cited essays as "New Ethnicities" (1988) and "Cultural Identity and Diaspora" (1990), Hall addressed issues of diaspora directly, they could nonetheless also be found scattered and dispersed throughout his earlier works on the sociology of immigration, and in particular, "The Young Englanders" (1967) and "Black Britons" (1970). While these essays may now appear largely nation-centric, since they pinpoint a political breach between "formal acceptance and informal segregation" in British race relations, they were nonetheless framed against a broader critical examination of the historical conjunctures of immigration and colonialism (Alexander, 2009).

It is also important to note that Hall's earlier work on race was framed against the backdrop of the first wave of black immigration to Britain. Immigrants in the 1960s and 1970s were mostly preoccupied with the questions of settlement, attempting to realize the social and economic opportunities they had been promised, but which widespread racism had prevented them from realizing. In becoming black *and* British, they experienced the ambivalent push and pull factors of loyalties involved in multiple identifications. Memories of leaving were still quite important to them at the same time as they experienced the enigmas of arrival. This of course was not the case with second and third generation black Britons, who had to interpret and negotiate Britishness from the other end of the transnational chain. Hall was deeply conscious of these profound shifts, and wrote about them most eloquently in his essay "Gramsci's Relevance for the Study of Race and Ethnicity" (Hall, 1986). In it, he expanded his critique of Marxist ethnocentrism, turning his attention away from theoretical generality to the specificities of the history of Caribbean culture and society, and the ways in which they were transformed through "a diacritical conception of antagonism in which relations of power and resistance enter representation and consciousness unevenly" (Mercer, 2000, p. 238). In accounting for the volatile mix of cultural relations, Hall insisted that "race was a modality in which class was lived" in a postcolonial setting. It involved structural convulsions, he argued, whereby Britain 'became a multicultural society.'

Hall's analysis of diaspora is profoundly dynamic, always taking into account the changing circumstances of cultural formation in Britain, in an effort to provide a historically specific account of the more messy and ambivalent hybrid experiences between the global and the local. In the 1980s, through his association with iconoclastic black photographers, visual artists, and filmmakers, Hall explored the shifting contours of the black British diaspora, and his own diasporic formation. He insisted that "black had not ever just been there," it emerged through a political struggle (Hall, 1996, p. 501). As Mercer (2000, p. 235) notes, Hall's work tells:

> the story of how England became Other than what it always imagined it to be, and in a twist of sociology's immigration narrative, how third generation became 'black because they could not go back.'

Hall insisted on the internality of race in all social processes, and in turn viewed race as a lens through which broader social structures can be explored, rather than a thing in and of itself. As Grossberg (2007, p. 101) quotes Hall, "I have never worked on race and ethnicity as a kind of subcategory. I have always worked on the whole social formation which is racialized." For Hall, it is always important therefore to focus on transitions in both personal identity and the broader social, political, and cultural contexts in which they unfold.

In his essay, "New Ethnicities," Hall (1992) dealt with the major social transformations that were then taking place in Britain, as a result of the emergence of a black community. Never abstract, his account of these transformations addressed the specific ways in which black communities represented themselves in response to their common experience of racism and marginalization on the one hand, and their complex relationship to the processes of diasporization on the other. In asserting common experiences, they created, he observed, a "singular and unifying framework based on the building up of identity across ethnic and cultural differences between the different communities" (Hall, 1996, p. 441). At the same time, Hall presented diasporic identities as multiple and mobile with their own inner tensions, against the extraordinary diversity of subjective positions and social experiences. Over time, the black community could not be easily homogenized, with more creative, critical, and conflictual responses becoming possible. This created a challenge for the black community of how can a politics be constructed:

> which works with and through difference, which is able to build those forms of solidarity and identification which make common struggle and resistance possible but without suppressing the real heterogeneity of interests and identities. (Hall, 1996, p. 444)

Diasporic thinking

Hall argued furthermore that the possibilities engendered by rethinking identity in terms of fluidity, mobility, and hybridity (routes rather than roots) alters the ways in which identities are formed for all people within various locations, and not only just those who are constructed as "diasporic communities." Avtar Brah (1996, p. 209) has used the concept of "diaspora space" to draw attention to the fact that contemporary experiences of transnationality involve an intersection of borders where all subjects and identities become "juxtaposed, contested, proclaimed, or disavowed; where the permitted and the prohibited perpetually interrogate, and where the accepted and the transgressive imperceptibly mingle even while these syncretic forms may be disclaimed in the name of purity and tradition." Drawing inspiration from Hall, Brah insists that the transformative potential of "diaspora space" is potent not only for those within diaspora communities, but also those who are constructed and represented as local. This analysis is consistent with Mercer's (2000, p. 233) conclusion that Hall did not so much write about "diaspora as a discrete sociological object," as he wrote "*from* the social world of diaspora to produce knowledge as a situated practice of interruption." Hall thus opened up a mode of critical thinking that may be referred to as 'diasporic,' concerned with analyses of lived practices around the experiences of transnational mobility, border crossings, and interconnectivity.

Much of my own recent work on diasporic thinking (Rizvi, 2009, 2011) has been shaped by these insights which I have drawn from Stuart Hall. Central to the diasporic mode of thinking, I have argued, is a focus on the collective and critical understanding of the various forms of transnational interconnectivity that are increasingly shaping our social identities and practices. Such thinking requires coming to terms with our shifting situatedness in the world – situatedness of our knowledge and of our cultural practices as well as our unique positionality in relation to various networks, political institutions, and social relations that are no longer necessarily located within particular national borders, but potentially span the globe. This understanding is best achieved collectively in transcultural collaborations, in seeking to understand local problems comparatively, as well as in relation to each other. While such collective understanding might not always be possible, an examination of the hegemonic manner in which dominant modes of representation can hold us captive can nevertheless be interrogated, becoming a situated practice of interruption. The purpose of such interrogation should be to develop a different imaginary with which to think about our lives and life chances and options in the materiality of our collective and interlinked circumstances, and also to consider how things could be otherwise. This view is in line with Henry Giroux's (2000, p. 355) notion of public pedagogy, consisting in "a continual involvement with border crossings, transgressive in its challenge to authority and power, and intertexual in its attempt to link the specific with the national and transnational."

Diasporic thinking thus demands socially and politically networked learning, both formal and informal, working within and across difference. Such learning necessarily encourages thinking outside parochial boundaries and cultural assumptions, to consider how global processes affect communities differentially, and to examine the sources of these differentiations and inequalities. Instead of learning about cultures in an abstract manner, diasporic thinking requires an exploration of the crisscrossing of transnational circuits of communication, the flows of global capital, and the cross-cutting of local, translocal, and transnational social practices, and the differential consequences these have for different people and communities. In this way, such learning must consider the contested politics of place making, the social constructions of power differentials and the dynamic processes relating to the formation of individual, group, national and transnational identities, and their corresponding fields of difference. Such a focus on criticality should not, however, always imply an oppositional politics, but should also be directed toward an examination of the meaning of intercultural experiences, seeking to locate them within transnational networks that have become so much a part of the contemporary era of globalization. It should explore the nature of globally hegemonic configurations of economic and cultural exchange, how emerging forms of racism might be located within these shifting conjunctures and how it might be possible to imagine and enact more democratic and just modes of exchange.

In this sense, diasporic thinking suggests a new approach to learning about cultural formations in and through intercultural exchange, based on a set of "epistemic virtues" (Rizvi, 2009). I have used the phrase "epistemic virtues" to highlight both the cognitive and ethical dimensions of intercultural exchange, and to suggest that learning about others requires learning about ourselves. It implies a dialectical mode of thinking, which conceives cultural difference as neither absolute nor necessarily antagonistic, but deeply relational. In a dialectical approach, we understand others both in *their* terms as well as *ours*, as a way of comprehending how all representations are socially constituted. This suggests the importance of understanding cultural formations historically, recognizing that cultural attitudes and practices cannot be understood without reference to the historical exchanges and connection that produce them. We live in a world that is characterized by various global networks and flows of money, technologies, people, and ideas, and of their articulations to each other. But these networks have histories, without an understanding of which we cannot fully comprehend how people's sense of their collectivity, as solidarity in its positive manifestations and as marginalization in its negative, is forged. The past is thus linked to the present, and plays an important role in imagining the future. It is only through this realization that we recognize that our identities are forged in the history of contact between groups of people, where knowledge and resources are traded, borrowed, improved upon, fought over, and passed on to others. The notion of a pure culture, located within its own territory, has always been a myth because all cultures result through encounters with multiple others.

If this is so, then relationality is an epistemic virtue that underpins much of Hall's work. If we cannot learn about cultures in their pristine and authentic form, then our focus must shift to the ways in which cultural practices become separated from their 'homes' and are converted into new forms in their new contexts; and on how this changes both the places people leave and the places they come to inhabit. In a world in which flows of information, media symbols and images, and political and cultural ideas are constant and relentless, new cultural formations are inevitable, and are relationally forged. This focus on relationality must therefore replace approaches that treat 'other' cultures as entirely separable from each other or as categorical homogeneous entities. Other cultures can only be understood in relation to each other, historically formed and globally interconnected through mobility, exchange, and hybridization. A relational understanding of global interconnectivity and cultural exchange also points to the importance of another epistemic virtue: reflexivity. Reflexivity requires people to be self-conscious and knowledgeable about their own cultural traditions and how they are subject to transformation as a result of their engagement with other cultural traditions. Reflexivity invites us to challenge the taken for granted assumptions that are often found in popular discourse. Such reflexivity cannot be achieved, however, without a critical recognition of our own cultural and political presuppositions, and the epistemic position from we which speak and negotiate cultural differences. This must involve a realization that knowledge about cultures is never neutral and that our efforts to learn about and engage with other cultures take place within asymmetrical configurations of power. But these need not prevent us from continuing to explore, engage, and learn from other cultural traditions in an effort to transform our own.

Conclusion

In this article I have shown how over the many decades that Stuart Hall wrote about issues of identity, culture, and racism, his views evolved constantly, not only as a result of his refusal to take for granted any theoretical position as entirely settled, but also because of his conviction that theoretical work was always political, and needed to speak to the particular conditions that applied to different national contexts. So, for example, the cultural politics of race, he insisted, was performed differently in the UK, the USA, and the Caribbean, even if ideas and ideologies traveled across the transnational space. For Hall this implied the need to consider issues of diaspora in a range of historically and politically complex ways, which attended to the politics of identity, mobility, and difference. In the emerging circumstances of globalization, Hall would thus invite new ways of thinking about identity, culture, and difference. I have argued that my own thinking about race and racism (and education) has been deeply shaped by these insights, as I have worked across the continents, encountering race and racism differently, and how these differences and changing conditions have demanded different strategies of educational intervention. I have called Hall's methods of sociological analysis an invitation to diasporic thinking, which in an era of globalization, I believe, is more important than ever before.

Acknowledgments

I would like to thank Leslie Roman for her invitation to write this article, to her and Bob Lingard for their very helpful feedback, and to Nima Sobhani for his editorial assistance.

References

Alexander, C. (2009). Stuart Hall and race. *Cultural Studies*, *23*, 457–482. doi:10.1080/09502380 902950914

Blackburn, R. (2014). Stuart Hall, 1932–2014. *New Left Review*, *86*, 75–93.

Brah, A. (1996). *Cartegraphies of diaspora: Contesting identities*. London: Routledge.

Burawoy, M. (2004). For public sociology, 2004 Presidential Address. Retrieved January 2015, from http://burawoy.berkeley.edu/Public%20Sociology,%20Live/Burawoy.pdf

Danford, J. (1978). *Wittgenstein and political philosophy*. London: Blackwell.

Gilroy, P., Grossberg, L., & McRobbie, A. (Eds.). (2000). *Without guarantees: In honor of Stuart Hall*. London: Verso.

Giroux, H. A. (2000). Public pedagogy as cultural politics: Stuart Hall and the crisis of culture. *Cultural Studies*, *14*, 341–360. doi:10.1080/095023800334913

Gramsci, A. (1971). *Selections from the prison notebooks*. London: International Publishing Company.

Grossberg, L. (2007). Stuart Hall on race and racism: Cultural studies and practice of contextualism. In B. Meeks (Ed.), *Culture, politics, race and diaspora: The thought of Stuart Hall* (pp. 27–42). London: Lawrence & Wishart.

Hall, S. (1967). *The young Englanders*. London: Community Relations Commission.

Hall, S. (1970). Black Britons. *Community*, *1*, 3–5.

Hall, S. (1978). Racism and reaction. In B. Parekh (Ed.), *Five views of multiracial Britain* (pp. 56–70). London: Commission for Racial Equality.

Hall, S. (1980). Race, articulation and societies structured in dominance. In *UNESCO, sociological theories: Race and colonialism* (pp. 305–345). Paris: UNESCO.

Hall, S. (1983). The problem of ideology—Marxism without guarantees. In B. Mathews (Ed.), *Marx: 100 years on* (pp. 57–84). London: Lawrence & Wishart.

Hall, S. (1986). Gramsci's relevance for the study of race and ethnicity. *Journal of Communication Inquiry*, *10*(2), 5–27. doi:10.1177/019685998601000202

Hall, S. (1988). *Hard road to renewal: Thatcherism and the crisis of the left*. London: Verso.

Hall, S. (1990). Cultural identity and diaspora. In J. Rutherford (Ed.), *Identity: Community, culture and difference* (pp. 222–237). London: Lawrence & Wishart.

Hall, S. (1992). New ethnicities. In J. Donald & A. Rattansi (Eds.), *Race, culture and difference* (pp. 252–260). London: SAGE.

Hall, S. (1996). The formation of a diasporic intellectual: An interview with Stuart Hall. In D. Morley & K. H. Chen (Eds.), *Stuart Hall: Critical dialogues in cultural studies* (pp. 484–504). London: Routledge.

Hall, S. (2010). In conversation with Doreen Massey: Interpreting the crisis. *Strategic Practice*. Retrieved January 2015, from http://www.strategicpractice.org/commentary/hall-and-massey-interpreting-crisis

Hall, S., Critcher, C., Jeffferson, T., Clarke, J., & Robert, B. (1978). *Policing the crisis: Mugging, the state and law and order*. Basingstoke: MacMillan.

Heyes, C. (Ed.). (2003). *Grammar of politics: Wittgenstein and political philosophy*. Itaca: Cornell University Press.

Mercer, K. (2000). A sociography of diaspora. In P. Gilroy, L. Grossberg, & A. McRobbie (Eds.), *Without guarantees: In honor of Stuart Hall* (pp. 233–244). London: Verso.

Pitkin, H. (1972). *Wittgenstein and justice*. Berkeley, CA: University of California Press.

Proctor, J. (2004). *Stuart Hall*. London: Routledge.

Rizvi, F. (2009). Towards cosmopolitan learning. *Discourse: Studies in the Cultural Politics of Education*, *30*, 253–268. doi:10.1080/01596300903036863

Rizvi, F. (2011). Experiences of cultural diversity in the context of an emergent transnationalism. *European Educational Research Journal*, *10*, 180–188. doi:10.2304/eerj.2011.10.2.180

Rojek, C. (2003). *Stuart Hall*. Cambridge: Polity Press.

Williams, R. (1958). *Culture and society*. London: Penguin.

Wittgenstein, L. (1969). *Blue and brown books*. London: Blackwell.

Wittgenstein, L. (1974). *Philosophical investigations*. London: Blackwell.

Stuart Hall and the theory and practice of articulation

John Clarke

Faculty of Social Sciences, The Open University, Milton Keynes, UK

In this article, I argue that the idea of articulation links three different dimensions of Stuart Hall's work: it is central to the work of cultural politics, to the work of hegemony and to his practice of embodied pedagogy. I claim that his approach to pedagogy entails the art of listening combined with the practice of theorising in the service of expanding who belongs to the public. This involves the work of translation, finding ways of addressing different audiences. I treat each of these aspects in turn, drawing out the salience of articulation for each and suggest that these three dimensions are themselves articulated by Hall's commitment to the theory *and* practice of articulation.

When reading or listening to the many comments and commentaries on Stuart Hall's life and work that followed his death in February 2014, I was moved by how many paid tribute to his personal charm, his generosity in thinking and talking with others and his engaging and persuasive way of speaking. In this brief article, I will make speculative connections between these apparently personal characteristics and his orientations to theory, politics and pedagogy.[1] In this, I do not mean to suggest that the descriptions of his grace, generosity or compelling style of thinking and speaking are trivial, incidental or even wrong-headed. On the contrary, they consistently convey qualities that seem all too rare in the worlds of the academy and politics. This article asks what underlies this outpouring of tributes and their recurrent themes and offers an alternative reading of these 'personal qualities' and engaging style, explaining them as central to his embodied praxis of articulation. This paper will demonstrate how the concept of articulation works in three different and yet interrelated ways to organise his political, pedagogic and intellectual projects – as the work of cultural politics, the work of securing hegemony and the attentive listening necessary to the work of embodied pedagogy.

Turning to articulation

This paper will argue that Hall's engaging ways were more than merely personal, yet nor were they the result of the sort of careful calculation expressed in the contemporary academic obsessions with public engagement or the maximisation of 'impact'. Rather, they were the manifestations of a uniquely historically aware and forward-looking reflection about intellectual, political and pedagogic work within and beyond the academy. Hall's many political projects and commitments embodied personal, political and pedagogical dimensions. They were part and parcel of his conduct throughout his varied and intertwined career as activist, theorist, public intellectual and academic, and, for me, linked his public practice to the more intimate relationships of mentor, collaborator, colleague and friend. No one who spent any time with him was in any doubt about the sincerity of the warmth, interest and attention that were in play in such encounters.

It is not exactly news to claim that the concept of articulation was central to Stuart Hall's work (see, e.g., Slack, 1996). What is perhaps most striking is the multiple productive ways in which this idea worked for him: it linked his approach to thinking about social formations, his orientation to culture as the site of ideological and political struggles and the problematic politics of constructing counter-hegemonic possibilities in popular politics. The idea also linked his work on diasporic identities, popular cultural forms and aesthetic/cultural practices. In the following sections, I review some of these usages of articulation, before returning to the question of 'practising articulation'.

The starting point is the role that articulation plays in Hall's response to the problem of analysing social formations, even though this issue often disappears in account of articulation in the analysis of discourse, ideology and culture. It is, however, an important starting point because it locates articulation at the centre of his attempt to think about cultural studies in relation to Marxism and forms a critical hinge in his uses of Marx, Gramsci and Althusser during the 1970s and 1980s. He followed Althusser in refusing the view of the base/superstructure distinction (and the internal relations of determination between the two parts) that had dominated much Marxist theorising, not least for the room this created for thinking about the relative autonomy of social instances – and for 'culture', in particular. The idea of articulation provided a means for addressing the complex character of social formations (as articulated unities) rather than simple, or expressive, totalities. This Althusserian view of social formations which combined multiple modes of production with economic, political, ideological levels or instances in an articulated combination that was 'structured in dominance' rather than simply determined, coincided with Hall's reading of critical parts of Marx, notably the 1857 *Introduction to the Critique of Political Economy* or *Grundrisse* (Hall, 2003; Marx, 1993). He was taken with Marx's description of the circuit of capital as a complex totality, composed of different moments (productions, exchange, circulation, consumption, etc.) that together formed a 'unity in difference'.

This understanding of social formations as articulated structures was paralleled in his understanding of articulation as central to work on ideology, domination and hegemony. Here Hall moved between an Althusserian concern with ideology (not least the question of interpellation) and a Gramscian focus on hegemony and the organisation of consent (not least in the complex relations with the field of common sense). This engagement took place dialogically – not least through the conversations (in person and in writing) with Ernesto Laclau and Chantal Mouffe's work on hegemony (e.g., Laclau & Mouffe, 1985). In the development of articulation as an alternative to more reductive conceptions of ideology, we can see the characteristic subtlety of Hall's mobile theorising: working with and against other ways of thinking in a complex negotiation: Althusser allows us to see X but does not help us with Y. Or Foucault provides a way of approaching knowledge and power yet does not give us Gramsci's understanding of common sense and so on. I suspect that Gramsci provided the closest thing to a fixed point for this mobility, not least for his attention to the necessity of conjunctural analysis (see, e.g., Hall, 1986, 1987). But this mobile and exploratory understanding of theory – and of articulation in particular – is visible in statements like the following:

> By the term 'articulation', I mean a connection or link which is not necessarily given in all cases, as a law or a fact of life, but which requires particular conditions of existence to appear at all, which has to be positively sustained by specific processes, which is not 'eternal' but has to be constantly renewed, which can under some circumstances disappear or be overthrown, leading to the old linkages being dissolved and new connections – re-articulations – being forged. It is also important that an articulation between different practices does not mean that they become identical or that one is dissolved into the other. Each retains its distinct determinations and conditions of existence. However, once an articulation is made, the two practices can function together, not as an 'immediate identity' (in the language of Marx's '1857 Introduction') but as distinctions within a 'unity'. (Hall, 1985, pp. 113–114, footnote 2)

Here we can see some of the characteristic formulations of articulation – in particular, the view that connections or links are not 'necessarily given' as a fact of life or by law like correspondences. Hall returned time and again to the importance of the 'no necessary correspondence' between elements, while simultaneously refusing the other pole of 'necessarily no correspondence' (1985, p. 94). Instead, he insisted on the importance of analysing the specifics of particular articulations. This meant paying attention to both the conditions of their existence and the political-cultural work (practice) that went into making and sustaining specific articulations. No articulation – whether the combination of social instances in a social formation or a discursive alignment of meanings and politics – came with a 'lifetime guarantee'. Rather their internal organisation (involving potential disjunctures, contradictions, antagonisms and tensions) and their external conditions of existence created the possibility of 'disarticulation and rearticulation'. This understanding of articulation – combining both its contingency and the necessity of the work of production and maintenance – was a critical element in Hall's approach to cultural studies and established the ground on which other implications of articulation as a way of naming the problems of politics and pedagogy could be developed.

Articulation as the work of cultural politics

This leads me to the second way in which the concept of articulation was important to Hall's project for cultural studies – in resisting expressive or reductive conceptions of ideology (or culture or discourse) in which specific ideas or ways of thinking were identified with a particular class location. This was always one of the most contentious terrains for cultural studies, given the temptations to identify ideologies with particular classes or to think of cultures as coherent organic unities that condensed a whole way of life (of a class or community) in an anthropological model. As Jennifer Slack (1996) argues, articulation is one of the means by which Stuart Hall 'resists the temptation of reduction to class, mode of production, structure, as well as to culturalism's tendency to reduce culture to "experience"' (pp. 122–123).

In developing his work around the concept of articulation, Hall always emphasised a double meaning, in which the ideas of 'to give voice to' and 'to connect' are always implied and always co-present. In an interview with Larry Grossberg, Hall talked at some length about the concept and its significance for him, including these (much cited) observations:

I always use the word 'articulation', though I don't know whether the meaning I attribute to it is perfectly understood. In England, the term has a nice double meaning because 'articulate' means to utter, to speak forth, to be articulate. It carries that sense of language-ing, of expressing, etc. But we also speak of an 'articulated' lorry (truck): a lorry where the front (cab) and back (trailer) can, but need not necessarily, be connected to one another. The two parts are connected to each other, but through a specific linkage, that can be broken. An articulation is thus the form of the connection that can make a unity of two different elements, under certain conditions. It is a linkage which is not necessary, determined, absolute and essential for all time. You have to ask, under what circumstances can a connection be forged or made? So the so-called 'unity' of a discourse is really the articulation of different, distinct elements which can be rearticulated in different ways because they have no necessary 'belongingness'. The 'unity' which matters is a linkage between that articulated discourse and the social forces with which it can, under certain historical conditions, but need not necessarily, be connected. Thus, a theory of articulation is both a way of understanding how ideological elements come, under certain conditions, to cohere together within a discourse, and a way of asking how they do or do not become articulated, at specific conjunctures, to certain political subjects. Let me put that the other way: the theory of articulation asks how an ideology discovers its subject rather than how the subject thinks the necessary and inevitable thoughts which belong to it; it enables us to think how an ideology empowers people, enabling them to begin to make some sense or intelligibility of their historical situation, without reducing those forms of intelligibility to their socio-economic or class location or social position. (Grossberg, 1996, pp. 142–143)

The 'articulated lorry' metaphor is often taken up in terms of how different elements are articulated in a discursive or ideological formation, in which the elements have no necessary belonging – it is the way in which they are assembled together, the forging of specific links and connections that gives them their social, cultural or political force.[2] But less clearly visible in this argument is a question of political articulation – the ways in which an articulated discourse and a combination of social forces can (conjuncturally) be connected. It is the articulation of both a discourse and that discourse with 'certain political subjects' that constitutes the double movement of articulation. It is that second element that makes articulation more than a 'merely cultural' concept.

It is important to note that Hall's reference to 'social forces' condenses a whole series of analytical questions. Although the concept and its relatives (balance of forces, political forces, etc.) are taken from an orthodox Marxist framing, the uses Hall makes of them always involve an insistence that social forces are never simply classes (as derivatives of the social relations of production). On the contrary, social forces for Hall were always multiple, constituted by the varieties of domination and subordination that were in play in any specific conjunctural setting. It is this argument that organises the conjunctural analysis offered in *Policing the Crisis* (Hall, Critcher, Jefferson, Clarke, & Roberts, 1978/ 2013) in which the accumulating crises of the British social formation are understood as being articulated through 'race' (see also the elegant essay by Gail Lewis (2000), in which she dissects the displacement of 'race' in British social policy). I have argued elsewhere (Clarke, 2014a) that this conception of social forces was one of the (many) enabling roles that Gramsci's work played in the development of cultural studies. Gramsci's tendency, in *The Prison Notebooks* (1973), to write cryptically and elusively about 'social groups' combined with his concern with hegemony as the site of alliances and blocs to blur the classical simplicities of class relations of domination and subordination.

Articulation as the work of hegemony

His interest in the work of hegemony stressed articulation as a practice in the double sense that I have described above. At the core of this was an understanding of hegemony as the (contingent and conditional) construction of popular consent to the project and programme of a 'ruling bloc'. Again following Gramsci, Hall insisted on the importance of understanding this as a bloc – an alliance of class fractions and other social groups that aimed to provide social leadership – a project that could shape the direction of the social formation. Here is the first moment of connection/articulation – the construction of the (would-be) ruling bloc among potentially competing and conflicting interests (including among the capitalist class itself).[3] The second moment consists of the work of articulating the subordinate (or subaltern) groups through material and symbolic concessions in which they are 'taken account of' in such ways that they can come to identify themselves in the leading project.

This includes the elaboration of ways of addressing, appropriating themes attached to and speaking for subordinate social groups. This included – a central theme for cultural studies – borrowing and bending the forms and styles of popular thought. Here is posed the relationship between hegemony and common sense. For Hall, this was where cultural studies connected most powerfully with Gramsci's understanding of the relationship between hegemony and common sense. In Gramsci's view, we are always:

> the product of the historical process to date which has deposited in you an infinity of traces without leaving an inventory ... Moreover, commonsense is a collective noun, like religion: there is not just one common sense, for that too is a product of history and a part of the historical process. (1973, pp. 324–325)

This insistence on the fragmentary and heterogeneous formation of common sense identifies the work of political articulation that is required to articulate selected elements or fragments of common sense with dominant conceptions to create the appearance of a shared, unitary and coherent understanding of the world. It is important to emphasise the 'selected elements', since there are many 'common senses' and some of them, as Gramsci argued, contain 'good sense' that might be mobilised to build alternative hegemonies. For example, the Right – in Britain, the USA and elsewhere – has often borrowed common-sense discourses of nation, work and family to articulate a national-popular project. But they have also borrowed (and bent) apparently more egalitarian fragments of common sense, as in the recent uses made of 'fairness' as a popular British identification by the Conservative-led Coalition government. In this, 'fairness' is rearticulated to legitimate welfare cuts (in benefits and services) in the defence of being 'fair' to 'hard working families' (Clarke, 2014b). Writing in the 1980s, Hall argued for recognising Gramsci's importance for engaging with politics as an articulatory practice:

> Since, in fact, the political character of our ideas cannot be guaranteed by our class position or by the 'mode of production', it is possible for the Right to construct a politics which does speak to people's experience, which does insert itself into what Gramsci called the necessarily fragmentary, contradictory nature of common sense, which does resonate with some of their ordinary aspirations, and which, in certain circumstances, can recoup them as subordinate subjects, into a historical project which 'hegemonises' what we used – erroneously – to think of as their 'necessary class interests'. Gramsci is one of the first modern Marxists to recognise that interests are not given but have to be politically and ideologically constructed. (1987, p. 20)

This practice of articulation was, for Hall, a complex one, implying political work: selective work *vis-à-vis* the many common senses, involving both the selective mobilisation of some aspects and the obverse: the selective *demobilisation* of other elements by rendering them silent, ridiculous, unrealistic, out of time or place and so on. As Slack and Wise (2007) insist, this view of articulation as a practice is closely tied to Hall's understanding of cultural studies as a contextual and conjunctural way of working:

> These articulations are not fixed for all time; they do not remain permanently in place. They can and do change over time. But, here too, the speed and direction of change is contingent. Some articulations remain relatively tenacious; they are rather firmly forged and difficult to disarticulate. Hall called these 'lines of tendential force', which draws attention to their tendency to remain articulated. Others, however, might be more easily broken and thus subject to disarticulation. It all depends on the particulars of the nature of the articulations at any particular historical moment. (p. 128)

This view of articulation then underpins a reading of hegemony as not just as something to be established and maintained, a conception which implies a view of cultural studies as critique (widely held and practised) but also a concern with how to conduct alternative politics. This is the condition for his famous observation that popular culture is:

> one of the places where socialism might be constituted. That is why 'popular culture' matters. Otherwise, to tell you the truth, I don't give a damn about it. (Hall, 1981, p. 239)

In this sense, culture constituted a field of possibility in which relations of domination and subordination were inscribed, represented, refused and contested through articulatory practices. A critical part of his frustration at much of British (and beyond) Left politics was about the failure to take this field of possibility seriously (see *The Hard Road to Renewal*, Hall (1989), for example). Some of this concerned the lack of attention to the work of hegemony being performed in Thatcherism (and subsequent British versions of what he later called 'common-sense neoliberalism', Hall & O'Shea, 2013), but much of his frustration focused on the Left's failure to think about the other threads of common sense and how they might be worked with and on to create progressive blocs that spoke with and for the subordinated, marginalised and excluded. Such a view of articulation implies paying attention to common sense, its multiplicity, its fractures, the desires it voices, the silences it contains and more. Listening and paying attention is hard work, while shortcuts are easy and attractive – if not necessarily politically effective. This issue preoccupied him through to his last writings, for example, the essays on neoliberalism in *Soundings* (Hall & O'Shea, 2013) and *Cultural Studies* (Hall, 2011).

Articulation as embodied pedagogy

This understanding of articulation as a practice also underpinned Hall's approach to pedagogy. By pedagogy, I mean to refer to the many varieties of teaching in which he engaged: lectures, classes, workshops and the vast amount of individual and collective teaching material he produced while at the Open University between 1978 and 1997. The Open University is a distance teaching university, and he contributed to the making of a variety of courses in the form of TV programmes and DVDs, audio commentaries, editing and authoring written materials and more. The university also operates a model of the 'collective teacher': the course or module team that is responsible for preparing such teaching materials and Hall's presence in such processes was a powerful one: leading, enabling, supporting and developing, but always with a view to finding the right modes of address and engagement between the course and its students. He also took an active role in the week-long summer schools that the university ran and was a remarkable presence in the everyday tutoring, in the one-off evening lectures given by all members of staff, but – most of all – in the amount of time he would give to talking with students in groups and individually about their studies, their lives and the world in which they lived. Having seen him in these settings, I can only say that the gracious generosity for which he was well known was constantly visible (and was a constant source of delight for students) – and these qualities were matched by a seemingly boundless capacity to enter, continue and renew such conversations.

But this is not just a question of being nice: it reflects an orientation to pedagogy as articulation that runs throughout his work. The somewhat banal pedagogical principle of 'starting where the student is' takes on a rather different political and cultural significance in this light. Of course, 'where the student is' – from a cultural studies perspective – is rarely simple, singular or straightforward. On the contrary, 'the student' embodied all those things that Hall knew to be true about identities, common senses and the practice of articulation. Identities are multiple and rarely fixed; common senses are heterogeneous and fragmentary, and the work of articulation is to build connections that lead towards a set of new configurations and possibilities. Angela McRobbie (2000) has argued for the importance of viewing him as a teacher in contextually specific ways:

> Two things about Stuart Hall's career as a teacher as well as an intellectual are significant. First, his practice as a teacher has at every point departed from the university tradition embodied in the Oxbridge model. Second, in the British post-1945 context where the agenda for public intellectual debate remains firmly set by the standards and concerns of Oxbridge, and symbolized by the role of the BBC, Hall's field of influence is less in the establishment channels of the quality press and the portals of government, and more in the lecture theatres and seminar rooms of the redbrick and new universities, and, of course, in the late night broadcasts of the Open University. Stuart Hall has operated throughout his career as a teacher, and indeed as a certain kind of teacher. As he himself said in interview, 'Open university courses are open to those who don't have any academic background. If you are going to make cultural studies ideas live with them, you have to translate the ideas, be willing to write at that more popular and accessible level. I wanted cultural studies to be open to that sort of challenge. I didn't see why it wouldn't 'live' as a more popular pedagogy'. (Hall, quoted in McRobbie, 2000, p. 212)

This establishes a view of pedagogy as an engagement, a conversation and a process of collective discovery, rather than an act of masterly revelation. That implies hard work too and it inverts what has (too) often been a left or progressive view of the relationship between politics and pedagogy: that teaching is the site for doing or – more frequently – announcing politics. In this mode, the act of revealing truth tears aside the veil of ideology and allows people to see clearly (as if they had become Johnny Nash). This was not a model of politics or pedagogy (or ideology) that Hall thought was sustainable or productive. Nor did he think that critical work was about the deconstruction of common sense (in which common sense was intrinsically erroneous or false – bad thinking), which could be simply countered or displaced by correct knowledge. Certainly, he thought teaching was the site of politics (just like popular culture), but that telling people what was right or true in a loud voice was unlikely to be an effective form of political mobilisation:

I do think it is a requirement of intellectuals to speak a kind of truth. Maybe not truth with a capital T, but anyway, some kind of truth, the best truth that they know or can discover – to speak that truth to power. To take responsibility – which can be unpleasant and is no recipe for success – for having spoken it. To take responsibility for speaking it to wider groups of people than are simply involved in the professional life of ideas. To speak it beyond the confines of the academy. To speak it, however, in its full complexity. Never to speak it in too simple a way, because 'the folks won't understand'. Because then they will understand, but they will get it wrong, which is much worse! So, to speak it in its full complexity, but to try to speak it in terms in which other people who, after all, can think and do have ideas in their heads, though they are not paid or paid-up intellectuals, need it. (Hall, 2007, pp. 289–290)

This conception of 'how to speak' is a powerful one, expressing a responsibility to engage with the audiences or publics who 'need to know' in the appropriate terms. Such a view meant that teaching was necessarily an exercise in articulation in a heteroglossic context, such that 'starting where the student is' meant considering the array of voices and modes of thinking that might be encountered and might provide the point of departure for the work of 'thinking again'. Cultural and political contexts were necessarily heteroglossic (in Bakhtin's sense) and required attention to the shifting terrains of the popular and the varieties of common sense that were in play at any particular moment. Pedagogy meant the task of working with, and on, those varieties– seeking to articulate them into new possibilities, new alignments and new directions of travel. Hall's willingness to undertake this work of articulation was echoed, perhaps, in his ways of thinking and theorising such that teaching was not a separate domain. James Procter in his book on Stuart suggests that his practice of 'doing theory' can itself be understood as a practice of articulation:

Articulation, as a theoretical practice in Hall's writing, involves linking two or more different theoretical frameworks in order to move beyond the limits of either framework on its own. For example, at the centre of this chapter has been a discussion of Hall's displacement of the early theoretical assumptions of 'culturalism' through an encounter with the more recent 'structuralisms'. Within Hall's writings this displacement does not involve rejecting the former in order to proceed to the latter, but a coupling or articulation of the two in order to propose an alternative theoretical direction. This process of linkage is not fixed or final. … Articulations can only be made under a specific set of circumstances or, to adapt one final theoretical concept used by Hall, at a particular historical conjuncture. Hall's theorising is conjunctural in the sense that it is always informed by and articulated as a response to, events at a particular moment. (Procter, 2004, p. 54)

This is an interesting and suggestive view of Hall's theorising: evoking Hall as 'bricoleur' discovering necessary elements in many different places and seeing what might happen if they were put together to illuminate pressing analytical and political issues. It certainly captures something of the mobile and unfinished way in which he would work patiently with, on and against, particular theorists or parts of their work. There are many examples of this – for instance, the essays on Gramsci (1986, 1987) or Althusser (1985). During the essay on Althusser, he carefully distinguishes that which he hopes to rescue and take up from Althusser's work, whilst rejecting what he sees as overly structuralist tendencies. This approach underpins his response to E.P. Thompson's (1978) famous critique of Althusser in *The Poverty of Theory*. He argues that Thompson provides an 'undialectical reading' of Althusser which lists the errors and problems yet 'fails to recognize, *at the same time*, what real advances were being generated by Althusser's work' which establish 'a threshold behind which we cannot allow ourselves to fall' (1985, pp. 96–97). Here, too, is a characteristic double movement: the careful engagement with the analytical resources being developed by others combined with the identification of 'thresholds' or 'springboards' that would enable forward movement – to enable the task of thinking again and thinking better. He once argued that he tended to favour the 'middle period' of writers:

> Perhaps I ought to say in parenthesis that I do find an alarming tendency in myself to prefer people's less complete works to their later, mature and complete ones. I prefer *The Eighteenth Brumaire* to book II of *Capital*. I prefer Althusser's *For Marx* to *Reading Capital*. I like people's middle period a lot, where they have gotten over their adolescent idealism but their thought has not yet hardened into a system. And I like Laclau when he's struggling to find a way out of reductionism and beginning to reconceptualize Marxist categories in the discursive mode. (Hall, quoted in Grossberg, 1996, p. 146)

Here one might detect his own disposition to thinking and theorising as active processes (and his reluctance to 'Do Theory' on a grand and abstracted scale). This orientation to thinking makes so much of his writing feel like 'teaching' in the best sense. In many places, he displays – in the sense of making visible – the process of working through ideas, concepts and orientations. What we read – or what we hear (since many of his essays began life as talks) – is the process of thinking, rather than just the conclusions. They are, then, also invitations to think with (and against) both Hall and the people with whom he is engaged. It establishes an exemplary practice of how to talk or write about thinking (as opposed to 'undialectical' critique). I was taken by the efforts of Gregor McLennan to capture this sensibility and style of Stuart Hall in a piece written shortly after his death. He begins from a troubling question – how to explain to others:

> What was it about Stuart Hall, as a social scientist, that was so special?

> To answer this, I find myself reaching for a rather old-fashioned, almost absurdly abstract term: dialectics. Yet for me this gets us close to the essence of Hall's appeal as a thinker, teacher, mentor and friend. In so many people, in so many texts, and in so many addresses, seemingly contrary inclinations, arguments, traditions, political positions, and personal attributes jostle around awkwardly, never quite gelling into a final synthesis. But this was exactly the 'dialectical' quality and achievement of Stuart Hall's work – especially when articulated in person.

> Indeed, if dialectics comes across as abstract, this is because it is usually considered only at the level of pure understanding: the synthesis of generalised positions, theories, findings, and so on. Yet Hall had the rare gift and intelligence of expressing the dialectical movement of ideas and politics in his very character and presence. This was the way he worked with people, talked to (diverse) audiences, disputed and laughed his way through issues, and wrote up his (provisional, inclusive) solutions.

> Only in recent times have sociologists (re)discovered the significance of 'embodiment' and 'affect', and only even more recently have fans of these new 'vitalist' notions realised that they are not in fact necessarily opposed to old 'dry' notions like reason, knowledge and argumentation. Better to put it, again, more dialectically: ideas and politics don't lose their generality when they are 'fused' in and by particular situations and people, but they do seem to matter more because of this, gaining enhanced significance and buzz. And no one exuded this kind of embodied synthesizing intellectuality quite like Hall. (McLennan, 2014)

This is a wonderful evocation and analysis that grasps the sense of a person as an embodied practice. This was indeed 'the way he worked with people', and McLennan captures the sensibility of pedagogy as articulation that I have been trying to address – but even then I think there is one more element that needs to be added.

Articulation as the work of attention

The practice of articulation is not only the work of engaging, addressing and connecting. In a complex and heteroglossic context, crowded by many common senses, it also requires the work of listening: paying attention to what circulates, to what matters, to what connections are already being forged, to what threads are being forgotten and to what apparently natural and normal alignments of things are coming apart. This is, in part, the work of cultural studies as Hall envisaged it: the search for the past, present and future possible articulations that secured and might unlock relations of domination and subordination. How is domination secured? How is hegemony articulated? What are the conjunctural conditions under which hegemony is fragile, vulnerable to the loss of consent?

Hall's legacy involves both such questions and the commitment to doing the careful work of listening that can make such links and potential new alignments available to us. Hall practised what Les Back (2007) has called 'the art of listening': the dialogical capacity to hear what people are saying. Such an orientation refuses the more conventional monological mode of politics (and teaching, one might suggest) and opens the space of possibility for discovery. This is, as Back himself has argued, something other than the 'we're listening' mode adopted by political parties (New Labour's 'Big Conversation', for instance), government agencies or the marketing arms of corporations that seek our responses to their provisions. But only by listening was Hall able to find the links and the connections that might be built upon to enable a conversation that moved. That attention was both large scale (the moving terrain of British popular culture in all its transnational formations) and intimate (the immediate encounter always felt as though it mattered). As a result, he was able to map the possibilities – a mapping that always enabled him to speak compellingly, making those connections, forging those links and refiguring the field of possibilities – again on a range of scales.

What so many of us remember is the voice – impassioned, warm, probing, inquisitive, laughing and always generous in its offerings. Many of the tributes to him have evoked that experience. For example, Les Back (2014) observed that:

> Listening to Stuart Hall made us see the world differently and he had a gift that enabled us to understand our life anew. He seemed to be talking directly to you, even if it was through the TV screen or through the pages of one of his many influential essays.

A similar view is offered in Nirmal Puwar's commentary about 'meeting Stuart Hall's voice' (2014) – an image that grasps at the life in (and of) that voice. She recalls having first encountered him speaking in the early hours of the morning (on BBC transmitted Open University programmes) and goes on:

> There were many other occasions when I met Stuart Hall. Of course we meet him when we read, teach and debate his vast scholarship. To meet him as a reader is to find a form of speech which is always directly addressing you.

> One of the many reasons he will be missed is the highlight of hearing him present a talk. He slowly comes alive. The audience comes alive. The ideas build up to a crescendo. He offers ideas which set off a whirlpool of connections. He moves the room. His analysis sets forth a sociological imagination that shifts its cadence through the tension of connecting the micro to the macro, the everyday to the abstract, from theory to everyday practices, and never without attention to the political moment. (Puwar, 2014)

This, I want to suggest, is the embodied practice of articulation: the work of forging new connections in the pursuit of building progressive orientations and progressive alliances. In conclusion, I want to emphasise this as a *practice* for two reasons. The first is about not fetishising the 'Stuartness' of Stuart Hall: what he did – and the way that did it – are models of good practice (the practice of articulation) rather than just the unfathomable wonders of a unique figure. I say this despite my profound admiration for who he was and how he conducted himself. We might nevertheless learn lessons – about listening and its value, about developing engaging (rather than instructive) modes of address and about finding ways of working in and with heteroglossic contexts in which multiple varieties of common sense circulate. It is also the mode in which the personal and the political were articulated in Stuart Hall – a mode which we might strive to enact ourselves.

My second reason concerns the sense of loss that so many of us feel following Stuart's death. On several occasions, I have heard this manifest itself in the question 'what would Stuart have said about …?' I think that misses the point: far better to ask 'how would Stuart have thought about this?' This question would bring us to the work of articulation – to think in ways that are committed but open, that recognise the unfinished nature of the moment, that try to borrow and bend productive intellectual resources and that take seriously the collective and collaborative nature of social (and political) life. For me, that is the greatest legacy: that articulation is not just a theory or an analytic orientation but that – as embodied by Stuart Hall – it was also a pedagogic and political practice.

Acknowledgement

I am very grateful to the editors for the invitation to contribute to this special issue and to the anonymous reviewer and Leslie Roman for their thoughtful and constructive suggestions on the first draft.

Disclosure statement

No potential conflict of interest was reported by the author.

Notes

1. It is hard to write in the aftermath of Stuart's death, not least because of the suspicion that he would never have taken himself this seriously. One specific instance of this difficulty concerns the problem of nomenclature – should he be interpellated as Stuart Hall, Stuart, Hall or SH in the context of academic convention? This question remains unresolved – at least for me.
2. I must confess to finding the 'articulated lorry' illustration somewhat frustrating. Articulated lorries articulate as a design feature – the cab and trailer are built with parts that are intended to conjoin. As a result, this may underestimate the work that articulation requires – whether in the ill-fitting alignments of economies and cultures in capitalist social formations or the bending of forms of commonsense into would-be hegemonic projects. If only the parts were pre-designed for self-assembly …
3. The rise of neoliberalism as a critical concept seems to have largely buried the question of the capitalist class as a fractioned, fractious, competitive and conflictual entity that cannot be relied upon to know its own 'interests'. In contrast, Nicos Poulantzas (1973) argued that the state had to serve as the means by which 'general interest' of the capitalist class could be organised, while also providing the means of disorganising the subordinate classes.

References

Back, L. (2007). *The art of listening*. Oxford: Berg.
Back, L. (2014, February 16). Stuart Hall—A bright star. *Open Democracy*. Retrieved from https://www.opendemocracy.net/les-back/stuart-hall-bright-star

Clarke, J. (2014a). Conjunctures, crises and cultures: Valuing Stuart Hall. *Focaal: A Journal of Global and Historical Anthropology, 70,* 113–122.

Clarke, J. (2014b). Imagined economies: Austerity and the moral economy of 'fairness'. *Topia, 30–31*(Fall 2013, Spring 2014), 17–30.

Gramsci, A. (1973). *Selections from the prison notebooks* (G. Nowell Smith & Q. Hoare, Eds.). London: Lawrence & Wishart.

Grossberg, L. (1966). On postmodernism and articulation: An interview with Stuart Hall. *Journal of Communication Inquiry*. In D. Morley & K. Chen (Eds.), *Stuart Hall: Critical dialogues in cultural studies* (pp. 131–150). London: Routledge.

Hall, S. (1981). Notes on deconstructing 'the popular'. In R. Samuel (Ed.), *People's history and socialist theory* (pp. 227–240). London: Routledge.

Hall, S. (1985). Signification, representation, ideology: Althusser and the post-structuralist debate. *Critical Studies in Mass Communication, 2*(2), 91–114. doi:10.1080/15295038509360070

Hall, S. (1986). Gramsci's relevance for the study of race and ethnicity. *Journal of Communication Inquiry, 10*(2), 5–27. doi:10.1177/019685998601000202

Hall, S. (1987, June 16–21). Gramsci and us. *Marxism Today.*

Hall, S. (1989). *The hard road to renewal.* London: Verso.

Hall, S. (2003). Marx's notes on method: A 'reading' of the '1857 Introduction'. *Cultural Studies, 17*(2), 113–149. doi:10.1080/0950238032000114868

Hall, S. (2007). Epilogue: Through the prism of an intellectual life. In B. Meeks (Ed.), *Culture, politics, race and diaspora: The thought of Stuart Hall* (pp. 269–291). London: Lawrence & Wishart.

Hall, S. (2011). The neo-liberal revolution. *Cultural Studies, 25,* 705–728. doi:10.1080/09502386.2011.619886

Hall, S., Critcher, C., Jefferson, T., Clarke, J., & Roberts, B. (1978/2013). *Policing the crisis: Mugging, the state and law and order* (2nd ed.). London: Macmillan.

Hall, S., & O'Shea, A. (2013). Common-sense neoliberalism. *Soundings, 55,* 9–25.

Laclau, E., & Mouffe, C. (1985). *Hegemony and socialist strategy: Towards a radical democratic politics.* London: Verso.

Lewis, G. (2000). Stuart Hall and social policy: An encounter of strangers? In P. Gilroy, L. Grossberg, & A. McRobbie (Eds.), *Without guarantees: In honour of Stuart Hall* (pp. 193–202). London: Verso.

Marx, K. (1993). *Grundrisse: Foundations for a critique of political economy.* (Martin Nicolaus, Trans.). London: Penguin Books.

McLennan, G. (2014). On Stuart Hall. *Discover Society.* http://www.discoversociety.org/2014/03/04/focus-on-stuart-hall/

McRobbie, A. (2000). Stuart Hall: The universities and the 'hurly burly'. In P. Gilroy, L. Grossberg, & A. McRobbie (Eds.), *Without guarantees: In honour of Stuart Hall* (pp. 212–224). London: Verso.

Poulantzas, N. (1973). *Political power and social classes.* London: New Left Books.

Procter, J. (2004). *Stuart Hall* (Routledge Critical Thinkers Series). London: Routledge.

Puwar, N. (2014, February 16). Meeting Stuart Hall's voice. *Open Democracy.* https://www.opendemocracy.net/nirmal-puwar/meeting-stuart-hall's-voice

Slack, J. (1996). The theory and method of articulation in cultural studies. In D. Morley & K.-H. Chen (Eds.), *Stuart Hall: Critical dialogues in cultural studies* (pp. 112–127). London: Routledge.

Slack, J., & Wise J. (2007). *Culture + technology: A primer.* New York, NY: Peter Lang.

Thompson, E. P. (1978). *The poverty of theory and other essays.* New York, NY: Monthly Review Press.

The contribution of Stuart Hall to analyzing educational policy and reform

Luis Armando Gandin

Programa de Pós-Graduação em Educação, Universidade Federal do Rio Grande do Sul, Porto Alegre, Brazil

This article focuses on the contribution of Stuart Hall to the study of educational policy and reform, using the experience of the Citizen School initiative in Porto Alegre, Brazil as a concrete example. This experience was a participatory educational reform implemented during the 16 years of the Workers' Party tenure in Porto Alegre's municipal administration. Hall's concept of articulation and his particular use of concepts such as ideology, discourse, common sense, and hegemony lay the foundation for the theoretical framework that provides a potent lens to analyze the complexity of educational policy and reform. In particular, this assemblage of concepts offers a vantage point to understand a counter-hegemonic initiative such as the Citizen School, because it helps to situate this experience as a particular historical articulation of discursive practices both connected to the recreation of common sense and anchored in a particular material context. First, the article will briefly contextualize the Citizen School experience. It will then show how Hall's concepts develop a complex theory to analyze complex phenomena such as educational policy and reform, in particular the Porto Alegre experience.

In the process of researching the Citizen School experience in the city of Porto Alegre, I was confronted with the task of analyzing a complex social setting. Brazil was living through a period – the 1990s – in which neoliberal practices were being introduced at the federal level (a push for market-based management and assessment, devolution and decentralization, and reduction of investment in education) and, at the same time, a very different school system reform was being implemented in the city of Porto Alegre. In searching for theoretical tools that could help to analyze the contradictions of the phenomenon, I encountered the work of Stuart Hall. It would not be easy, at that point in time, to get to his work.

Hall's work was introduced in Latin America in the early 1990s, especially by scholars in the field of Communication. Several of his articles were translated into Spanish as early as 1993. In Brazil, it was not until 1996 that Hall's first text was made available in Portuguese (*Cultural Identity and Diaspora*). Nevertheless, in 1998, when I moved to the USA to pursue my doctorate and when I started researching the subject of education reform in Porto Alegre, Stuart Hall's work was hardly known and used in the field of Education in Brazil. It is important to point out that one year earlier, in 1997, some of my School of Education colleagues (Tomaz Tadeu da Silva and Marisa Vorraber Costa, to cite two) at Universidade Federal do Rio Grande do Sul published Brazilian translations of Hall's work – *The Question of Cultural Identity* (1997a) and *The Centrality of Culture: Notes on the Cultural Revolutions of Our Time* (1997b). Notwithstanding, these two specific papers were framed, in Brazil, within the emerging subfield of Cultural Studies and ·Education and they did not seem, at the time, to offer particularly useful lenses to my specific study of educational reform.

I was then exposed to the corpus of Hall's scholarship (at first through John Fiske and Michael Apple, and later in Brazil through Liv Sovik), encountering Hall's Gramscian reworking of the concepts of ideology, common sense, articulation, and hegemony. These offered me an extremely potent theoretical lens through which the particular field I was investigating could be understood without any simplification of its complexity.

Stuart Hall was an avid reader of Gramsci and his work was highly influenced by the Italian intellectual. Notwithstanding, Hall did not simply "use" Gramsci's (or other authors') work: he constructed a new theory that used Gramsci's insights and advanced them, making them potent in the particular context where he was operating. Hall is clear about this point:

> Gramsci's work often appears almost too concrete: too historically specific, too delimited in its references, too "descriptively" analytic, too time- and context-bound. His most illuminating ideas and formulations are typically of this conjunctural kind. To make more general use of them, they have to be delicately dis-interred from their concrete and specific historical embeddedness and transplanted to new soil with considerable care and patience. (Hall, 1996b, p. 413)

Hall's particular configuration of the concepts and the theoretical framework that he created by reworking Gramsci's formulations were the ones that guided my analysis of the experiences in the educational system of Porto Alegre, Brazil. What I set out to do in my research about the Porto Alegre reforms was precisely this: to use Hall's formulations and delicately disinter them, transplanting them with patience, recontextualizing them, so they could flourish and help me understand the complexities involved. This article, then, examines Stuart Hall's influence and direct contribution to the research on education reform and hopefully shows how immensely fruitful and powerful his work is for understanding not only how domination works in particular contexts but also how counter-hegemonic struggles are formed.

A little note is necessary, nevertheless, before I proceed. Even though it goes well beyond the scope of this article to evaluate Stuart Hall's contribution to the field of education in Brazil, it is crucial to mention that, in that context, Tomaz Tadeu da Silva and Marisa Vorraber Costa (in a recent article, Costa recounts, with two colleagues, the uses of Hall in the Brazilian education context; see Costa, Wortmann, & Silveira, 2014), just to cite two key scholars in education, were instrumental to make Stuart Hall's papers available in Brazil. Another crucial scholar made Stuart Hall's work known in Brazil: Liv Sovik (who researches in the Communications and Culture field). Among her many contributions, she published, in 2003, an incredibly successful book (its first edition was sold out in four months) with several chapters by Hall and some interviews with him, along with a generous introduction by her on his work (*Da Diáspora: identidades e mediações culturais*, Sovik, 2003). She continues, along with several other scholars, such as Ana Carolina Escosteguy and Rosa Maria Hessel Silveira, to use Hall's work in a very sophisticated way. Anyone interested in examining Hall's influence in Brazil would have to take into account the work of these scholars.

Before showing and analyzing the particular combination of Hall's contributions to my research, I first present, briefly, the educational policy and reform of Porto Alegre, in order to contextualize it and highlight its complexities and particularities.

Porto Alegre and the Citizen School project

Porto Alegre is a city of 1.4 million people, situated in the southern region of Brazil. It is the capital of the state of Rio Grande do Sul and the largest city of the region. From 1989 to 2004, it was governed by a coalition of Leftist parties (the Popular Administration), under the general leadership of the Workers' Party (*Partido dos Trabalhadores* or PT, formed in 1979 by a coalition of unions, social movements, and other Leftist organizations). The Popular Administration was re-elected three consecutive times, thus giving it and its policies even greater legitimacy. The coalition was defeated in the municipal elections in 2005, but some of the structures and principles of the proposals put in place in those 16 years remain in place, even though the majority of them were gradually changed by the administrations that governed the city since then.

Working with the excluded members of Brazilian society, the Citizen School project had a clear and explicit project of transformation of the educational system of the city. According to one of the mayors of the city at the time, this project:

> institutes the possibility for citizens to recognize themselves as bearers of dignity, to rebel against the "commodification" of life ... In the Citizen School, the conformist and alienating pedagogy that sustains the idea that history is a movement rigorously pre-organized towards the reproduction of capitalist needs is denied. (Genro, 1999, pp. 10–11)

The Citizen School project was built, by the teachers and activists who were working at the schools and at the municipal secretariat of education (SMED), explicitly as an alternative to the marketization ideology around education, and it is clear that the notion of citizenship is used overtly as a way of opposing the process that views knowledge merely as a commodity or aims at using market values at public education, something that will be examined later in this article.

In order to construct the principles that would guide the actions of the Citizen School, a democratic, deliberative, and participatory forum was created, called Constituent Assembly, which initiated with a long process of mobilization of the school communities and ended with the definition of the principles that would guide the policy for the municipal schools in Porto Alegre.

The concept of the Citizen School was to eliminate the separation between the determination of the goals and the creation of the mechanisms to implement these goals, and the Constituent Assembly was the means to achieve this goal. The Constituent Assembly elected the radical democratization of education in the municipal schools as the main normative goal of the Citizen School project. This radical democratization occurred in three dimensions: democratization of access to school (building new schools in the most impoverished areas of the city and working to keep the students in schools, with new relationships with the citizens of the neighborhoods), democratization of knowledge (having a curriculum, built by each school, that discusses what counts as knowledge, starting by research of the school communities and finishing with a meaningful school set of curriculum principles that guide the whole school), and democratization of governance (with empowered school councils and election of principals and curriculum coordinators). These three principles were the ones guiding every action in the municipal system of Porto Alegre. They had the impact of changing the structure of the schools and of the relationship between schools and the SMED and represented a viable alternative to the market-oriented schooling experience being proposed at the national and international level at that conjuncture in Brazil.

In order to examine how the Citizen School project was built as a concrete alternative to neoliberal and neoconservative tendencies in Brazil at that moment, the work of Stuart Hall was central. The two following sections show how, in my research, this assemblage of theoretical tools provided by Hall (and others, influenced by him) was created and how the analysis was performed, with the use of these lenses.

A complex theory for understanding a complex reality: hegemony, articulation, common sense, and ideology

In order to understand how the coalition of neoconservative and neoliberal discourses (in an alliance that Roger Dale (1989) has named "conservative modernization") was able to set the tone of the conversation about education in Brazil at that particular historical conjuncture, and how the alternative project of the Citizen School was able to establish itself as a viable alternative to this conversation, it was crucial to operate with the more complex concept of hegemony rather than with a monolithic concept of domination or dominant ideology.

While it was crucial to recognize and analyze the strength and the real consequences of neoliberal and neoconservative policies, it was also essential to understand the renegotiations that were made at regional and municipal levels. As Ball (1994) emphasized, "policy is ... a set of technologies and practices which are realized and struggled over in local settings" (p. 10). Thus, rather than assuming that neoliberal and neoconservative policies dictate exactly what occurs at the local level, we should study the rearticulations that occur at this level to be able to map out the creation of alternatives.

The notion of articulation helps us understand both the construction of hegemony and counter-hegemony. Categories such as "participation," "democracy," "collaboration," and "solidarity," which were historically connected with progressive social movements in education in Brazil, can be disarticulated from their previous meanings and rearticulated in the educational arena using the language and practices of marketization. Those categories can be stripped from the meanings that linked them to specific struggles for justice and equality in society in general and in education in particular, and connected with categories like "efficiency," "productivity," and "knowledge as commodity."

The concept of articulation is central here because it helps us to understand the "work" that has to be done to connect ideas and practices. The examples above illustrate this: to disarticulate a concept historically associated with counter-hegemonic movements and rearticulate it to the hegemonic discourse (or the other way around, as in the case of the Citizen School project) actually requires heavy lifting. Hall helps us to better understand what is implicated in (dis/re)articulation:

> An articulation is ... the form of the connection that *can* make a unity of two different elements, under certain conditions. It is a linkage which is not necessary, determined, absolute, and essential for all time. You have to ask, under what circumstances can a

connection be forged or made? So, the so-called "unity" of a discourse is really the articulation of different, distinctive elements which can be rearticulated in different ways because they have no necessary "belongingness." (Hall [interview] in Grossberg, 1996, p. 141)

The concept of articulation provides us with a tool to understand the complex and historical "work" involved in constructing and maintaining hegemony. It also helps us to understand that the apparent homogeneity and solidness of a given discourse is actually a historical construction, one that has to be constantly renovated. A connection that is established among groups and specific ideologies is not "necessary" or given; it cannot be easily deduced from a central dominant ideology. It is better understood as an articulation, a non-necessary and more or less contingent connection made possible in a specific context and in a specific historical moment.

In another passage, Hall further develops this concept of articulation:

By the term, "articulation," I mean a connection or link which is not necessarily given in all cases, as a law or a fact of life, but which requires particular conditions of existence to appear at all, which has to be positively sustained by specific processes, which is not "eternal" but has constantly to be renewed, which can under some circumstances disappear or be overthrown, leading to the old linkages being dissolved and new connections – re-articulations – being forged. It is also important that an articulation between different practices does not mean that they become identical or that the one is dissolved into the other. Each retains its distinct determinations and conditions of existence. However, once an articulation is made, the two practices can function together, not as an "immediate identity" (in the language of Marx's "1857 Introduction") but as "distinctions within a unity." (Hall, 1985, pp. 113–114)

A good example is the discursive articulation that has to be built to sustain conservative modernization, the alliance, mentioned above, between neoliberals and neoconservatives. Neither group is dissolved, nor their differences remain; but the alliance is guaranteed by the process of articulation.

Nevertheless, the idea that the discourses of this alliance represented a stable state of domination coming from a unique dominant ideology that, in turn, came, unmediated, from the dominant class, did not explain adequately the complex process of struggles for counter-hegemonic spaces that I was trying to understand in my research. To view those discourses as part of a hegemonic movement meant that a notion of ideology as false consciousness, present in some versions of Marxism, had to be challenged in order to capture the movements of the social phenomenon I was studying. It also required the construction of a theoretical framework in which discourse, hegemony, ideology, common sense, and articulation were used together to map the terrain of the struggles around education in Brazil.

Ideology has certainly been a central concept in the neo-Marxist tradition. The early use of this concept in education tended to have a deterministic approach. This conception theorized ideology "in singular": ideology appeared to be always composed solely of the ideas of the dominant class, something that does not capture the contradictions always present in the process of dominance. This notion of ideology does not allow space to understand what Hall teaches us: "there is never any one, single, unified and coherent 'dominant ideology' which pervades everything" (Hall, 1996b, p. 433). Furthermore, there seems to be no space here for any resistance or alternative-creation because ideology "has" agency, not the agents. Structure and ideology seem to be the entities that "act," not people.

Against this conception of ideology, one that does not consider contradictions and the mediation work that has to be done in order to "order and organize" civil society, Stuart Hall offers a different understanding, one that invites us to also focus on the concept of common sense and the elements of good sense inside it. More than any constituted and coherent ideology, common sense dictates the parameters of our practical lives, which need fast reactions and answers to the various problems experienced every day. In common sense resides the origin of the majority of daily life actions; it is formed by the beliefs – contradictory, most of the time, because beliefs from different historical moments and from different subject positions coexist in common sense – which constitute the foundations of the decision-making process in everyday life.

Hall shows that "… because … common-sense elements constitutes the realm of practical thinking for the masses of the people, Gramsci insisted that it was precisely in this terrain that ideological struggle most frequently took place" (Hall, 1996a, p. 43). This is why it is so important to study common sense. Understanding the common sense of a society in a particular period allows us to understand what the conceptions are that have become hegemonic. Hegemony comes precisely from the colonization of common sense.

Although common sense is usually viewed as a "natural or logical way" of thinking and acting, it is, in fact, an historical construction. The elements that constitute common sense in each specific period are constructed in the struggle over conceptions that try to "explain" and "make sense of" society and people's lives. Common sense is never totally converted into dominant ideologies. It always contains, at least residual elements of resistance, and because of that, it is always a site where different discourses struggle for the power of constituting meaning. Hence, in the attempt to construct a counter-hegemonic movement, the move should not be to dismiss common sense as false consciousness, but to find inside it what "makes sense" and why it does. In other words, it should be a positive endeavor, rather than a negative one.

As we can see, discourse is a central concept when we discuss common sense and its power. In the historic moment in which I conducted my research, neoliberalism was the prevalent discourse of the hegemonic alliance, and education was (and still is) one of the arenas where the confluence of state policies and market-driven discourses could be seen. One example is the attempt to articulate the idea of marketization of the educational institutions and relations to elements of the so-called progressive pedagogical discourse, which gave this discourse a point of connection and entrance to the schools. Hence, when we see neoliberals talking about "autonomy" and "collaboration," we are witnessing a process of articulation, of winning the consent of the educational agents. Those are concepts that have a specific meaning inside the pedagogical discourse, and by using them to implement their goals of preparing better workers to the new work order, and introducing market-based values to education, neoliberals were colonizing these concepts and imbuing them with new meanings.

A connection of the notion of discourse with the concept of hegemony can be very useful to better explain articulation, alliance formation, and the notion of common sense. How do some discourses become more important than others? How is it possible to use this theoretical framework and not be paralyzed by the notion of a discourse that occupies all the spaces? To better address these issues, Hall can again provide crucial arguments. He states that:

ideas only become effective if they do, in the end, *connect* with a particular constellation of social forces. In that sense, ideological struggle is a part of the general social struggle for mastery and leadership – in short for hegemony. But "hegemony" in Gramsci's sense requires, not the simple escalation of a whole class to power, with its fully formed "philosophy," but the *process* by which a historical bloc of social forces is constructed and the ascendancy of that bloc secured. So the way we conceptualize the relationship between "ruling ideas" and "ruling classes" is best thought in terms of the process of "hegemonic domination" … Ruling ideas are not guaranteed their dominance by their already given coupling with ruling classes. Rather, the effective coupling of dominant ideas *to* the historic bloc which has acquired hegemonic power in a particular period is what the process of ideological struggle is *intended to secure*. It is the object of the exercise, not the playing out of an already written and concluded script. (Hall, 1996a, pp. 43–44)

Here we can see that some discourses are more powerful than others in society because discourses are linked to material conditions. This hierarchy of discourses, though, is not produced by a one-way determination from the material conditions. Instead, Hall helps us to understand that this is a process of constant movement, where the hegemonic groups must struggle to establish their discourse as the dominant one. This is not automatically guaranteed by the fact that those groups have the economic power (especially because groups without economic power could be brought inside the dominant alliance). Hall defends a non-necessary correspondence between the economy and culture, between dominant classes and dominant ideology, and not a necessary non-correspondence, as some poststructuralist propose:

"Necessarily no correspondence" expresses exactly the notion … that nothing really connects with anything else … I do not accept that simple inversion. I think what we have discovered is that there is no necessary correspondence, which is different; and this formulation represents a third position. This means that there is no law which guarantees that the ideology of a class is already and unequivocally given in or corresponds to the position which that class holds in the economic relations of capitalist production. The claim of "no guarantee" – which breaks with teleology – also implies that there is no necessary non-correspondence. (Hall, 1985, p. 94)

Discourses do not free-float, but have a non-necessary linkage to structural conditions in societies. Through Hall's analysis, we can identify a permanent process of struggle from the dominant groups to maintain their dominance. Ideological struggle is a crucial part of this process. For Hall, the concept of ideology is a central one in understanding why some discourses carry more power than others. Hall wants, however, to confront the so-called "negative" notion of ideology, the one that defines it as "false consciousness." For Hall, it is necessary to overcome this negative notion because it assumes that people are basically "dupes."

In discussing this issue, Hall questions whether a worker who uses capitalist categories to understand capitalism has a "false consciousness." His response is:

Yes, if by that we mean there is something about her situation which she cannot grasp with the categories she is using; something about the process as a whole which is systematically hidden because the available concepts only give her a grasp of one of its many-sided moments. No, if by that we mean that she is utterly deluded about what goes on under capitalism. (Hall, 1996a, p. 37)

Rather than living under a false consciousness, Hall shows that the problem is the fact that this is an inadequate explanation, one that has "substituted one part of the process for the whole" (Hall, 1996a, p. 37), something that Marx has defined as fetishism.

Using Gramsci's concept of hegemonic bloc, Hall provides us with a much more powerful theoretical tool to understand hegemony and counter-hegemony. Although he recognizes the existence of a hierarchy among discourses and ideologies, he does not defend the idea of a dominant ideology directly linked to the dominant class with a single meaning. Not only is there not one single source where we can go to identify the dominant ideology, but also there is no single consequence caused by any single dominant ideology. Interpreting Hall, Fiske says that "ideology does not say the same things to the same people at the same time. Rather it works through cultural forms whose meanings and political effectivity are determined by how they are articulated with other forms" (Fiske, 1996, p. 218).

In Hall's theory we see a dynamic society; we see contradiction that can lead to transformation, to counter-hegemonic possibilities. But these contradictions are:

> deeply inscribed in the material conditions of existence in capitalist societies and in the power relations that structure those conditions. Meanings underpin or undermine any given social order, but they cannot exist independent of it. The people are neither cultural dupes nor silenced victims, but are vital, resilient, varied contradictory, and, as a source of constant contestations of dominance, are a vital social resource, the only one that can fuel social change. (Fiske, 1996, p. 220)

As I said above, common sense, even when articulated by the hegemonic bloc through the dominant discourse, has a potentiality to promote counter-hegemonic struggles:

> If common sense represents the minimum common denominator of what a group or a people believe, it has, because of that, a solidarity and transclassist vocation … If it is true that common sense is the mode how subordinate groups and classes live their subordination, it is not less true, as studies about subcultures indicate, that this experience, far from being accommodative, contains resistance elements which, given the circumstances, can develop and transform itself in weapons of struggle. (Santos, 1989, p. 37)

Here we again see common sense as a central concept to understand both how the conservative alliance achieves its victories and how the counter-hegemonic strategies can be constructed. Elements of good sense (Apple, 1993, 1999) inside common sense could be articulated to construct different projects. Popular memory of organization and politicization, of beliefs in the possibility of alternative social relations, repressed by the normalization of dominant discourses, could be recuperated in order to forge new counter-hegemonic alliances.

This discussion about ideology and discourse should not imply that discourses do not construct reality – they do. They do not do so because they are the best rational formulations, but because they carry with them social relations of domination/resistance. For Hall, "we are still required to think about the way in which ideological/ cultural/ discursive practices continue to exist within the determining lines of force of material relations" (Hall [interview] in Grossberg, 1996, p. 147). In a way, the concept of ideology keeps theory grounded. Hall's use of the concept of ideology contains the idea that "we formulate our intentions within ideology" (Hall, as cited in Larrain, 1996, p. 49). In Hall's theory, discourse is always formulated within specific and concrete social material conditions.

There is a famous quote from Margaret Thatcher, the former Prime Minister of the UK, which, in my opinion, summarizes the reason why it is so important to use all these concepts together in order to understand the movements of the hegemonic alliance. She said, "Economics is the method, the aim is to change the soul" (as cited in Apple, 1996, p. 98). This sentence, I think, summarizes the task of any researcher interested in social regulation and social transformation. It is necessary to address the structural conditions where the "economics" is established: the materiality still counts. But it is also necessary to understand how neoliberal and neoconservative groups gained hegemony and how this discourse articulates the fears and beliefs of the dominated groups. Finally, it is necessary to analyze how "souls" are being changed, how the most cherished beliefs are being reconstructed, how social memory is being erased, and how consent is being won sometimes not rationally, but through a politics of feelings and desire. This has to be done both to understand how hegemony is achieved and articulations are formed and also to envision alternatives and study the ways these alternatives can and are being constructed.

Constructing an analysis that pays attention to all these issues helps us to visualize the hegemonic bloc's project toward a conservative modernization as a contradictory alliance of dominant and dominated groups. This alliance articulates its unity around discourses that construct their own alliance and the "possible" and "impossible" practices in the social relations. However, it is also possible to theorize the counter-hegemonic forces and their constructions of alternatives in a similar way: they construct new common sense in a discursive struggle for meaning, but they also build new structures that show that a new way of organizing society is possible.

Using these concepts together, concepts so well laid out by Stuart Hall, can provide a theoretical framework that not only allows for a better understanding of how hegemony is achieved and maintained, but that also sheds light on how counter-hegemonic struggles are constructed by rearticulating elements of the popular memory in the creation of new forms of social interactions. Because this theory is still grounded in materiality and is very much interested in the way culture is articulated to maintain the *status quo*, it forces us not to be romantic about transformation, allowing for a better understanding of the real possibilities of exploring contradictions in the construction of alternatives.

I now examine the case of Porto Alegre as a sociological phenomenon through the lens of these very sophisticated theoretical lenses. As mentioned before, I do not enter, here, in a detailed description of the Citizen School experience (something I have done elsewhere – see, for example, Gandin, 2011), but rather analyze it as a policy and a reform that can be better understood with the potent contribution of Stuart Hall.

Examining the case of Porto Alegre's Citizen School policy reform through the lenses provided by Stuart Hall

In hegemonic discourses, the emphasis on education is related to the will to colonize this space and produce an educational environment more in tune with the economic needs of the market. However, when this global process – and its mediation through federal policies – reaches Porto Alegre, contradictions are created and a process of rearticulation is forged. If it is true that the hegemonic discourse tries to colonize the educational sphere, it is also true that it creates unintended spaces for alternative experiences, because the common sense idea that education will solve the problems of the country allows real investment in education. The Popular Administration used this space to prioritize education in a country where education for the poor had been neglected. Once the space is occupied by the rhetoric calling for more investment in education, the Citizen School can deploy its alternative project, with its realignment of priorities, and invest in a transformative project of education for the excluded. The Popular Administration could also start to recuperate and, at the same time, reinvent concepts such as "autonomy," "decentralization," and "collaboration," rearticulated by neoliberals. These concepts had a completely different meaning in the popular movements in Brazil and now had to be disarticulated from neoliberal discourse and rearticulated to the Citizen School project.

Taking advantage of the hegemonic decentralization discourse expressed in federal documents and in the Brazilian Education Law, the Popular Administration was able to construct a system that does not have to follow any federal curricular directives and can be structured in cycles of formation (abolishing traditional grades and reinventing assessment, without student failures), an option anticipated in the law, but very rarely used in school systems at that time. While the governments of other state capitals were complaining about the neoliberal effects of decentralization that gave them more responsibility without more resources, the Workers' Party in Porto Alegre, while strongly protesting the lack of resources, explored every aspect of the decentralization proposals and used them to construct a real alternative. Rather than performing only the minimum that the federal legislation demanded from municipal systems, Porto Alegre created a democratic Municipal Council for Education, able autonomously to regulate education in Porto Alegre and to explore every possibility that the law allowed in order to construct an alternative school structure and an alternative curriculum.

This does not mean that the Popular Administration won that battle. The hegemonic groups forged new articulations (which led to the loss of the election 16 years after the first mayor of that coalition took office) and education remained a site of struggle. However, the important point is that no hegemonic action can block all spaces simultaneously, and even its own discourse can be rearticulated to favor counter-hegemonic purposes. That is what the Citizen School project concretely accomplished.

The process of disarticulation/rearticulation (along with the concept of common sense) can also help us to understand the case of the terminology of *citizenship*. Certain concepts can acquire different meanings in different contexts. The concept of citizenship, central to the project in Porto Alegre, has a very specific meaning in contemporary Brazil. It was not a randomly chosen word; it actually symbolized the struggles against the attempts to introduce the market logic inside public spheres, such as education. Hence, to say that you want to form citizens inside public schools had to be read, in that particular Brazilian context, as a response to neoliberal discourses. The term "citizenship" was used as a discursive weapon against the rival notion of "client" or "customer" introduced by neoliberal discourses. It provided very different subject positions for agency than those offered by the idea of the consumer in a set of market relations. The political meaning of citizenship was rearticulated to a set of more socially critical ideas and practices, one that intended to construct a new common sense that was truly focused on collective as well as individual empowerment of the impoverished communities that surrounded the schools in Porto Alegre. Hall's anti-essentialism, claiming that signs do not have necessary class belongingness, but can be disarticulated and rearticulated, is a very important contribution here (Hall, 1996a, 1996b).

The concept of citizenship was also a form of connecting with the struggles of the social movements and unions. Brazil had a history of mobilizations and social movements, during and after the military dictatorship that ended in the mid-1980s, demanding exact citizenship, the right of being a full citizen. When the Citizen School project elected this goal, forming citizen in its schools, it was actually forming an articulation with popular memory of mobilizations, with the idea that there is a more just way to structure social life, where social exclusion is not a daily reality. The strong history of popular organization and politicization of the daily life is part of this popular memory, latent in the local common sense (due to the history of political and social engagement). The Citizen School project, with its repoliticization of the educational arena and activation of community participation, brought this popular memory to the foreground. To construct a project of education that emphasizes citizenship has to be seen, in this context, as a recuperation of this category and a rearticulation with counter-hegemonic struggles. This was a form of slowly (re)creating a common sense where social rights and participation were considered a new minimum for the relationship between state and communities.

This process of rearticulation is not a simple task, though. Certain discourses gain truth effects, while others do not have access to the channels of distribution, or, when they do gain access, they must struggle to rearticulate concepts that were already framed in a certain way. It is true that the fact that this was a municipal government with access to a great number of schools, which grants the project a different point of entry and represents not a voluntaristic experience, but one sanctioned by the municipal level of state. Again, this does not mean that the rearticulation goes smoothly. The hegemonic forces have constructed and maintained their hegemony exactly by their ability to restrain the spaces of visibility of alternatives. Opening up spaces is always a struggle and the case of Porto Alegre illustrates this.

A discursive struggle about education and its major goals was taking place in Porto Alegre. I already mentioned above that talking about "citizen" as opposed to "client" or "consumer" was a conscious move to bring "political" words to the arena of the discussion. There was also a clear attempt to bring to the center of the debate alternatives that were formerly marginalized. This was an attempt to bring, to the very center of the political debate, the idea that impoverished communities, contrary to "experts" claims, can participate in the definition of their social destiny. Thus, not only were concepts that were relegated to the margins being brought back to the public discussion, but also an entire group of people that was marginalized and excluded from the economic, social, and political goods of society was affirmed as having the right to space, to voice, to social existence. Moreover, there was a constant struggle to legitimize the experience of the Citizen School, to make it socially visible, to frame the discussion over education in different terms, to pull education from the technical realm, and put it to a more politicized one.

Another example of disarticulation/rearticulation is the case of national tests that began to be given to students in the 1990s. The municipal system of the city of Porto Alegre, as a state capital and one of the largest metropolitan areas in the country, was expected to comply and give the national tests to its students. Nevertheless, the local authorities in the city, during the Citizen School project, refused to implement the national tests. Their main argument was precisely the notion of decentralization, so prevalent in the national neoliberal discourse at the time. Disarticulating the notion of decentralization and devolution from the neoliberal conception, one that implemented disinvestment from the federal government, the Citizen School project leaders reaticulated the notion of decentralization to the empowerment of the autonomy of the educational systems and schools (in the Brazilian case, linked to the Freirian notion that curriculum had to be built with the active involvement of the school communities) and refused to apply the national tests in Porto Alegre. The local state sheltered the educational system of Porto Alegre from national policies interested only in measuring outcome, at least at that particular historical moment.

Finally, the progressive movements, which formerly criticized the problems of the bureaucratic tradition of the state when dealing with education, were now put into an awkward position because, due to the neoliberal attacks, they had to defend the public characteristic of the same system they used strongly to criticize. The challenge was not to have a romantic position of the educational system that was in place before neoliberal tendencies started to gain space. It was important to recognize, however, the kinds of victories the organized progressive movements had in the welfare state and to fight to maintain and expand them. If everything inside the preneoliberal public system of education were entirely favorable to the hegemonic groups, they would not have attacked it so furiously. Maintaining this balance – criticizing the elements that were not so democratic in the welfare state and, at the same time, attempting to preserve the more democratic elements in the popular memory as weapons against the thrust of the neoliberal project – was a fundamental move. Nevertheless, this was not enough; it was also necessary to forge alternatives that could function as viable counter-hegemonic thrusts against an apparently all-encompassing neoliberalism. The example of Porto Alegre was able to become a concrete example that another education was possible.

Final remarks

At the end of this article, I go back to a quote from Stuart Hall about Gramsci's work: the need to rework it in order to make it fruitful. This is the process that Hall would certainly like to see happen to his own work; that researchers take up and produce potent analyses that do not simplify the phenomenon they set out to study, but rather map out its complexities. The work of Stuart Hall has certainly helped me to analyze in depth the Citizen School experience in Brazil and its counter-hegemonic project. Its rigor and ability to analyze societies relationally will certainly continue to inspire and guide new generations of scholars.

Funding

This work was supported by Conselho Nacional de Desenvolvimento Científico e Tecnológico (CNPq – Brazil).

ORCID

Luis Armando Gandin ⓘ http://orcid.org/0000-0002-8219-2004.

References

Apple, M. W. (1993). *Official knowledge*. New York, NY: Routledge.
Apple, M. W. (1996). *Cultural politics and education*. New York, NY: Teacher College Press.
Apple, M. W. (1999). *Power, meaning, and identity*. New York, NY: Peter Lang.

Ball, S. J. (1994). *Education reform: A critical and post-structural approach.* Buckingham: Open University Press.

Costa, M. V., Wortmann, M. L. C., & Silveira, R. M. H. (2014). Stuart Hall: tributo a um autor que revolucionou as discussões em educação no Brasil [Stuart Hall: A tribute to an author who revolutionized the debates about education in Brazil]. *Educação & Realidade, 39,* 635–649.

Dale, R. (1989). The Thatcherite project in education: The case of the City Technology Colleges. *Critical Social Policy, 9*(27), 4–19. doi:10.1177/026101838900902701

Fiske, J. (1996). Opening the hallway: Some remarks on the fertility of Stuart Hall's contribution to critical theory. In D. Morley & K. Chen (Eds.), *Stuart Hall: Critical dialogues in cultural studies* (pp. 212–220). London: Routledge.

Gandin, L. A. (2011). Porto Alegre as a counter-hegemonic global city: Building globalization from below in governance and education. *Discourse: Studies in the Cultural Politics of Education, 32* (2), 235–252. doi:10.1080/01596306.2011.562669

Genro, T. (1999). Cidadania, emancipação e cidade [Citizenship, emancipation and the city]. In L. H. Silva (Ed.), *Escola Cidadã: Teoria e prática* [The citizen school initiative: Theory and practice] (pp. 7–11). Petrópolis: Vozes.

Grossberg, L. (1996). On postmodernism and articulation: An interview with Stuart Hall (L. Grossberg, Ed.). In D. Morley & K. Chen (Eds.), *Stuart Hall: Critical dialogues in cultural studies* (pp. 131–150). London: Routledge.

Hall, S. (1985). Signification, representation, ideology: Althusser and the post-structuralist debates. *Critical Studies in Mass Communication, 2*(2), 91–114. doi:10.1080/15295038509360070

Hall, S. (1996a). The problem of ideology: Marxism without guarantees. In D. Morley & K. Chen (Eds.), *Stuart Hall: Critical dialogues in cultural studies* (pp. 25–46). London: Routledge.

Hall, S. (1996b). Gramsci's relevance for the study of race and ethnicity. In D. Morley & K. Chen (Eds.), *Stuart Hall: Critical dialogues in cultural studies* (pp. 411–440). London: Routledge.

Hall, S. (1997a). *Identidades Culturais na Pós-Modernidade* [Cultural identities in post-modernity]. Rio de Janeiro: DP&A.

Hall, S. (1997b). A Centralidade da Cultura: notas sobre as revoluções culturais do nosso tempo [The Centrality of Culture: notes on the cultural revolutions of our time]. *Educação & Realidade, 22*(2), 15–46.

Larrain, J. (1996). Stuart Hall and the Marxist concept of ideology. In D. Morley & K. Chen (Eds.), *Stuart Hall: Critical dialogues in cultural studies* (pp. 47–70). London: Routledge.

Santos, B. S. (1989). *Introdução a uma ciência pós-moderna* [Introduction to a post-modern science]. Porto: Afrontamento.

Sovik, L. (Ed.). (2003). *Da Diáspora—Identidades e mediações culturais* [On diaspora—Identities and cultural mediation]—*Stuart Hall.* Belo Horizonte: Editora da UFMG/UNESCO.

Index